The Quest for Home

The Household in Mark's Community

Michael F. Trainor

A Michael Glazier Book
THE LITURGICAL PRESS
Collegeville, Minnesota

www.litpress.org

A Michael Glazier Book published by The Liturgical Press

Cover design by David Manahan, O.S.B. Photo Courtesy of FLAT EARTH PHOTOS.

Unless indicated otherwise, the Scripture quotations are the author's translation.

1   2   3   4   5   6   7   8

Library of Congress Cataloging-in-Publication Data

Trainor, Michael R., 1950–
    The quest for home : the household in Mark's community / Michael F. Trainor.
       p. cm.
    "A Michael Glazier Book."
    Includes bibliographical references and index.
    ISBN 0-8146-5087-2 (alk. paper)
    1. Home in the Bible. 2. Households in the Bible. 3. Bible. N.T. Mark—
Criticism, interpretation, etc. I. Title.

BS2585.6.H627 T73 2001
226.3'06—dc21   00-062423

For Jack (1932–1996) and Cathy

Contents

Abbreviations

ABD	*Anchor Bible Dictionary*
ACR	*Australasian Catholic Record*
B.C.E.	Before the Common Era
BR	*Biblical Research*
BRev	*Bible Review*
BTB	*Biblical Theology Bulletin*
CBQ	*Catholic Biblical Quarterly*
C.E.	Common Era
CIL	*Corpus Inscriptionum Latinarum*
EDNT	*Expositor's Dictionary of the New Testament*
Int	*Interpretation*
JBL	*Journal of Biblical Literature*
JSNT	*Journal for the Study of the New Testament*
JSOT	*Journal for the Study of the Old Testament*
NJBC	*New Jerome Biblical Commentary*
NTS	*New Testament Studies*
RB	*Revue Biblique*
TDNT	*Theological Dictionary of the New Testament*
TLNT	*Theological Lexicon of the New Testament*
WBC	*Women's Bible Commentary*
RestorQuart	*Restoration Quarterly*
RSV	*Revised Standard Version*

1

The Quest for Home

In recent years we have been reminded of the need that every human being has for a home, a place to belong for refuge and safety. The images that flashed across our television screens over Easter 1999 of the tens of thousands of fleeing ethnic Albanians driven from their residences in Kosovo are an ironic reminder of how homelessness and forced exile reveal the deep urge for a home.

At the height of the tragic events of Bosnia, a photograph appeared on the front page of our local newspaper. A young mother and her daughter were locked in tearful embrace just prior to the small girl's departure to the safety of Sweden. The news report about the war which accompanied the photograph was factual, even clinical. The report was in stark contrast to the tragedy and tenderness written on the faces of the child and her mother. Here was the real meaning of the war—a story of suffering too deep for words. Their embrace spoke of the pain of separation and loneliness it would bring, of the desire for the lasting intimacy of the familial bond and the possibility of tenderness in the midst of the surrounding violence. It spoke of their desire for a place where they could live securely.

This black-and-white photograph was an icon of tremendous beauty and power. It invited the viewer into the warm embrace between the mother and her child, to feel the pain of separation experienced in families victimized by violence. This tragic yet moving icon is a potent reminder of the meaning of true intimacy and the universal longing for community.

The learning about community and our need for home was reinforced in an experience I had once in Sydney. While not as dramatic as the ones I have referred to above it provoked a similar conviction in me.

I had arranged to meet a friend at a shopping complex in the heart of the city. Being a visitor to Sydney and unsure of the bus timetable or the exact location of our rendezvous, I arrived very early—earlier than I wanted.

So I found a bench in a shopping mall close to where I thought our meeting would occur, pulled out a book, and started reading. About three paragraphs later, I sensed that someone had come and was sitting beside me.

I glanced across and noticed a man in a suit, about the same age as myself, staring into the middle distance and licking an ice cream. My eyes were drawn back to him several times as he sat oblivious to me. I noticed his blue soiled shirt, a wide-green, loose tie; a small tear near the left shoulder pad of his smudged brown coat; well-worn tan shoes with their souls lifting, and a vinyl brief case balanced on his lap and coming apart at its corners. His shabby neatness was in contrast to my own and to the customer in the exquisite jewelry shop opposite us. He finished his ice cream, got up and, walking deliberately, disappeared into the crowd— leaving me alone at our bench.

After he left I realized that I had been unusually captivated by this visitor. While I started thinking about the circumstances that might have brought him to our seat I found myself surprised that this nameless encounter had stirred me so deeply. Then it dawned on me. His harmless, unassuming presence had touched my soul. Irrespective of whether my visitor was homeless or not, he touched my own desire for community— to be in a personal space where my deepest dreams and longings could be realized.

These experiences—the images of fleeing refugees, a photograph of the tender embrace of a mother and daughter in Europe and the resting figure of an anonymous middle-aged man in a large, Australian city—illustrate different aspects of a deep-rooted longing for companionship expressed in authentic community. They clearly reveal the universal quest for what I call a "home." Obverse experiences also reveal the "underside" desire for community and a place to belong. Those among us who have experienced physical and sexual abuse in relationships, for whom "the home" has been a negative experience of destruction and personal violation will not warm easily to the idea of the domestic quest. Experiences associated with it are too painful or soul-destroying. The associated pain provoked by the household imagery features because the ideal is unrealized. The distress is evidence of the deep, existential desire for the ideal to be humanly experienced and felt. It is the ache for an authentic home.

Our Longing for Authentic Community

This overarching, all pervasive human desire for a home is further evident in two phenomena—one clearly community and the other oriented in experiences that underscore our fragility as a society. The first is seen in the observable social activities of people. It is most obvious, for example, in our local situations where people form clubs, societies and groups of local interest, or when people gather together to address a common concern. At times of national or local disasters or crises our gregarious spirit is most transparent. We are, by nature, social beings. Many of us consciously and explicitly seek community; others enjoy the hermitage and retreat. There in solitude we recognize our deepest connection with other human beings. The sense of ourselves as religious is enhanced when this social dimension is honored in the Christian setting. This is revealed in our liturgical or worship gatherings and the growth in neighborhood church groups or "basic ecclesial communities"—to name but two obvious indicators of the community aspect of Christian life.

A second indication of the quest for home is found in a range of social experiences which remind us of our fragility, limitations and ecological connection. The last half of the second millennium has been an age of enormous change accompanied by great social change. Coupled with this has been a growth in ecological sensitivity and a realization of the destruction that has been done to our planet in the name of progress or development. This growing recognition of our ecological interconnectedness—that what happens to our land, plants and animals affects us as human beings— and our environmental sensitivity nurtures our social consciousness and community awareness. The development of this ecological mindfulness has also been paralleled by a burgeoning of technological complexity.

We are the most technologically advanced and sophisticated people in human history. Yet, although we have access to great resources and an ability to address the most difficult human situations on our planet, millions still suffer and die through famine and disease. Undoubtedly, advances in technology and medicine have helped the human predicament. But despite the best technology which the human brain can engineer, people still have the potential to be profoundly confused and directionless. Technical advances, hailed by some as the great panacea to the social problems afflicting human beings, have not yet rescued us. We still suffer from isolation and estrangement; we long for a home.

In the country from which I write mobile phones have been most successfully marketed. Almost one in two Australians carry them or have them strapped to their hip—the antipodean equivalent to the American holstered gun. No one can doubt the benefits they provide their owners: portability, the sense of security and the obvious ease of communication. However, when I saw three people having lunch at a local cafe with one another—that is, they were the only ones sitting at the same table—and each of them on their mobile phones, another thought popped into my head. "Could they possibly be . . . ?" I instantly dismissed the question.

The image of the three mobile phone lunchtime companions, however, reminded me of the difficulty we sometimes experience in being with people; we long for friendship and community.

We look for an environment where we can feel whole and healed, and despite voices to the contrary, a community that can lead us beyond ourselves to experience the possibility of the transcendent and realize the spiritual urge deep within our beings. This does not mean that we want to leave our world as though to shun the exigencies of the present or regard the present demands and challenges as barriers to what is true, beautiful or good. Rather than seeking a sectarian-style of insular living disconnected from what is going on around us and with our feet firmly rooted on this planet, we desire a place where social equality and human respect is lived out in practice regardless of people's economic conditions or status. In other words, the growing sense of powerlessness and isolation that many feel from technology only serves to highlight our need for authentic community and our desire for a real home.

This human urge for a home is not unique to our time. It is expressed in every culture and age. It was particularly evident among the first Christian communities and revealed in the writings of the Second Testament[1] which emerged from their experience. As the first generations of disciples wrestled with the implications of following Jesus in a Greco-Roman world, some were misunderstood, suspected, and sometimes ostracized by those in the wider society unsympathetic to the Christian movement. This social exclusion forced some Christians to see themselves as a sect—separate from the recognized, socially confirmed, and civilly acceptable religions of the Greco-Roman world.[2]

---

[1] I use this expression "Second Testament" to designate those writings that emerged out of the Christian communities in the first and early second centuries C.E. This distinguishes these writings from those of the Jewish or Hebrew communities, the "First Testament." Both terms recognize the priority of the Hebrew Bible in witnessing to God's action and fidelity to the Jewish people. The writings of the Hebrew Bible are a first witness or testament inherited by Jesus and his followers. Those writings that emerged from the Christian communities became further reflections, a second witness or testament, to God's ongoing faithful action in the ministry of Jesus and the communities formed in his name.

[2] The "sectarian" nature of the Christian communities is discussed, among others, by J. H. Elliott. *A Home for the Homeless: A Social-Scientific Criticism of 1 Peter, Its Situation and Strategy* (Minneapolis: Fortress Press, 1990) 35–40; J. H. Elliott, *What is Social Scientific Criticism?* (Minneapolis: Fortress Press, 1993) 33–34; J. H. Elliott, "The Jewish Messianic Movement: From Faction to Sect," *Modelling Early Christianity: Social-Scientific Studies of the Second Testament in its Context,* ed., P. F. Esler (London: Routledge, 1995) 75–95; P. F. Esler, *The First Christians in their Social Worlds: Social-scientific approaches to New Testament Interpretation* (London and New York: Routledge, 1994) 12–18; B. Holmberg, *Sociology and the New Testament: An Appraisal* (Minneapolis: Fortress Press, 1990) 10–11.

In this kind of sectarian atmosphere the desire to create an environment where they could be sustained became increasingly pressing. The need was for a physical place ("house") that was also a nurturing space ("home"). The two could never be divorced from each other. A place was needed that provided the space necessary for disciples to immerse themselves again in the story and teaching of Jesus and where they could seek ways to allow this story speak freshly into a new culture and time never experienced or directly addressed by the historical Jesus and his disciples.

In the pages ahead I seek to unpack one Christian community's insights into how it sought to address this desire for home. The need for such reflection is most pressing among Christian churches. Today a common agenda seems to be emerging within our churches. We seek to make Christian life more relevant in the midst of the complexity of social issues that seem to engulf us; we want answers to the theological and educational concerns that surface within our faith communities. As we turn more to discover ways of living authentic religious lives there seems to be an accompanying desire to renew the very heart of what it means to be a faith community. Many Christians are looking for a church that is authentic and a witness to the values of Jesus. They search for a religious community in which they can experience being "at home," in a space which addresses the deepest longing for real, warm community.

The "House" in the Second Testament

This "turn" towards community among contemporary Christians can be assisted by the insights of the first Christian communities. The desire for "home" was fundamental amongst the earliest generation of disciples. This is reflected by the prominence of the household theme in their writings, the use of architectural language connected with house, and the frequency of Greek expressions that have "house" or "household" as their root.[3] It is also important to acknowledge, though, that our post-modern experience of home and its function for social growth and cohesion is different from the first-century C.E. Mediterraneans. This does not prevent their insights illuminating our quest.

---

[3] For these reasons I argue the importance, even predominance, of houses and households in the life of the first generations of Christians that is at variance with the position adopted by J. J. Meggitt, *Paul, Poverty and Survival* (Edinburgh: T. & T. Clark, 1998). Meggitt seeks to critique what he calls the "new consensus" adopted by some Pauline commentators, especially those coming to the biblical text from a social-science perspective. Meggitt's overriding thesis is that Paul and his audience were the poorest of society and generally did not live in or own houses.

Paul assumes that the house is the setting for the Christian gathering.[4] This is particularly obvious in his Corinthian correspondence when the very nature of the Christian "household" is under fire from internal division when it gathers for the Lord's Supper (1 Cor 1:16; 11:22, 34; 14:35; 16:15, 19) By the time he writes his Letter to the Romans the Christian house gathering is now called "church" *(ekklêsía)* (Rom 16:5).

The gospels are filled with references to houses and household activities. In the gospels of Mark, Matthew, and Luke the house becomes the setting for Jesus' ministry, his preaching of the good news about God's reign, healing, and instruction of the disciples.[5] It is the place of meals, where the social misfits find a welcome and the religious authorities have their style of leadership critiqued. Each of these three gospels uses the household setting in a particular way.

With Mark,[6] the house becomes the architectural indicator for the discipleship gathering in companionship with Jesus. As will become clearer, in a gospel that emphasizes Jesus' solitude and the disciples' incomprehension and dismay at Jesus, the house is the place of intimacy and becomes an overarching structure for reading and organizing the gospel.[7]

For Matthew, the house is the setting for the renewal of Israel gathered around the teaching Jesus (Matt 9:10, 28; 10:12-14; 13:36; 21:13).[8]

---

[4] V. Branick, *The House Church in the Writings of Paul* (Wilmington, Del.: Michael Glazier, 1989); J. Murphy-O'Connor, "Prisca and Aquila: Travelling Tentmakers and Church Builders," *BRev* (Dec. 1992) 40–51, 62; R. Banks, *Paul's Idea of Community: The Early House Churches in their Historical Setting* (Homebush West, N.S.W.: Lancer Books, 1981); R. Banks, *Going to Church in the First Century: An Eyewitness Account* (Parramatta, N.S.W.: Hexagon Press, 1985). In the Greco-Roman context of Paul's correspondence, it has been argued that Paul presents himself as the *paterfamilias* or leader of those Christian households that he founded or helped establish. See S. J. Joubert, "Managing the Household: Paul as *Paterfamilias* of the Christian Household Group in Corinth" in *Modelling Early Christianity: Social-Scientific Studies of the New Testament in its Context,* 213–23.

[5] For an overview of the frequency of the terms for "house" and "household" in the gospels, with a focus on Mark and the alterations which Lk and Mt make see P.-Y. Brandt and A. Lukinovich, "οἶκος et οἰκία chez Marc comparé à Matthieu et Luc," *Biblica* 78 (1997) 525–53.

[6] As a way of honoring the difference between the actual writer of the gospel and the text itself, in what follows I distinguish between the historical gospel writer (by using Mark, Matthew, Luke, and John) and the evangelist's writing (through use of the abbreviations Mk, Mt, Lk, Jn).

[7] In what follows, I choose to distinguish between Gospel and gospel. The "Gospel" is Jesus, his ministry, and revelation of God's decisive compassion for humanity. The "gospel" is the particular expression of the Gospel represented in the writings of the evangelists.

[8] M. Crosby, *House of Disciples: Church, Economics, and Justice in Matthew* (New York: Orbis, 1988) especially 21–48; S. L. Love, "The Household: A Major Social Component for Gender Analysis in the Gospel of Matthew," *BTB* 23 (1993) 21–31.

Luke builds on Mark's architectonic house-schema. In Luke's first volume, the gospel, the house is a place of gathering, healing, and teaching as in Mk (Lk 4:38; 5:24-5; 7:6; 8:51; 19:5f.). It is also the place of mission for Luke's missionary-oriented community (5:29; 7:6; 8:39; 9:4; 10:5-7; 19:5f.). Characteristically for Luke, the house is principally the place of celebration and feasting (Lk 7:36f.; 14:1f.; 15:6; 19:5f.). While the image of "temple" frames Luke's first volume, that of "household" frames the second.[9] After Jesus returns to God, the community of disciples return to the upper room of their Jerusalem house (Acts 1:13). At the end of the Acts of the Apostles, Paul is found under house arrest in Rome (Acts 28:16-31). From here he teaches, encourages the Roman Christians and his preaching is described by Luke as "unhindered" *(akôlútôs)*—the final word in Luke's two volumes and an obvious clue to the ongoing fruitfulness of the household mission in the Gentile world.

In John's gospel references to house are mostly associated with its connection to God. The house in Jn is predominantly God's. Its purification and renewal among the Jewish people fires the passion of the Johannine Jesus and brings him into conflict with its earthly guardians (Jn 2:17; 14:2). The Letter to the Hebrews also adopts the language of household in reference to the house of God (Heb 3:2-6; 10:21).

In the later Second Testament writings household language is prominent. Many commentators have noted how the writers of the Pastoral Letters (Titus, 1 and 2 Timothy) and 1 Peter were influenced by the prevailing cultural understanding of households and the importance of order and stability.[10] This order was ensured in households where the authority of the household-head prevailed and other members were subordinate. Second Testament writers adopted these cultural understandings and described their Christian communities accordingly (Titus 2:1-10; 3:3; 1 Tim 3:4-15; 5:1-17; 2 Tim 3:6; 1 Pet 2:13; 3:1-7). Alongside the writers' use of these culturally conditioned images was the conviction that the Christian community was God's household expressed in concrete form in the local situation (Titus 1:11; 1 Tim 3:15; 2 Tim 1:16; 4:19; 1 Pet 2:5; 4:17).

---

[9] J. H. Elliott, "Temple versus Household in Luke-Acts: A Contrast in Social Institutions," *The Social World of Luke-Acts,* ed., J. H. Neyrey (Peabody, Mass.: Hendrickson, 1991) 211–40.

[10] For example, D. Balch, *Let Wives be Submissive: the Domestic Code in 1 Peter* (Chico, Calif.: Scholars Press, 1981); E. Schüssler Fiorenza, *In Memory of Her: A Feminist Theological Reconstruction of Christian Origins,* 2nd ed. (London: SCM Press, 1995); R. F. Collins, "Marriage (New Testament)," *The Anchor Bible Dictionary,* ed., D. N. Freedman (New York: Doubleday, 1992) 4:569–72; J. H. Elliott, *A Home for the Homeless;* C. S. Keener, *Paul, Women & Wives: Marriage and Women's Ministry in the Letters of Paul* (Peabody, Mass.: Hendrickson, 1992); C. Osiek, *What are They Saying about the Social Setting of the New Testament?* rev. and expanded ed. (New York and Mahwah: Paulist Press, 1992).

Throughout these writings of the Second Testament, two Greek words are used to identify the house or household, *oikos* and *oikía*. The first occurs 115 times; the second, 93. Many scholars suggest that the terms be used interchangeably to mean either the physical place where the family gathers or the gathering of people that make up a household. My own preference, which is determined from the context and implied meaning in the text, is that both terms can be used interchangeably as "house-hold," though generally *oikos* is weighted in the direction of house-hold (the "residents") and *oikía*, household (the "residence").[11]

As noted above, place cannot be divorced from the human need for familial space. The terms which the Second Testament writers use for house and household are not purely architectural ones. They are also highly symbolic and theological. Contemporary studies for local church and small Christian communities need now to take into account the insights and contributions which the Second Testament communities can offer us. As we shall see in the study of one of the Second Testament writings, the Gospel According to Mark, the evangelist's use of domestic language reveals much about the story of Jesus and the meaning of discipleship for the writer's audience. The context of this language provides important clues to the reader for interpreting Jesus' ministry and noting the function which the "house" is to play in Mark's day.[12] The wisdom gleaned from Mark's gospel community can enhance the growth of smaller Christian communities today, suggest angles and insights into how we might go about developing basic ecclesial communities, and encourage us in our struggle to develop authentic Christian communities.

Four further observations are in order. First, I do not see the following as a commentary on Mark's gospel—at least "commentary" in the classic sense. Rather it is a reading of the gospel from a particular perspective. I will follow Mark's narrative unfolding of the story of Jesus that leads to the climactic final chapters using the domestic imagery of "house"

---

[11] For an alternative view see Brandt and Lukinovich, "οἶκος et οἰκία chez Marc," who argue that generally *oikía* is the place of welcome for the journey and *oikos* the actual building and space. Other frequent expressions in the Second Testament which have *oikos/oikía* as their root include: *oikodomeo* ("to build a house," 38 times); *oikodoméô* ("the act of building," 34); *oikodespótês* ("master of the house," 12); *oikónomos* ("managing a household or family," 10); *oikouménê* ("world," 15); *oikonomía* ("household management" 9) and *oikétês* ("inmate of a house," 4). Parenthetically, in the First Testament, the Hebrew "house" or "household" *(beyth)* occurs almost 2,000 times.

[12] While there are "readers" of the gospel today, originally the gospel was meant to be proclaimed and heard. In this setting, "auditors" would be a more accurate description of those who first received the gospel. In describing Mark's audience as "readers," this other sense of "auditors" or "hearers" is also intended.

and "household" as a reading lens. While I do not attempt to offer another commentary on Mark, I do work through the text—perhaps at times at a far too rapid a pace—to highlight or isolate those sections of the gospel that are important for the evangelist's household presentation. This will mean skipping over key sections quickly to focus on those parts of the gospel that I think are important to this domestic reading.

Second, in offering this reading I am conscious that I draw on the work of several scholars. There is a growing body of literature concerned with the social world of the Second Testament period, particularly on the nature, structure and function of households in the ancient and Mediterranean world. The insights of this scholarship enable us to appreciate the cultural context of the biblical world in general and Mark's gospel in particular. An exegetical reading with this social-science, domestic sensitivity will bear fruitful insights in our contemporary quest for home in our faith communities and wider society. The groundwork for such a domestic and second-level reading of Mark has been laid earlier by Struthers Malbon.[13] In what follows I seek to marry the contribution of social science scholarship with her spatial enquiry of Mark's gospel in an attempt to offer a fresh reading of the gospel.

Third, it is evident that apart from Mark's preoccupation with christology and presentation of Jesus, the second most important theme concerns discipleship. Struthers Malbon has also helped me to look freshly at the language and motifs in Mark's gospel that revolve around disciples, discipleship, and the community of disciples. The language that I shall be employing in the pages ahead to explore the role of the disciples and the function which the community of disciples plays in the gospel narrative will be couched in terms of "householders" and "household." I believe these terms more accurately reflect Mark's narrative plan. They might also contribute to a better appreciation of ancient biblical texts written in a society whose worldview was essentially clan and kinship linked.

One of the difficulties for post-modern readers attuned to the value of individualism and concerned about the importance of the reader as "subject" is an unwitting disregard for the social dimensions of a first-century C.E. text. It is possible that the important discipleship theme could be read through subjective, individualistic eyes. In such an interpretation of the gospel, the single disciple's relationship to Jesus becomes important. The wider community of believers is played down and a privatized religiosity

---

[13] E. Struthers Malbon in *Narrative Space and Mythic Meaning in Mark* (San Francisco: Harper & Row, 1986) investigates the geopolitical, topographical and architectural space of Mark's Gospel employing Levi-Straus' analysis of myth. Especially pertinent for this essay is her examination of Mark's spatial presentation of houses (106–40).

fostered. Hopefully, the use of household-language might offer an alternative socially conscious way of examining Mark's key discipleship theme.

The recognition that our worldview affects the way we read Mark's gospel brings me to a fourth point. While I believe that a meaningful conversation can take place between Mark's world and our own through the gospel—and this has been its basis as a source of nourishment for disciples in every era of history—it is important to recognize the limitations of this dialogue. My world is simply not that of a Mediterranean first-century Greco-Roman. Language and terms derived from my experience of living in a house or community as a white Australian male are not easily transferable to the first century. My understanding of domestic terms like "house," "home," or "household" needs to be broadened so that I can appreciate better how first-century Mediterranean people understood these terms. This is the intention behind Part One. Here, the social context and domestic architecture of Mark's audience, and the way "household" was understood by Greek and Roman writers is explored.

All this provides the ground for a domestic reading of Mark's gospel in Part Two where, when necessary, I offer my own translation of Mark's Greek text. For those seeking a more "streamlined" reading, the next chapter is important background that will elucidate my approach in reading Mark's gospel in Part Two. The two subsequent chapters (chs. 3 and 4) which are slightly more technical and philosophical, and offer an understanding of households from Greek and Roman writers may be omitted and returned to at a later time. Throughout, footnotes have been kept to a minimum, though recognition is given to those scholars with whom I am in dialogue and upon whom I have depended for developing this idiosyncratic and, I hope, exhilarating reading of Mark's gospel.

The lives, stories, and insights of my colleagues at the Adelaide College of Divinity and the School of Theology of Flinders University, South Australia, and the people from the Catholic community of Salisbury among whom I live have indirectly, and even unwittingly, helped me construct the domestic lens for reading Mark's gospel. There are a few I would like to especially acknowledge. I am aware of the inclusive household that I shared with Denis Edwards and Kevin O'Loughlin as we engaged in our respective ministries while living in community with them at North Adelaide. I value their friendship and wisdom. These continue to sustain me as our ministries and households take fresh and complementary directions. Denis also read an initial draft of this book and offered, as he usually does with what I write, several helpful critical suggestions for improving the text. I also wish to acknowledge the open hospitality and empowering ministry that I now share with Jim O'Loughlin in the Catholic community of Salisbury.

Our mutual intent to form a new household of disciples in the midst of the ministries which engage us has created a nurturing environment from which I write. I am indebted also to Robert Karris, friend and mentor, who generously read the manuscript and offered encouragement and a balanced critique of it in his characteristic sanguine style. I will always remember Justin Taylor's encouragement, kindness, and practical help in the time I was at the Ecole Biblique in Jerusalem. He offered suggestions and corrected errors in what became chapter 4. I am grateful too for other friends and colleagues at the Adelaide College of Divinity. I thank James McEvoy in reading and offering helpful insights that enabled me to clarify key sections in the final draft.

I am particularly grateful to Beth Prior, a fine librarian with a quick eye and enormous energy. Beth located relevant bibliographic material and, besides offering critical suggestions, spontaneously and generously helped to prepare the final manuscript for publication. I wish to thank The Liturgical Press for its willingness to publish this book and the ease with which they made it possible.

Finally, I wish to thank Cathy Jenkins, Australian religious publisher, friend, and co-conspirator. As I began exploring the possibility of this idiosyncratic reading of Mark's gospel some years ago, Cathy steered me towards the shape this book finally took. Her kindness and wisdom and, in a quiet but powerfully influential way, that of her father, Jack, reveal to me something of those qualities which Mark encourages disciples in Jesus' household to emulate. To Cathy and Jack this book is dedicated.

Part One

The "House" in the Ancient World

2

Mark's Social and Architectural Setting

The earliest Christians were members of households and gathered in houses to ponder the story of Jesus and its implications for their lives in the Greco-Roman culture in the late first century C.E. As we have seen, the Second Testament writings reflect this interest and context. In the pages that follow I seek to expand on the summary comments above in a reading of the Gospel of Mark.

I focus on Mk for two reasons. First, a study of all the Second Testament writings read through a lens that is sensitive to the domestic, Mediterranean world of the first century C.E. can bring fresh insights to our need today for community and our desire to renew ecclesial structures. However to do this adequately would be beyond the scope of one book. To focus on one writing, the Gospel of Mark, makes a domestic reading of the gospel more realistic and practical. There is a second reason for focussing on this gospel. Mark seems to show a keen interest in the "household" of Jesus. This becomes the setting for his healing and teaching and offers a contrast to the growing opposition from his antagonists. Mark's narrative portrayal of Jesus and his disciples makes a domestic reading desirable.

As we shall see when we look more closely at Mark's story, the evangelist is keen to assist the gospel audience reflect on its own human foibles and struggles mirrored in the gospel's battling characters. The growth in discipleship blindness, separation and ultimate failure is accompanied by the figure of Jesus seeking companionship and intimacy. Both portraits, of the disciples and Jesus, are assisted by the primary role which the "house" plays in Mark's narrative landscape. Mark's emphasis on Jesus' growing isolation throws up in sharp relief the evangelist's concern about community—the setting in which loneliness can be addressed and intimacy experienced. The struggle for intimacy in the midst of failure and betrayal becomes recognized and addressed in the house.

If "house" and "household" are prominent themes for appreciating Mark's Gospel, what kind of audience was addressed by them and how would these themes be understood by this Greco-Roman audience? These two important questions invite us to consider the socio-historical world Mark's audience. It is this context which can ground our reading of the gospel in the culture that the writer presumes but is unfamiliar to technologically proficient Westerners. This investigation will also help us appreciate the nature and function which house/households played in the Mediterranean world and the reason that Mark employs the house as a powerful narrative symbol.

Mark's Social Context

Mark's gospel is a cultural product. It was born out of particular historical and social setting. Mark's presentation of Jesus (Mk's "christology") and the gospel's narrative structure were shaped by the social and historical situation facing Christian disciples in a new cultural context. While there never has been a scholarly consensus about this setting, the recognition that the text emerges out of a late first-century Greco-Roman, Mediterranean context helps to root the gospel in the real struggles of believers. What follows, then, is not fanciful though it is speculative. This admission recognizes that we will never know what Mark's community was exactly like, but we can offer a speculative reconstruction based on the best available scholarly, archaeological and literary evidence. It is important to attempt such a reconstruction, even granting its limitations. Such an attempt comes from my conviction of seeking to link the situation encountered by Mark's listeners with our own. This means that the gospel cannot remain locked in history or address only its original or intended ancient Mediterranean audience. It also has the power to address a postmodern, scientifically inspired audience.

It is generally accepted that the gospel was written some forty years after the death and resurrection of Jesus to a community undergoing severe testing and suffering. Mark's audience can be located somewhere in the Roman Empire around 70 C.E. The gospel presumes a Greek-speaking audience not conversant with Hebrew or Aramaic and, although familiar with some Jewish customs which would have been known amongst non-Jews, unfamiliar with the details of Jewish purification rites. Mark's readers were living in a part of the Mediterranean world geographically and chronologically removed from the original historical event of the Jewish Jesus that gave birth to the Christian movement in Palestine. Jewish disciples of Jesus might have even first preached to Mark's people. Over time, within a generation, this original and formative Jewish influence expanded to embrace a non-Jewish, Gentile world into which the original story of Jesus and his disciples needed inculturation. The values, teaching and key themes associated with Jesus in this Jewish preaching were retranslated by Mark in a gospel addressed to a Greco-Roman audience. One of these themes inherited from the original story of Jesus was that of "house."

Gospel Latinisms (Latin terms or words transliterated into Greek) suggest that the audience was familiar with Latin or living in a Latin-speaking area even though Greek was the dominant language.[1] This further confirms that Mark's community members would have been truly "Greco-Roman." Though residents of the Roman Empire, they would have still been strongly influenced by Greek culture. Several geographical regions have been proposed for the community, including Northern Palestine, Syria, Egypt, and Asia Minor. A popular, current opinion still favors Rome as the provenance of the gospel, albeit anywhere in the Roman Empire would be suitable.[2] Although Rome will be used as the hypothetical urban locale for Mark's audience, the insights from archaeology and Greco-Roman literature about houses and their application in reading Mark's gospel could be extrapolated to any urban center of the later first-century

---

[1] For example, Mk 4:21; 5:9, 15; 6:27, 37; 7:4; 12:14, 42; 15:15, 16, 19, 39, 44. See F. Blass and A. Debrunner, *A Greek Grammar of the New Testament and Other Early Christian Literature* (Chicago: University of Chicago Press, 1961) 4–6.

[2] The most vigorous contender for the Roman setting has been M. Hengel, *Studies in the Gospel of Mark* (Philadelphia: Fortress Press, 1985) who argues to this position from, among other things, linguistic evidence and the tradition of Mark's Gospel linked to Peter as held by Papias. Also D. Senior, "'With Swords and Clubs . . .'—The Setting of Mark's Community and His Critique of Abusive Power," *BTB* 17 (1987) 10–20; J. R. Donahue, "Windows and Mirrors: The Setting of Mark's Gospel," *CBQ* 57 (1995) 1–26. R. E. Brown and J. P. Meier concede that "internal evidence is not unfavourable to the tradition that Rome was the place of provenance for Mark" and that it "cannot be quickly dismissed as implausible" (*Antioch and Rome: New Testament Cradles of Catholic Christianity* [New York: Paulist Press, 1983] 197). For other positions on the Markan locale see M. D. Hooker, *The Gospel According to Saint Mark* (Peabody, Mass.: Hendrickson, 1993) 5–8. A good summary of the various opinions on Mk's site is offered by R. E. Brown, *An Introduction to the New Testament* (New York: Doubleday, 1997) 161–63; P. J. Achtemeier, "Mark, Gospel of," ABD IV, 541–57. Some have argued for a Palestinian/Syrian rural setting. H. C. Kee, *Community of the New Age: Studies in Mark's Gospel* (Philadelphia: Westminster Press, 1977); C. Myers, *Binding the Strong Man: A Political Reading of Mark's Story of Jesus* (Maryknoll, N.Y.: Orbis Books, 1988); D. W. Chapman "Locating the Gospel of Mark: A Model of Agrarian Biography," *BTB* 25 (1995) 24–36; R. L. Rohrbaugh "The Social Location of the Markan Audience," *Int* 47 (1993) 380–95.

C.E. Greco-Roman world. The key point is that Mark is writing to a pre-industrial, Mediterranean, urban audience.[3]

Arguably, if Rome was the possible setting of the gospel and its community, the historical situation of Rome's Christians around the 70s could well be reflected in the narrative plot and character portrayals of Mark's gospel briefly described above.[4] The Roman Christian community in this period was severely divided. From the Roman historian Tacitus (*Annals* 15.44) and the second-century Christian writing of 1 *Clement* 5 we know that Nero blamed the Christians of Rome for the fire of 64 C.E. It is possible that the gospel's audience experienced martyrdom at the hands of the Roman religious and political officials, and was affected by apostasy from within its ranks. Many Christians denounced other Christians to the Roman authorities. In this social, political and religious climate of Rome, Christians' relationship with civil authorities and their genuine reception of apostates seeking reconciliation were two issues that needed addressing.

If Rome is the setting for the gospel, then this particular historical context would lend itself to explain further Mk's emphasis on inclusion as

---

[3] Rohrbaugh ("The Social Location") argues for a peasant class addressed by the gospel and presumes a location in rural Syria. He identifies the gospel's *real* audience with its *implied* audience. However, Rohrbaugh's presentation of Mk's social stratification, especially the urban elite, retainers, urban nonelite, degraded, unclean, and expendables (382–88) can arguably be presented in defense of an urban setting. See also Senior, "With Swords and Clubs," 13; W. A. Meeks, *The First Urban Christians: The Social World of the Apostle Paul* (New Haven, Conn.: Yale University Press, 1983); M. A. Beavis posits an educationally sophisticated, Greco-Roman audience for the gospel concomitant with an urban audience, in *Mark's Audience: The Literary and Social Setting of Mark 4:11-12* (Sheffield: JSOT Press, 1989); M. A. Tolbert, "Mark," *WBC,* 264; B. M. F. van Iersel, "Failed Followers in Mark: Mark 13:12 as a Key for the Identification of the Intended Readers," *CBQ* 58 (1996) 244–63; J. R. Donahue, "Windows and Mirrors: The Setting of Mark's Gospel," *CBQ* 57 (1995) 1–26. While I argue for an urban setting for Mark's gospel, this distinction between urban and rural settings cannot be drawn too tightly. Rather than arguing for the model of the ancient consumer-city which kept peasants barely subsistent, a more dynamic symbiosis between city and countryside is now acknowledged. This views ancient pre-industrial cities more like "service cities." See H. Moxnes, "He saw that the city was full of idols" (Acts 17:16): Visualizing the World of the First Christians, *Mighty Minorities? Minorities in Early Christianity—Positions and Strategies,* eds., D. Hellholm, H. Moxnes, and T. K. Sein (Oslo: Scandinavian University, 1995) 110–11. This symbiotic relationship could explain the peasant and village imagery in a gospel destined for urban auditors/readers. Wayne Meeks is unambiguous in his belief that Christianity was predominantly an urban movement in *The First Urban Christians* (New Haven, Conn.: Yale University Press, 1983) 11. Also, R. Stark, *The Rise of Christianity: A Sociologist Reconsiders History* (Princeton, N.J.: Princeton University Press, 1996) 129–62.

[4] If Rome was Mk's setting, then it would have been one of the largest cities in the ancient world, with a population by the end of the first century C.E. of 650,000. See R. Stark, *The Rise of Christianity,* 131.

an overarching theme and the prominence of the house in the narrative. This small, fragile group of Christians, treated as resident aliens and divided by disloyalty within its ranks, would strongly resonate with Mark's portrayal of a fragile, frightened, divided, and uncomprehending community of disciples. For these disciples the Christian community or "household" would have been in crisis. The evangelist would have seen renewing the vision of Jesus and rehabilitating his household as a priority.

The understanding of house/household in the ancient world is not that of the contemporary Westerner. Mark's readers knew how fundamental the household was in their world. It was the basic social unit and the source of societal life and recognition. A person's link with a particular household provided identity, support, community, protection, status, wealth, and honor. How important it was is further reflected in the literature of the period. However, a study of archaeology and the literary heritage of Greek and Roman writers enables us to gain insight into the value placed on the household by Mark's audience.

Mark's Architectural Setting

Archaeology has been helpful for revealing the kind of physical structures in which first-century Mediterranean Christians would have gathered.[5] Space is a revealer of social habits and, if interpreted correctly, can also indicate the social values that influenced the layout and design of a space or structure.[6] We are able to know something of the possible social interaction that might have happened between the wealthy and poor of the city. One of the limitations of archaeological research, however, is that it is not "gender noisy."[7] It does not reveal the gender activities specific to inhabitants of buildings and users of artifacts uncovered. First-century C.E. Roman household sites like Ostia, Pompeii, and Herculaneum can offer some kind of imaginative reconstruction of their physical features. But we must be cautious in extrapolating from them to a definition of the "typical" household

---

[5] Moxnes, "Visualizing," 109–10. A fine summary of Second Testament period household archaeology is offered in C. Osiek and D. L. Balch, *Families in the New Testament World: Households and House Churches* (Louisville, Ky.: Westminster John Knox Press, 1997) 5–35, who study excavations in Palestine, Syria, Italy, and Ephesus.

[6] K. A. Kamp, "Towards an Archaeology of Architecture: Clues from a Modern Syrian Village," *Journal of Anthropological Research* 49 (1993) 293–318; S. M. Foster, "Analysis of Spatial Patterns in Buildings (Access Analysis) as an Insight into the Social Structure: Examples from the Scottish Atlantic Iron Age," *Antiquity* 63 (1989) 40–51.

[7] C. Meyers, "Women and the Domestic Economy of Early Israel," *Women's Earliest Records: From Ancient Egypt and Western Asia. Proceedings of the Conference on Women in the Ancient Near East. Brown University, Providence, Rhode Island, November 5–7, 1987,* ed. B.S. Lesko (Atlanta, Ga.: Scholars Press, 1989) 273.

in which everyone lived.[8] This does not prevent us from investigating the major household building styles and reconstructing from their archaeology something of the values and interrelationships of their inhabitants.

The other caution we must bring to our use of archaeological information is that the focus of research has been on the wealthy and elite. Their artifacts have remained and have been the ones almost exclusively studied. However, the advantage of imaginatively extrapolating from Roman urban archaeological finds of places like Pompeii and Herculaneum is that the destruction caused by the eruption of Mt. Vesuvius in 79 C.E. was not limited to the dwellings of one social group. The whole population irrespective of social standing was affected. Archaeological study of these urban centers has not been conducted solely on the domestic dwellings of the wealthy. The living spaces of artisans, merchants and the poor have also been studied.[9]

Mediterranean Dwellings

There were six types of housing in the first-century Mediterranean region: simple, courtyard, big mansion, farmhouse, house with shop, and apartment-styled dwelling.[10] Five of these (simple, courtyard, big mansion, shop house, and apartment) are important for our reflection on the Gospel according to Mark. What I will be arguing below is that the simple and courtyard houses enable us to reflect on the Galilean, rural ministry of Jesus; the big mansion, shop house, and apartment dwellings are the domestic settings of Mark's urban audience. The occupants of the first two types of structures were disciples of Jesus. Though his ministry was primarily to the peasant community and those victimized by the economic structures imposed from the social hierarchy, Jesus' disciples were also

---

[8] The "burnt house" in the Herodian Quarter of Jerusalem and other excavations of elite dwellings are examples of how archaeology can help in the reconstruction of first-century C.E. households. These reconstructions reflect Jewish households in the wealthy upper part of the city of Jerusalem and therefore would be typical only of a minority of the population. N. Avigad, *The Herodian Quarter in Jerusalem: Wohl Archaeological Museum* (Jerusalem: Keter Publishing House, n.d.) presents the archaeological finds of the "burnt house" and the "Herodian Quarter in Jerusalem." These urban dwellings were the victims of the Roman destruction of Jerusalem in 70 C.E. and the archaeological remains can be accurately dated by coins found in the excavations. The reconstruction of the houses gives us an accurate picture of urban planning and life in the Upper City of Jerusalem, the residential area of the religious aristocracy of the Jewish people. These residences represent about 5 percent of the population at the time of Jesus, and do not offer us a picture of the life of the peasant majority.

[9] Moxnes, "Visualizing," 113.

[10] S. Guijarro, "The Family in First-Century Galilee," *Constructing Early Christian Families,* ed. H. Moxnes (London and New York: Routledge, 1997) 42–65.

from wealthier situations. This background was inherited by Mark's community and written into the gospel of a different time and culture. In our study of the big mansion, house shop and apartment dwelling, we move more obviously into Mark's era, geography, and urban location.

These three types of domestic structures are familiar to the Markan audience and, I would argue, are read back into Mark's Gospel of Jesus. An appreciation of these Roman domestic structures should illuminate our reading of the gospel. The only dwelling that is not discussed below is the farmhouse. This is not to say that it was not an important residential structure or a place of later Christian evangelization. But this kind of dwelling does not seem to be the focus or setting of Jesus' direct ministry or the usual residence of Mark's audience.

1. The simple house was the most common dwelling for peasants in agrarian communities. It was made of mud-brick, rock, or stone. Examples of rock and stone houses still survive (at Gamla, Meron, and Nazareth)[11] though examples of the most common and frequent construction (the mud-brick house) have not. Generally, the house was structured as a "four-room" house (though variations of "three-room" and "two-room" houses have also been found) with a main boardroom at its rear (Room 1, below) which probably served as the main sleeping and living quarters for the family.[12]

This structure varied and was expanded to accommodate family needs with the addition of the married son's family. Before such an expansion, the size of these houses was originally designed to accommodate a small family of approximately four to six people (mother, father, dependent children, slaves, or servants).[13] The house structure architecturally accommodated the "household"—all living beings that sheltered within it. This included not only what Westerners would call the nuclear family, but their dependents (slaves) and animals. The simple house structure architecturally also illustrates the close and intimate bonding that the peasant family would experience. The house would have been clustered with other houses from the same kinship or clan group, reflecting the patrilocal residential pattern of the extended family common in the ancient world.

The temporary nature of the mud-brick peasant houses also symbolizes something else about the world of their inhabitants. The house's impermanence and fragility typified the life of a peasant majority subject to the natural and economic factors that would have impinged on their world.[14] The

[11] Guijarro, "The Family," 50.

[12] J. S. Holladay, "House, Israelite," *ABD III,* 308–18.

[13] Ibid., 315.

[14] The estimated population of Jerusalem in the latter part of the first century C.E. varied from 25,000, to 82,500, to 220,000 in a total population of around two million. Ac-

peasants were victims of the elements. Good harvests, the essential commodity for the survival of the peasant family, depended on good rains. Grain was also an essential trading and taxation commodity. Without it the agrarian family was forced into debt. Members then needed to borrow from extended family members or other kinship members from the same village region. Taxation was the scourge of these people.

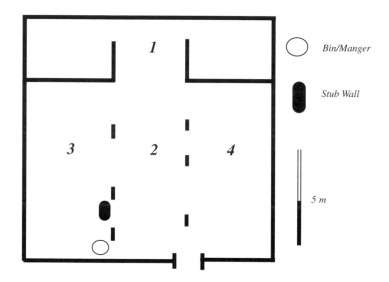

A floor plan of the "four-room" house typical of the peasant family in the ancient world modeled on an eighth-century B.C.E. house at Tel el-Far'ah about ten kilometers north east of Nablus on the Nablus-Tubas road.[15]

In first-century Palestine, as in all parts of the Mediterranean world, the land which produced the crops was the peasant's sign of wealth and status. Land had been inherited and kept within the family group for gen-

---

cording to Meeks (*The First Urban Christians,* 34) in the first century some five to six million Jews were living in Diaspora and the Jewish population in the Mediterranean cities was about 10 to 15 percent of a total population of a city. See Joachim Jeremias, "Die Einwohnerzahl Jerusalems zur Zeit Jesu," *Zeitschrift des Deutschen Palästina-Vereins* 66 (1943) 24–31; Magen Broshi, "La Population de l'Ancienne Jérusalem," *RB* 82 (1975) 5–14; L. H. Feldman, "How Much Hellenism in Jewish Palestine?" *Hebrew Union College Annual* (1986) 91. According to Guijarro, "The Family," 58, usual estimates place peasants at around 75 percent of the population.

¹⁵ After Holladay, "House," 311. See also E. Stern, ed., *The New Encyclopdedia of Archaeological Excavations in the Holy Land,* vol. 2 (New York: Simon & Schuster, 1993) 440.

erations. Barter and reciprocal kinship exchange were the primary economic practices among them. In the late first century a dramatic economic crisis developed, forced by the growth of a specialized market economy. This resulted in increased taxation and the burden of reshaping their ancient farming practice to incorporate the production of goods for the specialized market, not necessarily for their region.

This new market economy moved the base of economic power and decision-making more squarely into the hands of the elite, away from the rural sectors where the majority lived. Peasant families who were agrarian producers for centuries were unable to adapt to this newer form of economic strategy. They found themselves more and more unable to meet the economic demands placed on them. Mutual or reciprocal economic exchange, the basis of peasant life and honor among equals for centuries, was no longer seen by the elites as essential. Market forces dictated a new approach.[16]

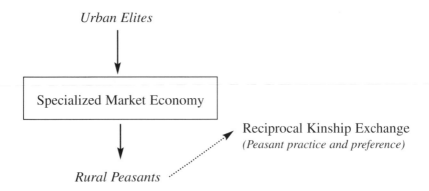

A specialized market economy propelled by the urban elite forces rural peasants into a form of economic practice to which they are unable to adjust and away from reciprocal kinship exchange, their ancient practice and preference.

As peasant families failed to adapt to changing manufacturing needs and a specialized economy they went into greater debt. To overcome debt peasants would borrow money either from their own clan members, if that was possible or, more commonly, from official money lenders using their

[16] There is a growing body of literature that supports this view. For example, H. Moxnes, "What is Family? Problems in constructing early Christian families," ed. H. Moxnes, *Constructing Early Christian Families: Family as Social Reality and Metaphor* (London and New York: Routledge, 1997) 25.

land and household property as guarantee. Most in this predicament were unable to get out of the debt trap and finally were forced to relinquish their farms. These were taken over by the urban elite as absentee landlords or patrons of moneylenders.

Some peasants from confiscated lands found that they could stay and work these properties, though most were forced to the urban centers in search of work. When these groups of estranged peasants were added to those who had no support from relatives or kin and to those regarded as socially unclean, degraded and expendable, it's not hard to imagine that a sizeable proportion of the population would have been homeless.[17] This final observation cannot be emphasized strongly enough. Along with the peasant majority, the homeless have little or no archaeological data that records their existence, social habits, or thoughts.

Jesus' Galilean message was first preached to the peasant community, the owners of simple houses, the homeless and the socially expendable. Debt-ridden peasants expelled from ancestral lands, overburdened by taxation and economic demands and victimized by a civil and religious elite minority from the major urban centers heard Jesus' message of a joyful and liberating God. In a culture in which religion was embedded with politics and economics, this message of God's renewed reign *(basileia)* was more than a theological one. It was a conviction that God was involved in and cared about their lives. This proclamation of the presence of God's *basileia* that echoed in the ministry of Jesus was heard with economic and social ears. In Jesus' community of disciples, the model of a renewed Israel, the peasant "household" was also renewed. In such a house where mutuality and inclusivity were the community's characteristics, the ancient practice of reciprocal kinship exchange was also encouraged. In this situation it would be easy to see how the religious and political leaders interpreted the Jesus movement as a social and economic threat.

The above analysis of the structure of the simple "four-room" house and the suggested interpretation of the economic and political factors that influenced the lives of the Mediterranean peasant majority is important for reading Mark's Gospel. By the time Mark comes to write, the cultural and social circumstances have altered from the original context of Jesus' message. The same message that Jesus preached, though, of God's liberation for an oppressed people, also needed to be echoed in Mark's Roman community. Mark translated Jesus' preaching to an urban setting. New cultural and economic concerns could also be addressed by Jesus' original vision and teaching. For Mark, what was needed was also a renewed household—the houses of Mark's community differed in style from those of Jesus' first disciples.

---

[17] Guijarro estimates 15 to 20 percent, "The Family," 58.

2. The courtyard house was a refinement of the simple house. As the family grew and expanded through the marriages of sons who incorporated wives and children into the patriarchal family structures, either the simple house was expanded to include the expanding family, or other houses were added and connected by a common courtyard. The courtyard house allowed several families from the same clan group to cluster together, to preserve their kinship bond and to support one another in solidarity, especially in cases of need. The structure also provided a better means for the clan to diversify in its production of goods. This meant that the families were geared more to surviving the changes of a specialized market economy that had plagued the residents of the simple mud-brick house. In the central, common courtyard domestic and agrarian duties were performed.

The courtyard house was typical in Palestine and Herodian-period houses and has been excavated at Dor, Bethsaida, and Caphernaum.[18] Though some courtyard-style houses are found in peasant communities, their majority are located in more well-to-do settings. A study of the size of courtyard houses from Bethsaida and Caphernaum,[19] and the implements found in them are indicators of the relative wealth of their occupants. At Bethsaida excavators found lead for weighting fishing nets, a needle and an anchor. Such finds would be expected in Bethsaida and Caphernaum which are both fishing villages. They also underscore the relative wealth of these families that relied on the fishing industry for income.

Unlike the peasant farmers who were subject to the marketing whims of the social elite, fishing families were supported by a more gainful resource. They were not the only owners of these courtyard houses. Those who benefited from the surplus of wealth and goods from the elite (called "retainers"), priests, military officers, landowners of modest means, and tax-collectors could conceivably be owners of the courtyard house. What characterizes all these people was their capacity to accumulate a little wealth from their industry. They were small in number,[20] not as powerful or wealthy as the elite upon whom they relied for their income, but capable of living a relatively comfortable life. That is, they lived above the level of bare subsistence experienced by the peasant community. This study of the courtyard house and its occupants is important for understanding the ministry of Jesus and reading Mark's Gospel.

---

[18] Ibid., 52.

[19] Ibid., 52–53; R. Arav and R. A. Freund, eds. *The Bethsaida Excavations Project Reports and Contextual studies* (Kirksville, Mo.: Thomas Jefferson University Press, 1995) (approximately between two hundred and three hundred square metres).

[20] Guijarro suggests around 9 percent of the population, "The Family," 58.

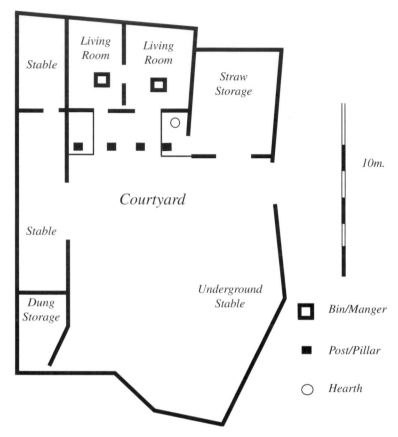

Floor plan of a peasant courtyard-styled house from Hasanabad in W. Iran for one or two families.[21]

As noted above, most of Jesus' followers came from the rural, peasant segment of Jewish society. But Jesus' community was not composed solely of the peasant poor. If there is any historical basis for the story of the calling of the first disciples, of Simon, Andrew, and the two sons of Zebedee (Mk 1:16-20; Mt 4:18-22; Lk 5:1-12) from their fishing cooperative to discipleship, then these four could well represent a more well-to-do wider group of disciples. The gospel image of them leaving behind their boats and nets, and two of them their immediate family, does suggest that a new, redefined family and "economic"[22] household waited. This does not mean, though, that they also left behind their business acumen with their fishing

[21] After Holladay, "House," 313.
[22] Throughout this book, the term "economic" is used in its specific and original sense. In the ancient, pre-industrial world, the household *(oikos/oikia)* was the place where the

nets on the boat. They would have had an ability to organize, recognize potential and create structures (households) that would bring about "success" (that would turn out to be different from what they had anticipated). These were some of the characteristics that made them leading disciples and foundational for the Twelve—a symbolic group representative of the widespread renewal that was to happen among the twelve tribes of Israel through the ministry of Jesus and the missionary activity of his disciples.[23] How these discipleship structures were to develop depended on the particular geographical and cultural situation in which the Gospel was preached.

In Mark's community a generation later the household design in the Roman world had been altered, architecturally determined by the population needs (and wealth) of the new situation. The three dwelling types that we will now investigate, the big mansion (or *domus*), tavern houses *(tabernae)* and the apartment-styled buildings of an *insulae,* retained something of the house designs we have already seen but had important distinguishing features. What this new Christian community had learnt from the story of Jesus was that the gospel was not exclusively for the poor. It could include and embrace all, including people from those higher up the social ladder. The fishing background of some of the Twelve and Jesus' residence in the courtyard-styled houses of Caphernaum confirm this.

3. The big mansion *(domus)* was the typical house of the elite in the Greco-Roman world. It was one of two types of housing that dominated the Roman urban landscape and was popular in Mark's day. Along with the house-apartment/shop, the *domus* could well be read back into Mark's story of Jesus. Several examples of the big mansion are found throughout the Mediterranean, in Israel, Syria, Turkey, Egypt, Greece, and Italy.[24] The archaeological house excavations at Pompeii and Herculaneum south of Rome are particularly enlightening for a domestic study of Mark's Gospel. They are from the same Mediterranean region as Mk, if we accept a Roman origin for the gospel, and date from approximately the same time.

---

family was nourished. The *oikos* was the place where practical and spiritual sustenance of the family took place. Using images drawn from our world, the household was the church, bank, factory, and school combined in one. In this material sense—seen as the manufacturing center where goods were produced and used for battering—what happened in the *oikos* was economically related. This required a particular form of administration for the household to function productively. The Greek word given to the art or skill of enabling the household to operate harmoniously and productively was *oikonomía),* the basis for the English word "economy."

[23] E. P. Sanders, *Jesus and Judaism* (London: SCM Press Ltd, 1985); R. Horsley, *Sociology and the Jesus Movement.* 2nd ed. (New York: Continuum, 1994).

[24] The literature on this is massive. Some pertinent texts include Osiek & Balch, *Families,* 11–24; Hasat Kitabevi, *Ancient Ruins of Turkey* (Ankara: Türk Tarihi Kurumu Bastmevi, 1985) 203–7, 370–82.

The chief characteristic of the *domus* was its central courtyard *(atrium)*, surrounded by rooms, eating and public gathering area, living and sleeping quarters. Under Greek influence, a peristyle courtyard was added which gave the building more space and elegance.[25] Originally one storey, in time a second storey was added which was associated with the dining area and given the name *cenacula*.[26]

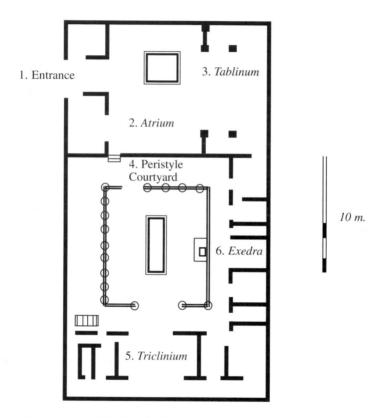

Plans of a domus *modelled on the House with the Mosaic Hall in Herculaneum. The entrance (1) leads into the* atrium *(2) with its impluvium for collecting water. To the top right is the* tablinum *(3), where the household head received visitors, stored documents, and studied. This adjoined the Greek-influenced peristyle courtyard (4) which was surrounded by sleeping quarters, the dining room* (triclinium-5) *and the* exedra *(6), an open room for relaxation and conversation.*[27]

[25] O. Seyffert, *The Dictionary of Classical Mythology, Religion, Literature, and Art* (New York: Gramercy Books, 1995) 309–10; Osiek and Balch, *Families,* chapter 1.

[26] Seyffert, *Dictionary,* 311.

[27] After A. Maiuri, *Herculaneum* (Rome: Istituto Poligrafico dello Stato, Libreria Dello Stato, 1977) 28.

There are five features about the Roman *domus* that are important for our reading of Mark's Gospel. First, the *domus* was the residence of wealthier families, and presumably some members of Mark's community were owners of such dwellings.[28] At the same time, it is important to point out the scholarly consensus that by the later half of the first-century C.E., there is no evidence of the existence of Christians from the highest and lowest levels of society.[29] This is not to say that they did not exist in fact. If any historical reliability can be attributed to the writings of Paul and the Acts of the Apostles, Christians were owners of houses in which other members met. This means that while Christians may not have been from the wealthiest of the elite group, there were some who had enough means to own houses large enough in which a significant number of co-religionists could gather. The style of architecture of these larger houses would have been along the lines of the big mansion. The other usual architectural space for Christian gatherings (and perhaps the most common) would have been the house-shop.

Second, the Roman house, unlike its Greek counterpart, was designed for welcoming the invited guest.[30] The Greek house was designed to protect privacy; the Roman house, on the contrary, for public display and a large group. People could enter into the *atrium,* be received in the *tablinum* and move into the courtyard. The only spaces designated as private were the sleeping and eating areas. Public use of the *domus* might explain one of the characteristics of Mark's house. As we shall see, the house envisaged in Mark's gospel is one that is open to public scrutiny and contestation from religious and political officials. Into this house the disenfranchised were welcome. Those who enter it have the invitation to become members of the

---

[28] Contra Meggitt, *Paul.* Meggitt's analysis of the overwhelming poor and homeless condition of Paul's audience (and even Paul himself) stems from a rereading of the biblical material from the perspective of extant inscriptions and Greek and Roman writers. He comes to suspect the "household" language and allusions of the Second Testament material.

[29] E. Judge, *The Social Patterns of the Christian Groups in the First Century: Some Prolegomena to the Study of the New Testament Ideas of Social Obligation* (London: Tyndale Press, 1960) was one of the first to critique the accepted position that Christians were from the lowest rung of society. See also J. G. Gager, *Kingdom and Community: The Social World of Early Christianity* (Englewood Cliffs, N.J.: Prentice-Hall Inc., 1975) 106–7; W. A. Meeks, *The First Urban Christians,* 51–52; B. Holmberg, *Sociology and the New Testament: An Appraisal* (Minneapolis: Fortress Press, 1990) 21–76; Osiek & Balch, *Families,* 96–102.

[30] See A. Wallace-Hadrill, *Houses and Society in Pompeii and Herculaneum* (Princeton, N.J.: Princeton University Press, 1994) 38–61, who offers a fine chapter on the way the articulation of the house reflected the social values of its occupants, the public nature of the house and the house as a center of commerce and activity. He also offers an analysis on the use of wall decoration as an indication of the function of the room. Form and decoration guide the "social flow" in the house.

household. Unlike the *domus* which is open to invited guests, Mark's household challenges the social conventions of status and expands the boundaries of those who are welcome.

Another aspect of the grand Roman mansion connected to its public nature concerns privacy. The construction of the house for public use did not rule out the possibility of the guest being invited into a great degree of privacy with the household head. This was symbolized by the part of the house in which social exchange occurred between guest and resident:

> The pattern of Roman social life, admitted numerous and subtle grades of relative privacy, in which it must be apparent, greater privacy represented not a descent but an ascent in privilege, an advance toward intimacy with the paterfamilias. . . . The *triclinium* will be private relative to the main circulation and open reception areas; yet the *cubiculum* is private relative to the *triclinium,* and this is a place not only for rest ("bedroom") but for the reception of intimate friends and the conducting of confidential business—and even for emperors conducting their notorious trials *intra cubiculum.*[31]

The degree of privacy as a sign of intimacy with the household head is reflected in Mark's gospel household. As we shall see, in the later part of the gospel, Jesus turns to instruct his disciples and the house becomes the setting in which this happens "in private." This privacy would undergird the intimacy that Jesus seeks with his disciples and their recognition of the privilege and honor they have in Jesus' eyes.

A fourth important feature of these houses was their size. The *domus* was designed to allow a large group of invited guests to gather and for a larger than nuclear family to be housed. Unlike the modern church building in today's parish, if the Roman *domus* was the envisaged gathering place for the Markan community, then the size of the gathering would be limited. A reasonable estimate of the numbers in each of Mark's household communities might be around fifty persons.[32] If this is the case, then it is feasible to conclude that the size of Mark's community would have been large, but not too large, perhaps three or four *domus*-house communities.

A final characteristic of the grand Roman house concerns the way the articulation of the *domus* reflected and reinforced the conventional social practice of patronage-brokerage. The entrance of the house led through into the *atrium* to the *tablinum* where the household-head received clients in the early mornings and late afternoons. Here the head would grant

---

[31] Wallace-Hadrill, *Houses and Society,* 17.

[32] J. Murphy-O'Connor, *St. Paul's Corinth: Texts and Archaeology* (Wilmington, Del.: Michael Glazier, 1983) argues for around fifty people in the average size *triclinium* and *atrium* (158). Also, Banks, *Paul's Idea of Community,* 40–50.

benefices to his clients who, in turn, would reciprocate with expressions of honor. The design of the house, the beauty of its murals and the gracefulness of its garden sculptures reflected the status of its occupants and the honour due to them. Mark employs a similar understanding in presenting the household of Jesus' disciples. Honor and status become motivating preoccupations of the disciples profoundly critiqued by Mark's Jesus.

4. The final two types of dwellings, houses with shops *(tabernae)* and apartment-style blocks of residences *(insulae),* were the most common dwellings in the Greco-Roman cities and possibly the most typical residences for Mark's audience.[33] These were the dwellings of non-elite people who represented about ninety percent of the urban population—artisans, city workers, retainers, and the poor. Often the apartment buildings were above or behind these shop houses.[34] In comparison to the *domus,* these two types of dwellings were small, overcrowded, noisy, and unhygienic.[35] While the occupants of the grand Roman house were catered for within their own dwelling, the poorer urban dwellers relied upon the public amenities of their street—fountains, shops, and latrines. The lack of urban sanitation and poor living conditions brought disease and contributed to the high incidence of mortality among infants and the failure of many adults to reach old age.[36]

Herculaneum, Pompeii, and Ostia provide many examples of these poorer dwellings. A study of the types of dwellings in Herculaneum and Pompeii reveals that the wealthier larger style *domus* of the city's wealthier citizens existed alongside the house-tavern and apartment dwellings of the poorer citizens. This pattern is consistent in both cities.[37] What distinguished the rich and poor, besides other obvious social characteristics, was the size and elegance of their dwellings. These reflected their status. The poor relied upon the public areas of the city; the elites were enhanced by their *domus.* While physically both groups lived side-by-side, the poor were socially unrecognized and silent, the elite honored and eloquent.[38]

There is one section of the Herculaneum excavations that is worthy of closer scrutiny, especially for the way it provides us with the possibility of an imaginative reconstruction of Mark's community.

---

[33] See Banks, *Going to Church;* Banks, *Paul's Idea of Community.* Murphy-O'Connor, "Prisca and Aquila," who argue for a *taverna* setting for Christian gatherings in Rome.

[34] Guijarro, "The Family," 55. Osiek and Balch, *Families,* 31.

[35] For a helpful reflection on the overcrowded nature and chaos typical of the Roman city, see Stark, *The Rise of Christianity,* 147–62.

[36] Osiek and Balch, *Families,* 32.

[37] A. Wallace-Hadrill, "Houses and Households: Sampling Pompeii and Herculaneum," *Marriage, Divorce and Children in Ancient Rome* (Oxford: Clarendon Press, 1991) 204.

[38] Wallace-Haddrill, *Houses and Society,* 13–14.

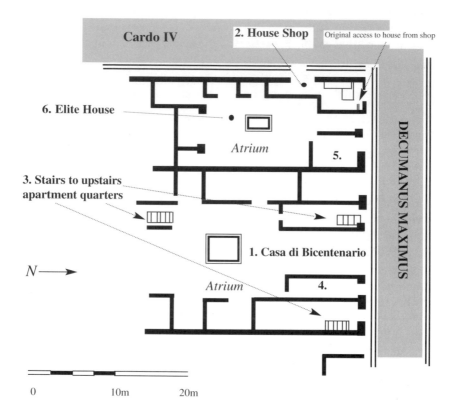

Part of a plan of Insula V, *a northern section of the Herculaneum excavations on the De-*
cumanus Maximus.[39] *Three types of dwellings coexist, reflecting the three major housing*
styles discussed—(1) the mansion house (named by excavators as the Casa di Bicentenario), *(2) the house-shop* (taverna) *and the apartment houses. Access to these apart-*
ments is provided by three sets of stairs (3). Originally the structures were part of the
large Casa domus *that was gradually altered and reduced to accommodate more people*
and create shops as the population increased and for economic reasons. At least one of
the rooms (4) at the entrance to the Casa, *and one (5) at the entrance of the elite house*
were altered for commercial reasons. The apartment dwellings were in a second storey
above the tavern and Casa. *A fourth house of a wealthier family (6) is located between*
the Casa *and the house shop. Entry from the shop to this "elite house" is marked.*

Herculaneum was an agricultural and fishing city, given its strategic position near the fertile volcanic slopes of Mt. Vesuvius and on the Naples gulf
coast. It was also the town to which many Roman officers retired. Its popu-

[39] After Maiuri, *Herculaneum,* 2.

lation was economically mixed, with some relatively wealthy families of the Roman elite, and others who were artisans, merchants, fishing people and day laborers. Like Pompeii, Herculaneum was the victim of a series of earthquakes in the first century C.E. In the midst of its restoration after one such earthquake (in 62 C.E.), Herculaneum was finally destroyed by the eruption of Vesuvius in 79 C.E., around the time or not long after Mark's Gospel was penned. The mud-lava that flowed from the crater submerged the whole city, encasing and freezing it in time. The excavations which began in the mid-eighteenth century have revealed a Roman city of the first century, the lifestyle of its habitants, and the kinds of houses that they occupied.

In the northern part of the excavations, where the major road leading to the Forum *(Decumanus Maximus)* is met by a north-south road *(Cardo IV)*, in the north-west corner of *Insula V*, lay a series of dwellings and shops. The area is typical of Herculaneum—a Roman *domus (Casa di Bicentenario)* is situated next to a smaller house owned by a well-off family and joined to a corner shop. Stairways lead to upper-level apartment houses. The two-storey structures and the variety of dwellings at this street corner reflect the way that the wealthier and less prosperous lived side-by-side, a common feature in Greco-Roman cities. There is an access from the shop to the smaller *domus* which once connected by a passage way to the larger *Casa*. These connections suggest that the *Casa di Bicentenario* dominated the area but was altered to provide more dwellings and incorporate at least three shops. This might have happened when the dwelling changed hands and parts of the building were converted into rented lodgings. This corner section of the Herculaneum excavation reflects the economic and residential interests of its population. It also illustrates a close-knit, Roman city populace that was a mixture of backgrounds and wealth. The domestic architecture caused the wealthier and less prosperous to intermingle—albeit along the lines of Roman protocol. The well-to-do lived in the two grander and more spacious houses; the artisans and merchants crowded into the three shop houses and several apartments positioned around and above the two *domus*.

This excavated section of Herculaneum is an excellent illustration of the kind of residential complex in which Mark's Gospel audience lived. Elite and non-elite Christians would have gathered in this kind of setting, probably in the *domus* that could take their numbers.

There is something else about the *Casa di Bicentenario* that is noteworthy. In the last years before the eruption of Vesuvius, it seems that the original owners abandoned the building, and its upstairs rooms were converted into rented apartments and humble living quarters. In one of these upstairs rooms and facing its entrance, excavators found the impression of a cross, originally of wood, in a stuccoed panel that seemed surrounded by a supported wooden frame. Beneath the cross stood a cupboard like a wooden shrine with a kneeler or footstool.[40]

The meaning of the find is not clear. However, if the cross is the Christian symbol popularized in the second and third centuries and the cupboard a *prie-dieu,* then the dwelling was also a place for prayer and worship. This might be the first evidence we have of the "apartment church" and the remains of the earliest known Christian symbol, dated to 79 C.E. Whether they are or not, their possibility raises a further point. Christians did not seem to be any different from the rest of the urban population. Apart from this one example, disputed as it might be, there are no other signs of Christian art or iconography from this period. In other words, Mark's community were probably no different from the rest of the people among whom they lived. They gathered in apartments or the larger houses to celebrate their communion with Jesus in the Lord's Supper and remembered the stories of his teaching, preaching, and healings. They had no special buildings in which they gathered. They were regular city dwellers of the Roman city and their congregation mirrored its social and economic mix—the kind of mix imaginatively reconstructed from the ruins of Herculaneum.

Summary

The study of these five styles of houses in the Mediterranean world has enabled us to reflect on the kinds of people who originally gathered around Jesus in Galilee and formed the community addressed by Mark's Gospel a generation later. I have looked at the architecture and construction of these houses as a way of reconstructing the social context and values of the various groups of disciples who were influenced by the story of Jesus—first in Israel and then later in Italy. Each of the house structures shows us how people interacted with each other and what was important for their living together. This has emerged from a conviction that archaeology and ancient domestic architecture are never "silent." They do speak to us about what was important and valued by ancient people.

The insights from the simple and courtyard house have been used as a way of understanding the creative and challenging ministry of Jesus in Galilee among peasants when market forces were splitting up families, creating a loss of home and security. In this economic and social mess, the rural peasants felt a sense of divine abandonment. Jesus' preaching and

[40] Maiuri, *Herculaneum,* 45–47; G. Giubelli, *Herculaneum* (Naples: Carcavallo, 1995) 28–29.

healing reminded these people that God's *basileia* was present and active among them. They were not abandoned and they were being invited to gather as members of a renewed house of disciples.

The study of the big mansion, the *domus,* the shop, and apartment-styled dwellings moved us firmly to another era and into the Greco-Roman world. The similarities and differences of these Roman houses highlighted the importance of the Greco-Roman conventional values of honor and status and the complexity of the urban setting. The style of these houses, the kind of public and private interaction that surrounded them, and the aspects of public life connected to these urban structures and settings (like health and longevity) caution the contemporary Western reader of Mark's Gospel. We have to read this gospel from the perspective of a first-century Mediterranean city dweller, with an appreciation of its domestic architecture and the social values inscribed in it. This study of the domestic Mediterranean world also alerts us to reading Mark's gospel with an awareness of the various social groups that are narrated. Just as one house style was not used by all—for various economic and social reasons—so too, not one socio-economic group is reflected in Mark's story world. A careful reading of the gospel requires sensitivity to this social diversity.

A study of archaeology and the domestic architecture of the ancient Mediterranean world is not the only way to come to an appreciation of the Greco-Roman household presumed by Mark. This study is filled out by the literature from Greek and Roman writers.

3

The "House" in the Greek World

A focus on ancient domestic architecture provides one piece of information for understanding the importance of the house in Mark's world. The evangelist's Greco-Roman audience would have also been shaped in their appreciation and understanding of the house by a literary and philosophical heritage from Greek and Roman writers and philosophers—a heritage that stretched back to the sixth-century B.C.E. and a Greek philosophical tradition inspired by Pythagoras.

Two methodological caveats must be first acknowledged that indicate the limitations of any literary study from Greek and Roman writers. The first concerns the gender bias of such writing. Males are the authors of ancient literature (in the form of plays, treatises, dialogues, histories, poems, and inscriptions). Except for a few poems and sepulchral inscriptions in Rome, male perspectives and concerns stamp the literature. We have no direct access to what women think. The literature does not reflect their interests. This recognition of the gender bias of the literature is not a moral evaluation of the literature. It is simply a recognition of its limitation.[1]

A second issue in the study of documents for deriving insight is the social specificity of documents, literature, and extant inscriptions. Most extant Greco-Roman writings are from the social elite; the elite remained their interest group. As a result we have little material on the general population and

---

[1] For example, there are frequent lists of the qualities which were considered important for women, but there is no such similar list written by women for men, see J.A.R. Shelton, *As the Romans Did: A Source Book in Roman Social History* (New York: Oxford University Press, 1988) 45. The most frequent situation when women are the subject of literature comes from sepulchral inscriptions. These inscriptions are helpful for offering us a glimpse at the social world of Roman men *and* women and the values considered important. These values, though, were shaped by a standard formula of virtues available and from which the inscriptions were written. This colors the possible uniqueness of such inscriptions, even when they are about women.

still less specifically focused on the marginalized and poorer groups of the Greco-Roman world. The next two chapters will offer us insight into how some elite Greek and Romans regarded the household. Arguably they show us how at least some in Mark's community appreciated the household and its structures—that is, if we hold that the majority of the gospel audience were from the middle stratum of Roman society, and few from the upper-most and lowest strata.

Given these two limitations, what does emerge is the way that Greek and Roman writers considered the household and the relationships of the family. What they present are the boundaries and ideals of the household that all in society were expected to emulate, irrespective of social stand-ing. Whatever people's economic background or concrete household situation, this conventional wisdom would have influenced the way people sought to realize the function, management, and authority structure of the household. I shall argue later on that Mark's audience inherited this con-ventional domestic wisdom. It was also presented with an alternative style of household relations influenced by the story of Jesus and the first dis-ciples. This alternative created social conflict with those who held to the dominant Greco-Roman domestic conventions of order and subordination. However, it found support from themes of mutuality and partnership subtly present in the Greco-Roman literary tradition.

The great philosophical quest among the Greeks was for wisdom. They considered wisdom the key to happiness and the glue of society. One of the earliest exponents of how wisdom and happiness could be attained was Pythagoras (born ca. 570 B.C.E.). He developed a philosophical tradi-tion that laid the foundation for others, especially Plato and Aristotle, in their consideration of the Greek household.[2] A brief study of these three influential Greek philosophers provides further insight into how house-holds were regarded in Mark's Greco-Roman world.

---

[2] None of Pythagoras' writings survive. Most of his tenets are gleaned from the writ-ings of his biographers Iamblichus (ca. 240–325 C.E.) and Diogenes Laertius (ca. 400–325 B.C.E.). Diogenes Laertius' biography of Pythagoras in *Lives and Opinions of Eminent Philosophers Book VIII* also summarizes the work of early biographers of Pythagoras. Dio-genes also discusses whether Pythagoras left behind any writings in *Lives*, VIII: 6–11. On Diogenes Laertius see A. J. Malherbe, ed., *Moral Exhortation, A Greco-Roman Sourcebook* (Philadelphia: Westminster Press, 1986) 31–32; K. S. Guthrie, ed., *The Pythagorean Sourcebook and Library: An Anthology of Ancient Writings which relate to Pythagoras and Pythagorean Philosophy* (Grand Rapids, Mich.: Phanes Press, 1987). S. Treggiari, *Roman Marriage: Iusti Coniuges from the Time of Cicero to the Time of Ulpian* (Oxford: Oxford University Press, 1991) 200–1.

Pythagoras: The "Happy" Household

The foundation of Pythagoras' philosophy was his consideration of Number. He regarded this as the universal principle and foundation of everything, embracing the whole world.[3] Every human being was its miniature replica. Pythagoras gave the name "cosmos" to the universe revealed by Number because the world was "ordered"—or in Greek, *kosmiótês*, the same root word for *kosmos*. The language of "cosmos" and "order" underscored the divinely intended harmony observable in the universe and self-evident through contemplation. Such contemplation was the aim of the philosophical life, the goal of every educational and social institution—including the household. Or, as Pythagoras' biographer puts it, ". . . the purest and most genuine character is the one devoted to the contemplation of the most beautiful things."[4]

The search for inner harmony through a contemplative style of life was not intended to keep a person locked in pure speculation shut off from the world. It was intended to spill over into action, into the way a person lived in society and "become the citizen of a well-governed state."[5] Unfortunately, Pythagoras did not translate his insights into a fully developed political and domestic written code of ethics. This was undertaken later by Plato and Aristotle. However we do have some insight into how Pythagoras understood the function of the household, which comes to us sifted through the interests of one of his biographers, Diogenes.

Diogenes made two interesting comments about two members of Pythagoras' household. These comments may be the only evidence we have of how Pythagoras lived in his own house, in a way radical for its day. They also remind us that while there might have existed defined lines of authority and subservience typical of the culture of the day, other more egalitarian domestic themes were possible. These were in tension with the dominant cultural expectations. Diogenes' first comments concerns Pythagoras' desire to bequeath his writings to his daughter.

In the beginning of his biography on Pythagoras, Diogenes spends a great deal of space disproving those who insist "absurdly enough" that Pythagoras left no writings.[6] This comment "absurdly enough," serves only to reinforce in the mind of the reader the credibility of the contrary argument which Diogenes is contesting. What is more interesting is Diogenes' reason that some argue that Pythagoras left behind no writings. According

[3] Guthrie, *The Pythagorean Sourcebook*, 20–21.
[4] Iamblichus, *Life of Pythagoras*, chapter 12.
[5] Diogenes Laertius, *Lives*, Bk VIII, 8.
[6] *Lives*, Bk VIII, 6–11.

to him, Pythagoras bequeathed his writings to his daughter Damo and asked her to promise that she would never show them to anyone outside the household.[7] Pythagoras also had a son called Telauges and, in Greek law, the primary beneficiary of any inheritance (including any writings). Pythagoras' preference for his daughter as the recipient of his writings would have been unusual in a culture which favored sons over daughters.

There is a second comment that Diogenes offers that reinforces the image of Pythagoras' enlightened and "egalitarian" household. Diogenes comments that Pythagoras' wife Theano was literate ("Telauges wrote nothing, so far as we know, but his mother Theano wrote a few things") and able to give advice about marriage and the relationship between husband and wife.[8] This is all the more revealing given the general scholarly consensus that education was generally the privilege of males and women were confined to the inner household and never permitted to philosophize in public, especially on matters as intimate as the union between husband and wife.[9]

Diogenes' two comments about the female members of Pythagoras' household are important. They are the only reflections we have of the practical implications of Pythagoras' philosophy spelt out in his household. More startlingly, they reveal—at least from Diogenes' point of view—that the women of Pythagoras' household were independent, intelligent, and educated. One was entrusted with Pythagoras' memoirs, presumably because she could read and value them; the other was literate and could write (unlike Pythagoras' son who was expected to be the more educated). Diogenes describes both as lettered and that was apparently unusual for Greek women, even of elite households, in the sixth-century B.C.E. To Diogenes, Theano and Damo were tangible evidence of the fruit of Pythagoras' philosophy and lived in a "happy" household.

Plato: The "Subordinated" Household

Like his predecessor, Plato (428–328 B.C.E.) considered the importance of harmony and the soul's need for contemplation. Unlike Pythagoras, he developed these into an explicit political and domestic philosophy. Plato argued, like Pythagoras, that order was at the heart of the universe. But he considered that this order found in the universe and reflected in society (and, one could say, households) was unattainable without the key social virtues of communion, friendship, justice, and temperance. In his important work *Gorgias*, Plato wrote that

[7] *Lives*, Bk VIII, 43.
[8] *Lives*, Bk VIII, 43.
[9] Sarah Pomeroy, *Goddesses, Whores, Wives, and Slaves: Women in Classical Antiquity* (New York: Shocken, 1975) especially chs. 4 and 5.

where there is no communion, there can be no friendship. And the wise tell us that heaven and earth and gods and humans are held together by communion and friendship, by orderliness *(kosmiótês)*, temperance and justice; and this is the reason, my friend, why they call the whole world by the name of order *(kosmos)*, not of disorder *(ákosmia)* or dissoluteness.[10]

These two sentences are an important summary of Plato's ethical and political views. Happiness, in the context of Plato's *Gorgias*, was the fruit of friendship which came from human and divine communion. Though Plato maintained a dualism typical of the Greek cosmology of his day that separated the created world from that of the gods, the penetration of the divine world into the human was possible. But it required the cultivation of social and community virtues. The structure of the sentence above rhetorically demonstrates the very point which Plato was arguing. The hinge of the sentence is "orderliness," which depended on the presence within a society of communion and friendship, temperance and justice. All this had implications for households in which orderliness was essential. In a dialogue between Socrates and Callides, Plato reminded his audience ". . . if regularity and order are found in a house, it will be a good one, and if irregularity, a bad one."[11]

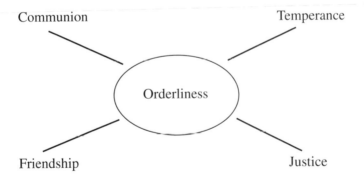

Significantly, Plato further explored how this orderliness might be achieved in households. Here we come to one of the most influential aspects of Plato's thinking that retained its impact into the first-century C.E. and on the writers of the Second Testament. Plato emphasized the role of the intellect in the quest for the ideal—whether that be truth, beauty, goodness, or order. By leaving behind the world of sensory objects which were

[10] *Gorgias,* 507d.
[11] *Gorgias,* 504a.

a shadowy reflection of the transcendent realm and moving through to the higher, purer forms of knowing represented in the intellect, a person could come to the transcendent ideal forms. Although Plato did not discard the sensual world of human experience, it was inferior to the world of ideas that came through the intellect and to which everything else was directed. Plato's predilection for the intellect removed from the encumbrances of the senses was expressed most dramatically through this question posed to Socrates in the *Symposium*:

> But tell me, what would happen if one of you had the fortune to look upon essential beauty entire, pure and unalloyed, not infected with the flesh and color of humanity, and ever so much more of mortal trash?[12]

Only through the intellect, freed of the infection of humanity and "mortal trash," could the ideal form "beauty" be contemplated and enjoyed. In the light of this, social and household order must be determined by laws prescribed by reason. Plato's logic was crystal clear: the capacity for reason to contemplate eternal truth was a reflection and gift of the gods. This gift was also present in its formulation of those laws which govern how order was to be determined within households and the city-state. Because these laws were derived from reason they were imbued with the same divine quality in which reason shared. Laws therefore demanded obedience.

When Plato applied his theory of knowing to human affairs, especially to the structure and maintenance of households, the cognitive hierarchy was translated into human terms. Hierarchy was seen as the logical structure which allowed the perpetuity of a divinely determined "order" in households. Hierarchy could not exist without subordination. So in households there was to be hierarchy and subordination for the achievement of order. According to Plato, who ruled and was ruled in the household was determined by nature. The superior was to rule over the inferior, the more perfect over the less perfect. In practice, this meant that males were the authoritative household heads. To them wives, children, and slaves were to give their obedience.

There is a final unfortunate opinion that Plato had about women that flowed from his conviction of male superiority. In Plato's anthropology, males represented the original state of perfection; the defective sign of degeneration that annihilated perfection was found in females. And "since human nature is two-fold, the superior sex is that which hereafter should be designated 'man' but those who have failed therein shall be changed into woman nature at the second birth."[13] Plato portrayed women as superfluous,

---

[12] *Symposium*, 212a.
[13] *Timaeus*, 42b.

or at least secondary in the act of reproduction in which "the female bears and the male begets."[14] Women were responsible for evil and distress and, in some cases, were the reincarnated bodies of men who behaved cowardly:

> According to the probable account, all those creatures generated as men who proved themselves cowardly and spent their lives in wrongdoing were transformed, at their second incarnation, into women.[15]

This last comment painfully illustrates the essential difference Plato saw between men and women reinforced in the Greek household. It further illustrates the unfortunate and inevitable conclusion of a philosophy in which human reason was invested with ultimate (and divine) authority. His presentation of family and the household was consistent with his epistemological logic of hierarchy and subordination. The male's unquestioned authority and the subordination of wife, children, and slaves to this authority were the pragmatic ways by which household order was to be maintained and happiness achieved. The implications of Plato's divinization of reason expressed by a household "orderliness" that relied on the subordination of one over another continued to have its impact well into the Christian era on some Second Testament writers. On the other hand, Mark's gospel presentation of the renewed household of disciples offered an implicit critique of this Platonic household and the one that was to be encouraged by Aristotle.

Aristotle: the "Partnered," "Mutual" but "Subordinated" Household

Aristotle (384–322 B.C.E.) built on Plato's thinking and explicated further the nature and function of the household and its relationship to the city-state. This evolved into a fully developed domestic philosophy. Part of the reason for this evolution was the effect which one of Aristotle's pupils had on the course of history. The Mediterranean conquest by Alexander the Great (356–323 B.C.E.) stamped Greek culture and philosophy—including that of Aristotle—on the Middle East. This effect was still obvious approximately three centuries later in the world of Jesus, his first followers, and the Christian movement that sprang from the Mediterranean soil and spread into Asia Minor, Greece, Africa, and Italy, and into the world inhabited by Mark's audience.

Like Plato, Aristotle was concerned about happiness, the political structures necessary to nurture it, and the kinds of human virtues in which people must be educated to achieve happiness. The basis of his reflections on these

---

[14] *The Republic*, Bk V, 454d.
[15] *Timaeus*, 90e–91a.

deep philosophical issues was his understanding of the human person. He defined the human person as a "political animal"[16] who needed the support of the city-state *(polis)* and at the local level, households. The nature of these organizational or political structures was expressed by what Aristotle called "partnership" *(koinônía)*. "Partnership" was the foundation of Greece's political system. As he wrote in the opening lines of his major work *Politics*:

> Every city-state *(polis)* is as we see a sort of partnership *(koinônía)*, and every partnership is formed with a view to some good (since all the actions of everyone are done with a view to what they think to be good). It is therefore evident that, while all partnerships aim at some good, the partnership that is most supreme of all and includes all the others does so most of all, and aims at the most supreme of all goods; and this is the partnership entitled the city-state *(polis)*, the political partnership.[17]

A careful reading of this text indicates the pervasiveness of the term "partnership" *(koinônía)*. In Aristotle's political philosophy *koinônía* was a form of collective harmony that looked towards the good or welfare of those who formed the city-state. Every social institution, including the household, was to be infused with it.

A considerable section of Book I of Aristotle's *Politics* is taken up with a discussion about the household under the heading "household management" *(oikonomía)*. In it he reinforces the importance of *koinônía*. While Plato (and his predecessor Pythagoras) regarded "orderliness" as central for people coming to happiness, for Aristotle it was *koinônía*. "Partnership" rather than "orderliness" was the basis of so much in the city-state; it was key for understanding a whole range of political alliances and associations that could exist in a society, from the all-encompassing city-state to the individual or basic units (households and families) that constituted it. In his preference for "partnership" Aristotle did not dispense with the hierarchical perspective inherited from Plato. The city-state was composed of villages made of households; within each there existed relationships and authority structures so that "the good life" could be enjoyed. The "good life" was a consequence of *koinônía*. More significantly, the basis for *koinônía* to form an association within society was found within the very nature of the human person. It was a natural impulse or urge.

Therefore the impulse to form a *koinônía* of this kind is present in all people by nature; but the one who first united people in such a *koinônía* was the greatest of benefactors.[18]

---

[16] *Politics*, I.1.9.
[17] *Politics*, I.1.1.
[18] *Politics*, I.1.12.

Here we also see the reason for Aristotle's definition of the human person as "a political animal." The natural tendency or "impulse" to be in *koinônía* with others led people to form associations—first the primary association of men and women, which created households, then the clustering of these households into villages, finally the gathering of villages which formed the city-state. The city-state was the fullest and most perfect expression of the minor alliances and associations. For Aristotle this was the political entity that best enabled human beings to experience the "good life."

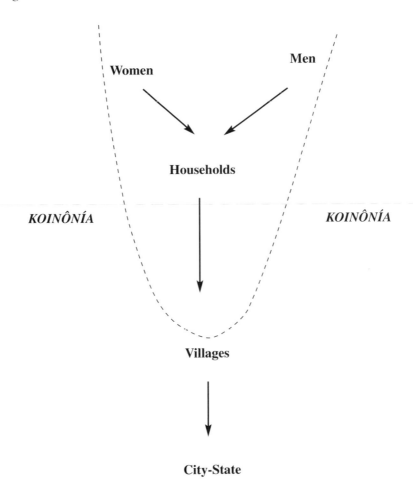

Aristotle's understanding of the relationship of the major social institutions bound together through koinônía. *The household is the primary and basic association; the city-state, the most perfect form.*

Aristotle further explored the nature of the relationship between the household and the city-state in a section of *Politics* entitled "household management" *(oikonomía)*. Here he reasoned that as the city-state could be divided into its various component parts, a similar division could be considered in the management of the household. In this domestic division, Aristotle distinguished three kinds of relationships:

> Household management *(oikonomía)* falls into departments corresponding to the parts of which the household in its turn is composed the primary and smallest parts of the household are master and slave, husband and wife, father and children. We ought, therefore, to examine the proper constitution and character of each of these three relationships, I mean that of mastership, that of marriage—there is no exact term denoting the relation uniting wife and husband—and thirdly the progentitive relationship—this too has not been designated by a special name.[19]

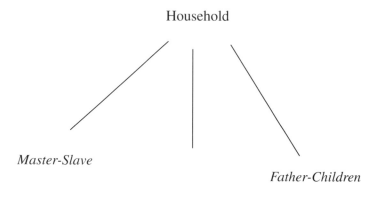

Household

Master-Slave

Father-Children

Husband-Wife

There are several things worth noting in this statement. These reflect the style of life of the Greek household which influenced the Greco-Roman world of the first century C.E.:

- The discussion is concerned about "household management," *oikonomía* in Greek which is related to the English word for "economics." The expression is used in a functional sense and linked to the actual running of the household. However it is also concerned with the relationships essential to the household. Aristotle is con-

[19] *Politics*, I.2.1-2.

cerned with both the practical and relational aspects of the household. Second Testament writers focused on the relational dimension of the Christian household.

- The household includes the natural family unit (husband, wife, and children) and the house slaves. This means that slaves were considered intrinsic in a household that generally excluded members of the wider family.[20] Slaves were part of the Greco-Roman household of the first century and were also members of Second Testament Christian households.

- Aristotle's discussion about household management flows out of his previous reflection on the city-state. He investigates each discrete unit of the household and considers in turn its three fundamental relationships: master and slave; husband and wife; father and children. These three relationships dominate subsequent descriptions of households which are eventually fashioned into a household "code" of conduct and are presumed by Second Testament writers.

- There is a set order in the discussion of the relationships. The first to receive attention is that between master and slave. This is the one that is said to express the household "in its perfect form."[21] This perfection probably stems from the way that Greek society was divided into the free and slave. If the association between master and slave was secure then the protection of the household and the city-state could also be assured. The relationships between husband and wife, and parents and children flow on naturally from this first relationship guaranteeing household protection and security. In the Second Testament the relationship between the one considered "free" and those regarded "slaves" is reflected upon. The way this is discussed, particularly in Mark's Gospel upsets the conventional expectations of leadership, control, and service.

- Aristotle recognizes that there is no set language for the marriage relationship. Perhaps this mirrors the cultural perception that at marriage the wife became part of the groom's family. Rather than

[20] This point was previously made by Plato when he recommended that after the marriage ceremony, the son (with his wife) leave the family home and live, as it were, in "exile" (". . . the married pair must leave their own houses to their parents and the bride's relations, and act themselves as if they had gone off to a colony, visiting and being visited in their home, begetting and rearing children, and so handing on life, like a torch, from one generation to another, and ever worshipping the gods as the laws direct" —*Laws*, Bk VI, 776b.)

[21] *Politics*, I.ii. 1.

seeing a completely new family or household coming into existence, the lack of a language suggests that the moment of what could be called marital cohabitation was regarded more of an expansion of the groom's family. This also reflected the preference for the patrilineal relationship through the absorption of the wife into the husband's family.[22] The world of the Second Testament is also androcentric and patriarchal with the household's focus on the male head. However, Mark's presentation overturns the traditional lines of authority in the Christian household.

- A similar difficulty of description applies to the "progenitive relationship." Aristotle's acknowledgement of this problem of language betrays a recognition that the relationship between husband and wife was more than simply a generative, purely functional production of children for the city-state. Their relationship was more dynamic and nurturing for the education of children in the regulated household.

All these points derived from Aristotle's presentation of household management in *Politics* also summarize the central features of the Greek household: it was a functional institution that involved three sets of patriarchal relationships (master-slave, husband-wife, father-children). Like Plato, Aristotle used anthropology to validate this androcentric hierarchy. He argued that the difference between men and women was physical and essential. Difference was at the essence of being human. Aristotle argued that some people by their nature were made to rule (masters, husbands, males, fathers); others to be ruled and dominated (slaves, wives, women, and children). Men and women possessed virtue, temperance, courage, and justice. However, the quality of their possession differed according to each gender's nature that reinforced the natural hierarchy of power and subordination. "The male is by nature superior," wrote Aristotle, "and the female inferior, the male ruler and the female subject."[23] Aristotle further contended that the male was intellectually and physically superior.[24]

Aristotle's contention about the superiority of the male and the subordination of the slaves, women and children in the household is not surprising. It follows logically from the groundwork already laid by his former teacher Plato, and it builds on an anthropology that presumes the

---

[22] P. S. Pantel, ed., *A History of Women in the West,* Vol. 1, *From Ancient Goddesses to Christian Saints* (Cambridge, Mass.: The Belknap Press of Harvard University Press, 1992) 250–52.

[23] *Politics,* I.ii.12.

[24] *Generation of Animals,* 716a; 775a. See also *Politics* I. V. 8; VII, xiv, 4.

inferiority of certain people in the city-state. What is surprising is a second aspect that Aristotle presents about nature of the relationships of those in the household. Aristotle raises the possibility of equality and mutuality characterizing relationships in the household. These are in tension with the dominant submissive theme that we have already seen.

Aristotle derived this theme of household mutuality from a consideration of the governance of the city-state. This governance was of two types, according to Aristotle. The first was "monarchical" in which there was only one ruler who exercised authority of the ruled; the second was "republican." This was the exercise of political power that respected the freedom of people and different from the authority of the master over the slave.[25] The first was appropriate between father and children;[26] the second between husband and wife:

> It is true that in most cases of republican government the ruler and the ruled interchange in turn (for they tend to be on an equal level in their nature and to have no difference at all) the male stands in this relationship to the female continuously.[27]

In acknowledging this "republican" relationship his language shifts from the hierarchical, unilateral description of the master's control over the slave to a more interactive, almost egalitarian description of what occurs between husband and wife. The shift indicates Aristotle's desire to resolve one of the tensions inherent in his political philosophy: At the beginning of *Politics*, Aristotle identified the "partnership" *(koinônía)* as the basis of every institution. The identification of two types of government or authority (monarchical and republican) allowed partnership to co-exist in a society that presumed slavery as a fact and necessity, and it supported the familial household relationship between husband, wife, and children.

In household government, interchange between husband and wife was based on their natures being "on an equal level." This equality did not stem from the exercise of power—"for the male is by nature better fitted to command than the female."[28] It originated rather from a mutual commitment to be in "partnership," the capacity of both to realize this partnership and to make the household a reflection of the partnership needed in the city-state. Aristotle argued that this mutual and reciprocal

[25] *Politics*, I, ii. 22.
[26] The "monarchical" relationship between father and children does not rule out the possibility of affection. As Aristotle states in *Politics*, I. v. 2, ". . . the rule of the father over the children . . . is that of a king; for the male parent is the ruler in virtue both of affection *(philiá)* and seniority, which is characteristic of royal government."
[27] *Politics*, I. v, 2.
[28] *Politics*, I. v, 2.

relationship between husband and wife preserved and enhanced the city-state.[29] Such a relationship was enhanced by a bond of affection and a "friendship" based on a "natural instinct."[30] For, "friendship *(philiá)* is the greatest of blessings for the city-state."[31] In other words, while the household had clear lines of authority stemming from the male head, Aristotle argued in his domestic philosophy for the necessity of a more mutual relationship between husbands and wives expressed through affection and friendship.

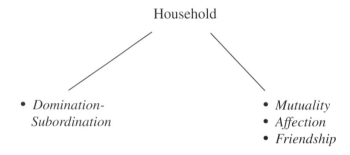

Household

- *Domination-Subordination*

- *Mutuality*
- *Affection*
- *Friendship*

Aristotle's domestic philosophy: He describes household relationships in terms of domination-subordination. Within such a structured household, relationships based on mutuality and affection are possible to enable its occupants to know "friendship," the "greatest of blessings."

Summary

Any discussion about households in the Greco-Roman world, and particularly Mark's, must take into account the contribution of the key Greek philosophers. Their insights were influential in the world of Jesus and Mark. There are several points that emerge from this study of the domestic philosophy of Pythagoras, Plato, and Aristotle.

First, the Greeks began their discussion on households from the premise that the human person was a "political" and "social" being. This meant that every person was so influenced by their social world that their identity as communally related beings was derived from other citizens. Membership in the city-state meant that the city-state fashioned people's identity. Likewise, the household played an important and indispensable

---

[29] "Reciprocal equality is the preservation of the city-states" (*Politics* II. i, 5).
[30] *Nicomachean Ethics*, VIII. xii. 7.
[31] *Politics*, II. i 16.

role in shaping the identity of its inhabitants. Whatever the social structure, their key concern was that Greek citizens be happy.

Second, Plato and Aristotle identified the cardinal qualities foundational for the city-state. For Plato, it was "orderliness"; for Aristotle, "partnership." To insure order and partnership both argued for the perpetuation of patriarchal institutions based on relationships of domination-submission. They reinforced their argument for this institutional hierarchy from an anthropology that presented the male as naturally superior and the female inferior. It is noteworthy how much this superior-inferior description has permeated all subsequent understanding of the nature of household relationships. It has also been responsible for an essentialist argument that presents women as fundamentally different (and usually inferior) to men, perpetuated in patriarchal and hierarchical structures.

Third, alongside the presentation of the prevailing style of relationships characterized by domination and submission, another theme also surfaced in the domestic philosophy of Pythagoras and Aristotle. The story from Pythagora's biographer Diogenes, of Theano and Damo, and Aristotle's presentation of the two styles of governance offered a more mutual style of household relationships. For Aristotle, affection and a "natural instinct" for friendship influenced this partnership between husband and wife.

This brief review of the domestic philosophy of Pythagoras, Plato, and Aristotle illustrates how influential the description of household relationships was in terms of domination-subordination/superiority-inferiority.[32] It was also the paradigm that controlled the description of households used by the Second Testament writers.

In the Second Testament this Greek tradition about household order and authority is found in the Pastoral Letters (Titus, 1 and 2 Timothy), 1 Peter, Colossians, and Ephesians. Their writers literally applied the Greek understanding to Christian households, especially the household codes of conduct. While there was some reshaping of these codes to balance lines of responsibility, their adoption among Christian authors indicates the ongoing influence into the late first century C.E. of the Greek philosophical tradition that produced them. The incorporation of these household codes of conduct into these writings suggests something further. The Christian communities from which these writings originated were not impervious to or isolated from their cultural world. This world was still heavily influenced by Greek traditions adopted by Roman society. Some Second Testament writers tried to show

---

[32] This is not to say that Aristotle was the first to describe household relationships in terms of domination-subordination or that his description was prescriptive for subsequent households. The reality in some cases was quite different. See W. C. Lacey, *The Family in Classical Greece* (London: Thames & Hudson, 1968).

how the Christian movement was culturally in tune with Greco-Roman society. Christian households were no different from any other. They blended
in with the rest of the Greco-Roman urban landscape.

It is important to note that, given the predictable description of
households in terms of authority-subordination, there are indications that
Second Testament communities sought to ameliorate this pattern. How
Mark contributed to this will become clearer in Part Two.

4

The "House" in Mark's Roman World

Mark's community inherited attitudes about the household from the Greek world. These are reflected in the domestic philosophy of Pythagoras, Plato, and Aristotle. I have also proposed that Mark's audience was steeped in the Roman world, with a possible location for the gospel at Rome. The Greek understanding of household therefore needs to be balanced and filled out by the way that first-century C.E. Romans regarded the house. Both perspectives will provide us with a greater sensitivity for reading Mark's Gospel. I propose to look at some of the most important literary descriptions of Roman households relevant to this period that reveal something about the function of households and their internal relationships.

Cicero: Political Philosopher

In 46 B.C.E. the famous Roman orator Cicero (106–43 B.C.E.) wrote the treatise *De Beneficiis* ("On Duties"), in which he explored the relationship between the household *(domus)* and the city-state. His primary aim was to set out a self-evident political philosophy that would strengthen people's commitment to the structures of the Roman Republic and affirm the benefits and privileges that flowed to its citizens.

Cicero's essay emulated the Greek philosophical tradition reminiscent of Plato and Aristotle. He presented what he considered the undeniable truths held by all as a way of exploring other more particular and socially relevant truths. For him, the undeniable universal truth was that everyone belonged to the human race. Differences emerged in the particular expressions of this universal experience with the various nations of the world and the uniqueness of each city-state. Roman citizens, he argued, recognized that they had much in common with every other group of people. What distinguishes them was the close bond they have as a people. This bond, wrote Cicero, "sets them apart from that limitless society of the human race into one that is narrow and closely-defined." The most specific expression of human identity, Cicero considered, was found in the Roman household established through marriage.[1]

Cicero's recognition of the centrality of the household in the structure of the city-state echoed his Greek heritage. He sought to spell out the structure and relationships that typified the Roman household: the domestic unit consisted of husband, wife, and their dependents. Those who made up the household included children born to the couple, children of previous marriages, current and former slaves (freedmen and freedwomen), and their children. All were members of the *domus*. This corresponded with Roman law that understood the *familia* (the family) in two senses: (1) people bonded to one another through *kinship*,[2] or (2) in a strict legal sense "a number of people who are by birth or by law subjected to the *potestas* [power] of one man, e.g., *paterfamilias* [father of a *familia*], *mater* [mother of a *familia*], son or daughter of a *familia*, and so on in succession."[3]

"Family" in Roman Law

This second legal definition illustrated three elements from Roman law which impinged on the way the family and household were viewed:

- Males were favored over females. In practice this meant that husbands and sons were legally more privileged (and protected) than wives and daughters.

- Everyone in the Roman city-state was subject to an ultimate authority. In the household this was the *paterfamilias*; in the city-state it was the Emperor as the *paterfamilias* of the Roman family. The authority (called the *potestas*) exercised by the *paterfamilias* was definitive. It distinguished the master from the slave, the honorable citizen from the one deserving least honor. It also helped to galvanize the prescribed ranks of status into its various social classes.[4]

---

[1] Cicero, *On Duties,* 1, 53–54. See J. F. Gardner and T. Wiedemann, eds., *The Roman Household: A Sourcebook* (London and New York: Routledge, 1991) 2.

[2] Kinship meant that members of a household could be patrilineally linked. They were connected biologically or through marriage to the father.

[3] *Digest* 50, 16.195 (Ulpian); Gardner, *The Roman Household,* 3–4. The *Digest of Justinian* was a juridical document of 533 c.e. While the *Digest* is much later than the period, we are considering it summarizes the earlier legal treatises of the Republican Period.

[4] R. P. Saller, *Patriarchy, property and death in the Roman family* (Cambridge: Cambridge University Press, 1994) 72.

• Roman law was specific about the order and hierarchy of authority. Authority descended from one generation to the next via males. It passed next to the females: the wife after the husband, the daughter after the son, then to the nearest *agnates*.[5] The authority of the household head institutionalized in the *potestas* and exercised by the *paterfamilias* was so binding in the *domus* that it was not until the death of the *paterfamilias* that the married children could form their own household. The death of the father was a definitive moment in the realization of a new *domus*.[6]

In summary, the Roman household, like its Greek counterpart, was regarded as a reflection of the city-state. Roman law reinforced the cultural expectation that males would be the public figures of power in Roman society. This reinforcement was reflected in the way households functioned. Domestic power dynamics mirrored those of the city-state.

Household Order and Stability: *Potestas*

In a society that lacked a police force or judicial system the absolute and unquestionable authority of the male household head, legally enshrined in the *potestas,* guaranteed social order.[7] Two examples illustrate its use. The first from the Roman historian Valerius Maximus illustrates how *potestas* had such legal protection even when its extreme use was fatal:

> Egnatius Maecenius killed his wife by beating her with a stick for being drunk on wine. Not only was he not summoned to court for doing this, but he was not even criticized by anyone: all right-thinking men considered that she deserved what she got because of her lack of self-control. It is agreed that any woman who drinks without restraint puts any virtue she may have at risk and risks falling prey to every vice.[8]

In general, Valerius would have been naturally inclined to support the husband in his use of jurisdiction over his wife. In this particular case, however, he seems to have a more sympathetic outlook towards Egnatius' wife. He is surprised at the lack of any legal action and the social complicity in Egnatius' conduct. Valerius' commentary suggests that Egnatius' cruel action deserved redress and that "all right-thinking men" may have

[5] *Agnates* were those who could prove descent from a common male who was an ancestor to the deceased head.

[6] *Digest* 50, 16. 195 (Ulpian), section 2, i.

[7] The exercise of *Potestas* ranged from managing household to the education of house slaves. See Nepos, *Atticus* 13; Gardner, *Roman Household,* 10.

[8] Valerius Maximus was a Roman historian and rhetorician. The event is recounted (around 31 C.E.) in *Factorum ac Dictorum Memorabilium,* Bk. IX, 6, 3. 9.

actually thought differently. The reason that Egnatius killed his wife was not that she was actually intoxicated, but that she had compromised the honor of her husband and his household. The extreme, disproportionate action taken by an angry husband against his wife judged to be intoxicated dramatically illustrates the legal sanction that the exercise of the husband's *potestas* over his wife had. This sanction was seen to be necessary. It was considered to be a means to protect the integrity of the household and the male kinship line.

Valerius' story may be put alongside a second in which the use of *potestas* was curbed. Vedius Pollo was about to have his household slave hurled into a pond of savage fish for dropping and smashing a valuable drinking goblet. Vedius had legal *potestas* over his slave and could punish him in any way he thought fit. Emperor Augustus present at the dinner recognized the disparity between the punishment and the offense. He intervened on behalf of the slave and overruled Vedius Pollo.[9] In this example, Vedius' household slave received more protection (and was regarded as more "valuable") than Egnatius' wife. In the second example, Augustus was the *paterfamilias* of the whole Roman household which extended across the Empire and was the largest in the Roman world. Vedius' *potestas* and household was subordinate to and overruled by Augustus' *potestas* and household. This household included the emperor himself, his immediate family, relatives, friends, procurators and governors, slaves, and freedmen and freedwomen.

Different Households: Elite and Rural

Apart from information regarding the size of the imperial household and of larger households and estates, farms and holiday villas of the Roman elite, there is virtual silence about rural households—save for one description from Ovid.[10] In *Metamorphoses,* Book VIII, Ovid describes the earthly journey of two gods, Jupiter and Mercury, the grandson of Atlas, and their frustrating search for hospitality from humans. After being rejected by a thousand households they are finally warmly welcomed by a peasant couple, Baucis and Philemon. Ovid describes this peasant household:

---

[9] The story is found in *Cassius Dio* 54, 23.1ff.; Seneca *On Anger,* 3, 40. 2. See Gardner, *Roman Household,* 14.

[10] A fine description of an elite household comes from Pliny (*Natural History,* 33, 47/135). He describes the household of Caecilius Isidorus, who died in 8 B.C.E., and he left behind him a retinue of 4,117 household slaves. See Gardner, *Roman Household,* 7. See also Pliny's description of his villa at Laurentum in *Letters* 2.17, in Shelton, *As the Romans Did,* 76–80.

Still one house received them, humble indeed, thatched with straw and reeds from the marsh; but pious old Baucis and Philemon, of equal age, were in that cottage wedded in their youth, and in that cottage had grown old together; there they made their poverty light by owning it, and by bearing it in a contented spirit. It was of no use to ask for masters or for servants in that house; they two were the whole household, together they served and are ruled.[11]

Ovid's story concludes with the gods punishing the inhospitable and rewarding the peasant couple.

Roman Marriage: The Ideal and the Reality

The romantic picture that Ovid paints of the couple is idealized and is painted by one from a superior social position. This bias notwithstanding, Ovid offers us with a description of an ideal marriage. It is one in which the monogamous couple have grown old together. They are welcoming to strangers, content with what they have; are without children or slaves and have a spirit of equanimity in which "they served and are ruled." If this is the only kind of household that can welcome the gods of Ovid's poetry, then it is the one in which an emphasis on the *paterfamilias* and his use of *potestas* is surprisingly absent. Whether such households actually existed in Ovid's time is, from one point of view, irrelevant. What is described is the ideal household and marriage relationship that Ovid considered worthy of divine blessing.

A comparison of Ovid's ideal to the reality gleaned from the literature and sepulchral inscriptions of the period, highlights some notable differences. Instead of the complementarity evident between Baucis and Philemon, an extensive social gap separated women and men. Women were confined to the household. They were officially excluded from holding any public office, sitting on juries, exercising a civic magistracy, taking legal action on behalf of themselves or anyone else. Before the law they were *impotestas*,[12] without power or authority, and ranked by marital status.[13] The only kind of status independent of their household confinement came from their participation in private associations, some oriental cults (like Isis and Osiris) and mystery religious (Eleusis and the Olympian deities) or through the public honor of becoming a vestal virgin.[14]

---

[11] Ovid, *Metamorphoses,* Bk. 8, 630ff.

[12] *Digest* 50, 17.2 (Ulpian) in Gardner, *Roman Household,* 7.

[13] Women were ranked according to whether they were young virgins, celibate adults, wives, wives married only once (called *univira*), and widows. See Pomeroy, *Goddesses,* 206.

[14] For the privileges and restrictions of vestal virgins see B. Rawson, "The Roman Family," in *The Family in Ancient Rome: New Perspectives,* ed. B. Rawson (Ithaca, N.Y.:

The most famous expression of the household and marriage ideal is found in what has been called the *Laudatio Turiae* (Eulogy of Turia), a second-century B.C.E. funeral oration delivered by Quintus Lucretius Vespillo, the husband of the deceased Turia. In his praise of Turia, Quintus also acknowledges the qualities necessary for a happy and enduring marriage.

He praises her for the way she and her sister sought justice, in the absence of their husbands, for the murders of her parents. The primary intention for justice was family honor, not personal pride. The oration continues:

> Rare indeed are marriages of such long duration, which are ended by death, not divorce. We had the good fortune to spend forty-one years together with no unhappiness. I wish that our long marriage had come finally to an end by *my* death. . . . We longed for children, but spiteful fate begrudged them. If Fortune had allowed herself to care for us in this matter as she does others, we two would have enjoyed complete happiness. But advancing old age put an end to our hopes for children. . . . You were depressed about your infertility and grieved because I was without children. . . . You spoke of divorce and offered to give up your household to another woman, to a fertile woman. You said that you yourself would arrange for me a new wife, one worthy of our well-known love, and you assured me that you would treat the children of my new marriage as if they were your own. You would not demand the return of your inheritance; it would remain, if I wished, in my control. You would not detach or isolate yourself from me; you would simply carry out henceforth the duties and responsibilities of my sister or my mother-in-law. . . .[15]

The oration presumes a social context in which the couple come from a wealthy, elite, and politically involved background.[16] The speech confirms several features of Roman marriage: (1) Vespillo recognizes the uniqueness of his marriage to Turia which was terminated by her death, rather than by the more customary practice of divorce. (2) He also acknowledges the social importance of a fruitful marriage, the value placed on fertility and children, and the lengths to which some couples would go for the household to have legitimate heirs. Their absence laid acceptable grounds for divorce among the Roman elite. Vespillo's oration reveals the

---

Cornell University Press, 1986) 22–23 and Pomeroy (*Goddesses,* 220–23) who also includes an analysis of the benefits that Osiris, Isis, and the Olympian deities could bring to Roman women.

[15] *CIL* 6. 1527, 31670 (*ILS* 8393); Shelton, *As the Romans Did,* 293–95.

[16] Vespillo acknowledges the assistance that Turia gave him when he was considered a political opponent to Octavian and Marc Antony.

self-sacrificing lengths to which Turia would go to ensure the continuation of her husband's family line. (3) Turia's suggested solution with its pro-creative emphasis presumes the importance of this patrilineal line.

In his *Laudatio,* Vespillo praises Turia for:

> your modesty, obedience, affability, and good nature, your tireless attention to wool making, your artless elegance and simplicity of dress . . . your af-fection towards your relatives, your sense of duty *(pietas)* toward your fam-ily. . . Why recall the countless other virtues which you have in common with all Roman matrons worthy of that name?

The style of the oration and the virtues for which Turia is acclaimed are borrowed from a *topos* in which certain virtues were expected of women and for which they were esteemed.[17] The *topos* is concerned with household management and the virtues necessary to bring the household honor. The standardized virtue list characterized the Roman matron and cultured noble woman of an honorable household. It is clear from the *Lau-datio* that Turia exemplified them impeccably, with the most important being the last mentioned, *pietas*. This was the devotion, duty, and loyalty that a woman showed to her husband, family, and nation. Essential for a harmonious household, it was the basis for the reverence that children had towards their parents.[18] Vespillo implies that it was Turia's *pietas* that led her to seek justice for the murders of her parents and indicates the kind of relationship she had with them. While the *patria potestas* shaped the style of relationships within the household, between parents and children, Turias' *pietas* for her parents suggests these relationships could also, at times, be intimate. Even Seneca (ca. 4 B.C.E.–65 C.E.) comments, "A father's power is most forbearing in its care for the interests of his children and subordinates his own to theirs."[19]

---

[17] Virtues of women are often found on funeral epitaphs. Women are frequently praised for hard work, fidelity, chastity, for "staying at home" *(domiseda)* and "serving at home" *(domum servavit).* Cf. *ILS* 8402 = *CIL* 6, 11602; *ILS* 8403 = *CIL* 1, 1007; see also *ILS* 8450, 8456, 8437, 8444, 1218.

[18] See Cicero *De Oratore* 2.168; *De Finibus* 3.62.65; Plutarch, *De Amore Prolis,* pas-sim. A helpful exposition of *pietas* is found in R. Saller, "Corporal Punishment, Authority, and Obedience in the Roman Household," in *Marriage, Divorce and Children in Ancient Rome,* ed. B. Rawson (Oxford: Clarendon Press, 1991) 147–50; also Saller, *Patriarchy,* 102–32; Treggiari, *Roman Marriage,* 209.

[19] Seneca, *De Clementia* I.14.2. See E. Eyben in "Fathers and Sons," in *Marriage, Di-vorce and Children in Ancient Rome,* who argues that the father sought to strike a balance between harsh discipline and indulgent permissiveness with his children, even though there are examples of the extremes of treatment of children that by today's standards might be called "child abuse." Eyben also illustrates the way the father took care of the moral edu-cation of the sons from fifteen to thirty years of age (114–43).

In investigating Roman literature about households and marriage an important point emerges. From the literature it is clear that alongside stories of the extreme and sometimes cruel use of power by the household head, there coexisted other more humane, affectionate themes reflecting a household and marriage ideal. This is summed up in Tacitus' observation about the change in the way husbands treat wives: "It is a good thing, a cause for rejoicing, that much of the ancient harshness [of husbands towards their wives] has changed. . . . Wives share most aspects of life with their husbands, and that is no impediment to peace [in the provinces]."[20]

Tacitus applauds the change towards a more harmonious common life shared between married couples. More significantly, such an alteration has compromised neither the security of the Roman world nor the harmony so valued in the city-state. Tacitus' assent to the social value of a more reciprocal relationship between husbands and wives turns us to another important household theme explored by Cicero.

Cicero: Households and "Communion"

In his treatise *De Finibus Bonorum et Malorum* ("Concerning the Final Things That Are Good and Bad"), Cicero sought to outline his own ethical and philosophical views in dialogue with the most prominent ethical systems of his day.[21] His inspiration came from Aristotle who posed the key ethical challenge in two questions, the second an expansion of the first: "What is the ultimate aim of human existence?" "Where are ultimate good and well-being to be found?"

In *De Finibus* Cicero attempted to answer these two questions by drawing on Aristotle and highlights his admiration for Aristotle and the whole Greek philosophical tradition. This connection is important to note because it indicates, at least in Cicero, the heritage and influence of the Greek philosophical tradition on the Roman world of the first century C.E. Cicero was in debate with his contemporaries about the answers to the great ethical questions of his day. He drew on what he regarded as a revered philosophical tradition to formulate his responses. As he noted in his preface to *De Finibus,* his treatise was an important attempt to give popular access to the wisdom of the Greek philosophers: "Yet even supposing I have a direct translation of Plato or Aristotle, exactly as our poets have done with plays, would it not, pray, be a patriotic service to introduce those transcendent intellects to the acquaintance of my fellow citizens?"[22] Cicero saw his task more than sim-

---

[20] Tacitus, *Annals* 3:33-34.
[21] Epicureanism, Stoicism, and Antiochus' Academy.
[22] Cicero, *De Finibus,* 1.7 (my translation).

ply translating Plato and Aristotle into Latin. He wanted to communicate their spirit so that his own people could appreciate them.

Towards the end of his work, Cicero described the social structures necessary for citizens to realize their ultimate good. This was based on his conviction that the pursuit of moral good and truth was something intrinsic to human beings from nature. Given this human predisposition, Cicero argued that "there is nothing more glorious nor of wider range than the communion *(coniunctio)* of humankind."[23] For Cicero "communion" *(coniunctio)* was the most important social value to which all other human activities were directed. In an importance sentence from *De Finibus,* Cicero defined its meaning and its impact on the whole of Roman society. What unfolds is a social philosophy parallel to the Greek tradition about "partnership" *(koinônía)* and a remarkable vision for Roman society and its constitutive households. "Communion," wrote Cicero, "is that form of solidarity *(societas)* and partnership of interests *(communicatio)* and the very affection *(caritas)* which exists between human beings. These come into existence as soon as we are born because children are loved by their parents and the whole household is bonded together *(coniungitur)* by the ties of marriage and parenthood."[24]

This compact sentence explores the basis for a cohesive society and co-operation among its members. In Cicero's vision of such a society, the household was central as the basis for human community and social moral good.[25] In its relationships between spouses and their children "communion" grows and, "gradually moves slowly beyond the home, first by blood relatives, then by those related by marriage, next by friendships, after that by neighbors, then by fellow citizens and those who are political allies and friends, then in embracing the whole human race."[26]

Cicero called "communion" the "affective dimension of the human spirit" and was expressed in the exercise of three virtues: *societas* (solidarity), *communicatio* (partnership) and *caritas* (affection).[27] These social virtues are not esoteric or unachievable. They are concretely realized in the Roman household *(domus),* in the relationship between spouses and their love for their children.

---

[23] Cicero, *De Finibus,* 5.65. *The Oxford Latin Dictionary,* P. G. W. Glare, ed. (Oxford: Clarendon Press, 1982) translates *coniunctio* as "the act of joining together," "a bond, mutual association, friendship, community" (408).

[24] Cicero, *De Finibus,* 5.65.

[25] Cicero's *coniunctio* is equivalent to the *koinônia* of his Greek predecessors, Plato and Aristotle.

[26] Cicero, *De Finibus,* 5.65.

[27] Here Cicero echoes Plato and Aristotle. For them orderliness was the fundamental link between members of Greek society and it was expressed through the virtues of temperance, communion, and friendship.

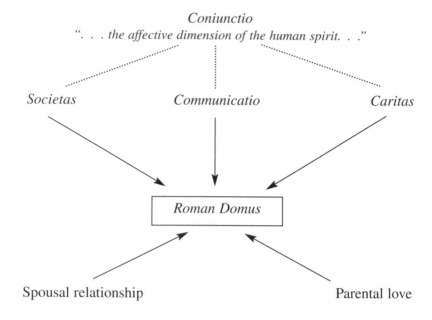

Coniunctio
". . . the affective dimension of the human spirit. . ."

Societas   *Communicatio*   *Caritas*

Roman Domus

Spousal relationship   Parental love

Cicero's vision of the Roman household: "Communion" (coniunctio), "the affective dimension of the human spirit," is foundational for society and households. This brings about "solidarity" (societas), "partnership" (communicatio) and "affection" (caritas). All these are central to the Roman domus. The most important relationships in the domus are those that come from marriage (husband-wife) and parenthood (parents-children).

Cicero's vision of the Roman household presented here is a counterbalance to the stereotypical, subordinate, hierarchical household that permeated the literature. He regarded the household as foundational for a community seeking to nurture a morally ethical citizenry with appropriate social virtues. Preeminent among these virtues was *pietas,* the attitude of respect that people have for each other, especially children for their parents.[28] *Pietas,* like "communion" originated in the spousal relationship of the household[29] and depended on affection. Because of *pietas* communion grew, justice permeated Roman culture, and citizens were nurtured in social virtues.

What emerges clearly from *De Finibus* is that Cicero regarded the household as the indispensable means for human beings to achieve moral good and realize their intrinsic worth. The household was more than sim-

---

[28] *Pietas* is the "attitude of dutiful respect towards those to whom one is bound by ties of religion, consanguinity, etc." (*Oxford Latin Dictionary,* 1378).

[29] The link which Cicero makes between *societas* and *pietas* parallels the link that the Greek philosophers saw between *koinônia* and *philia.*

ply a legal structure to protect the *potestas* of the *paterfamilias;* it was the place where the primary values for Roman society were formed. Cicero's insights add voice to a way of considering the Roman household and its internal relationships that seem to move beyond the mainstream of what can be gleaned from the literature of the Republican period. His appreciation of the household coincided with the household and marriage ideal described by Ovid in his story of Baucis and Philemon:

> This marriage and household ideal, of a permanent, more equitable marriage relationship based on affection had implications for the other members of the household, especially the children. Cicero explicated these implications also for the wider Roman society. Such households fostered *coniunctio,* promoted justice, and nurtured those social virtues which enhanced the Roman city-state.

The ideal to which Ovid and Cicero witness is all the more surprising given the culture in which the overriding structure of authority was expressed in terms of hierarchy and patriarchy. Its lines of power and authority were clearly delineated: the male was the dominant authority and females were subservient. This was reinforced later by the Roman legal system. Husbands ruled over wives; the household head, the *paterfamilias,* over the other members of the household, including the slaves. This authority structure shaped every political and legal system. It also influenced the practice of marriage and divorce.

Marriages seemed easily entered into and divorces arranged with little social stigma. Marriage was not regarded as permanently binding. This impermanence created new marital relationships and households. Caution needs to be exercised in trying to estimate the number of marriages and divorces. Nevertheless, couples would expect to go through at least a couple of marriages in their lifetimes, and children born of the union would know that the relationship between the parents could be severed most frequently by divorce, than by death or old age. The unromantic characteristic of marriage meant that the new alignments constantly undermined any sense of stability, particularly between the parent and child. In this setting, the child became more vulnerable.

The only stable figure possible in the Roman social set up was that of the father as household head.[30] The child in the elite household would always be linked to the father's house, though the mother might have died or been divorced. Only if the divorced mother was still alive after the death of the father could the child's link with the mother be restored. The overriding nature of the relationship between father and child was not one of

---

[30] K. R. Bradley, *Discovering the Roman Family: Studies in Roman Social History* (New York: Oxford University Press, 1991) 64f., 139f.

intimacy but authority. The authoritative control maintained by the father would have kept him at a physical and emotional distance from his children who would have been in the hands of child-minders.[31]

Alongside this picture of an authoritatively structured household dominated by a *paterfamilias,* alternative images of households and family relationships are offered which are more humane and affective.[32] They suggest that in the day-to-day life in households other attitudes were encouraged which ameliorated the submissive attitude expected of its members. As we have seen in Ovid and Cicero, it was possible for affection to be the basis of a husband's relationship to his wife and parents towards children. This also had implications for the relationship of the master to the slave.

When we turn to Mark's gospel, its audience would have been steeped in these insights, expectations, and experiences of the Roman household and its relationships as reflected in the writings of Cicero, Valerius, Ovid, Vespillo, and Tacitus. How much Mark's audience was encouraged to conform to the social conventions about the function and nature of the Roman household or live out a radical critique of it will be seen when we engage in a closer reading of the gospel.

---

[31] Ibid., 64.

[32] Also in the late Republican Period and for the first time in Roman history, women do not have to be handed over into the total power of another male in the institution of *manus.* She is able to retain her link to her original household and to the *potestas* of the *paterfamilias.* Other factors, like the rise in native and oriental religious practices offer ways for women to act independently of socially determined roles expected of them in the household.

5

A Summary of Mark's
Greco-Roman "House"

The insights about houses and households gleaned from a study of first-century C.E. domestic architecture, three key Greek philosophers (Pythagoras, Plato, Aristotle), and Roman writers (Cicero, Ovid, and Vespillo) can provide perspectives from which we can read Mark's gospel. They sensitize us to the way that Mark's audience could have heard the "house" in the gospel. In the very least, they warn us against imposing our contemporary experience of households and family on to the gospel. I am not suggesting from our brief survey of selected Greek philosophers and Roman writers that their insights were determinative or prescriptive of the way households were to be understood in Mark's Greco-Roman world.

I am suggesting, though, that their presentation on households is *descriptive* of how some interpreted their domestic situation. Their insights could well be representative of some, if not most, Greco-Roman householders in the late first century C.E. If this is true, then their presentation of houses, of what they considered the fundamental principles that constituted the household ("order," "friendship," "communion") and the dominant-submissive relationship that characterized the exercise of domestic authority, would be the culturally acceptable description of the house. How Mark uses these representative perspectives in the gospel story provides the reader with one set of narrative clues for understanding the gospel's christology and presentation on discipleship.

From a study of the archaeology and Greco-Roman literature, I suggest that five themes emerge that can be helpful in reading Mk: culture, similarity, difference, harmony, and nurture.

1. *Culture:* Mark's gospel is a cultural product. It is written from the perspective of a first-century C.E. Mediterranean author for a Greco-Roman

audience. This background has influenced the author's intention in composing the narrative. Narrative images, like house and household, must be read with the cultural world of the intended audience in mind. They must be interpreted with sensitivity to the socially constructed information of the gospel's intended auditors.

Reading Mk with a sensitivity to culture implies two further things:

- Contemporary gospel readers need to be cautious in interpreting the story so that our experiences and interpretations of narrative images (like houses and households) do not prevent us from "hearing" the biblical text from its original intended context.

- In reading Mark's story we must be careful that we do not presume that the story is an accurate reproduction of that world from which the original story emerged. Mk does not give us a direct line to the ministry of the historical Jesus and his first community of disciples. We have access to the original story (Jesus and his disciples) only through Mark's story fashioned for a people in a time and place removed from the original story. In practice, this means that we read the gospel text from the point of view of Mark's late first-century Greco-Roman audience, not Jesus' Galilean audience.

2. *Similarity:* In the previous chapters I emphasized how the audience of the gospel had an appreciation of the household which developed from their Greco-Roman culture. Their cultural worldview influenced the way Mark's people perceived the household. The writer is not seeking to invent a totally different household structure, but presumes certain specifics of the Greco-Roman household. These would have been familiar to Mark's audience. Some of these specifics include:

- the power or authority exercised by the household head, the *paterfamilias;*
- the exercise of authority in a hierarchical manner;
- the dominance of the male in the household;
- the variety of house structures (*domus*, shop house, apartment);
- the public and private aspects of the *domus*;
- the Roman house as a space into which one was invited;
- the importance of hospitality;
- the greater possibility of the guest being invited into the inner sanctum of the house to experience familiarity with the *paterfamilias*;
- the extensive and potentially inclusive possibilities of membership in the house.

3. *Difference:* The evangelist's appreciation of the house is not necessarily determined by or limited to the socially constructed understanding of houses and households. As a pastoral theologian and creative writer, it is possible that the evangelist could make the house a narrative symbol or vehicle for communicating deeper insights into the gospel's christology and story of discipleship. It remains to be seen whether there are differences between the conventional understanding of the Roman *domus* and Mark's story. Collectively, differences might indicate an important theological theme or motif which the reader or auditor is invited to consider. Together they compose a reading scenario that contributes to Mark's portrait of Jesus and the structure of his household of disciples.

4. *Harmony:* Drawing together the insights of some Greek philosophers and Roman writers, the household was seen as the place in which harmony was preeminently evident. The consistent term for this was "order." It was argued by Greek and Roman writers that if order could be attained in the smallest social unit, then it guaranteed social harmony and stability on a wider level. "Order" was the fundamental basis of the household and from it sprung "communion" (Aristotle) or "friendship" (Cicero). Each of these qualities were reflections of the harmony experienced by household inhabitants. It could be argued that each were aspects of the one reality—the experience of an internal household union between the members of the *domus*, which led to happiness, the ultimate meaning of the existence of the city-state or the Empire. It remains to be seen whether this concern about domestic harmony is important to the evangelist in presenting Jesus' household of disciples.

5. *Nurture:* The strongest image of the household among the Greek philosophers and Roman writers was the powerful authority exercised by the *paterfamilias*. This power seemed to dominate the entire structure and to it all relationships were subservient. The dominant-submissive themes evident in the ancient Mediterranean household overwhelm the modern reader. However, we also noted in the literature a subtler theme about relationships. In some cases, while the authority of the *paterfamilias* was undeniable, a balance was offered. This appeared in those spousal relationships that were described as "republican" (Aristotle) and coequal. A household ideal was presented where relationships were moderated by the criterion of nurture. This ideal was in tension with the overriding dominant expectation of members' submission to a *paterfamilias* who could act in a dictatorial and unilateral fashion. Mark's readers will see how nurturing Jesus' household is as it becomes a place in which people are explicitly healed, taught, and forgiven.

These five themes alert us to some of the ways that Mark's Greco-Roman audience might well have heard "house." They are reminders that Mark's gospel is culturally shaped and that its architectural spaces have the potential to be symbolic and metaphoric narrative indicators. How the evangelist chooses to use and adjust the received or conventional appreciation of the household helps the reader to value the narrative's twists and turns, and its portrait of key characters.

Part Two

Reading Mark's Gospel

6

An Overview

Let me sketch a general outline of the gospel's drama with an appreciation for the way Greek and Roman writers regarded the house and households.[1] Here I shall also suggest the way in which Mark's household theme functions overall and in subsequent chapters propose a more specific or detailed analysis of the gospel's domestic story.

The Prologue and Ending (1:1; 16:8)

The opening verse (1:1) presents an overview of the gospel in a theologically compressed and rich statement which summarizes the structure and christology of Mark's gospel. What is about to unfold in the remaining narrative is "a beginning." The opening verse leads to a prologue (1:2-13) which introduces the audience to the major christological motifs that shape the rest of the narrative. This prologue or gospel overture begins with the prophetic ministry of John the Baptist and includes Jesus' baptism and temptation. All the events that form the prologue are set significantly in the context of two narrative sites—"the heavens" (1:10-11) and the "desert" or "wilderness" (1:2, 4, 12). This second, as we shall see, is a deliberate thematic refrain to which Mark wants the gospel's audience to attend. This setting, it will be argued, is symbolic of homelessness; from it the Spirit initiates Jesus' ministry.

[1] M. Hengel, following the lead of F. G. Lang and others, describes Mark's gospel as a dramatic narrative that unfolds in a series of "acts" *in Studies in the Gospel of Mark,* 34–37. See also D. Rhodes and D. Michie, *Mark as Story: An Introduction to the Narrative for a Gospel* (Philadelphia: Fortress Press, 1982).

Both the opening verse and its subsequent prologue at the beginning of the gospel (1:1-13) find their parallel at the end in the final verse and the scenes which immediately precede it. These concern Jesus' death, burial, and the women's encounter with a young man in the tomb (15:21–16:8). The gospel referred to as "a beginning" (1:1) connects to the enigmatic last verse (16:8) in which the women fail to do the very thing the young man has commissioned them, namely, to proclaim the Easter message to Jesus' other disciples. Instead they flee and say nothing to anyone. The gospel ends in a strange silence about the possibility of an Easter announcement of discipleship rehabilitation and reconciliation in Galilee.

Mark's story of death and resurrection is the climactic moment of failure, desertion and loneliness. It is here that Jesus' identity is mysteriously revealed and enigmatically proclaimed to the Markan audience. The reasons for the appropriateness of this ending will be explored later, but the gospel audience knows that Mark's narrative, including the women's apparent failure, is "a beginning." Just as the first verse leads into the prologue with its emphasis on wilderness and allusions to homelessness, so the gospel's final verse is preceded by scenes dominated by images connected to the ultimate experience of homelessness—the cross and the tomb. Within this frame is the rest of Mark's gospel story and its quest for home (1:14–15:20).

Opening Verse (1:1)—*"A beginning . . ."*

> *The wilderness* (1:2-13)—Place of homelessness
>
> > *The quest for home—Mark's Gospel Story (Mk 1:14–15:32)*
>
> *The Cross* (15:33-39)—Ultimate Experience of homelessness

Concluding Verse (16:6)—*". . . they say nothing to anyone . . ."*

The First Half of the Gospel (1:2–8:21)

In the prologue, as Jesus surfaces from the baptismal waters a heavenly voice declares, "You are my Son, the Beloved; with you I am well pleased" (1:11). This divine designation offers a reading perspective by which the gospel audience can interpret the rest of Jesus' actions. From the outset the reader knows Jesus' identity. In the narrative which follows

(1:16–8:21) Jesus' identity is mysteriously hidden from all earthly characters in the story, even though they experience his deeds and words.

As Mark's gospel story dramatically unfolds from this point, Jesus' ministry is first focused on gathering together a group of disciples and forming them into a community which, for reasons that should become clearer below, I name a "household" (1:16–3:35). I shall suggest that it is this household that becomes the tangible locale of God's dwelling *(basileia)* as the narrative develops in the first half of the gospel. It offers an antidote to the experience of homelessness symbolized by the prologue's wilderness-motif. The community that forms into a household around Jesus becomes further identified, strengthened, and tested in Jesus' teaching in parables, a storm on the lake and various healing events (4:1–6:6).

As we move towards the gospel's center, a new moment occurs in defining who belongs to Jesus' household of disciples. In 6:7–8:27 it becomes clear that social, gender, and ethnic prescriptions of those who "belong" to Jesus are redefined and Mark's community is encouraged to reevaluate its missionary focus. Jesus' teaching about household purity in this part of the gospel (7:1-37) reinforced by his healing of the Syro-Phoenician's daughter and the deaf and dumb (7:24-37) illustrate the kind of reassessment necessary for Mark's readers to undertake. In the first half of the gospel (1:16–8:21), the circle of those who reject him steadily widens. The reader becomes aware of those "inside" Jesus' household and the "outsiders." The religious and political authorities, his townspeople, and even his relatives and family reject or seek to confine him. The scene in 6:1-6 dramatically illustrates this rejection. Here his hometown kinship group disbelieves and takes offense.

Over the first half of the gospel, Jesus' disciples, initially enthusiastic, slowly become perplexed. The growing disenchantment among Jesus' companions signals that all is not right in the household of disciples, nor, by inference, among Mark's householders. There is a final point that is important to note in the early chapters. Mark contrasts Jesus' house in which the disciples gather to the socially prescribed sacred gathering place, the synagogue. This is not to replace the conventional religious setting, but to offer an alternative.[2] Jesus' household is heralded as a legitimate alternative for those excluded from the traditional religious locale.

---

[2] Here I differ from the interpretation offered by several scholars who posit a replacement theme—the household replaces the Jewish institutions of synagogue and temple. See, for example, J. Painter, "When is a House not a Home? Disciples and Family in Mark 3.13-35," *NTS* 45 (1999) 498–513.

The Second Half of the Gospel (8:22–16:8)

In the second half of the gospel, the perplexity of the disciples turns to blindness. This is symbolized by two healings concerned with curing blindness. The first (8:22-26), clearly at the center of Mark's narrative structure, marks off an important literary segment (8:22–10:52) in which Jesus' attention turns more to his disciples and their instruction. Mark's Jesus wants the disciples to be forewarned of the impending suffering which awaits him and those who follow. But they seem deaf and blind even to the three moments of teaching on the passion that mark off this section (8:27f.; 9:30f.; 10:32). This is confirmed especially by the second healing of blindness (10:46-52), which closes this discreet literary section and prepares for the events about to unfold in Jerusalem. The three "predictions" of his impending passion and death in this section are strategically placed as he journeys with his uncomprehending disciples towards Jerusalem. This important teaching that flows from the second prediction and immediately precedes the third (10:23-31) is a final restatement of the nature of Jesus' household and its authority structure.

Throughout the last half of the gospel (8:22–16:8), a blinding, deep-rooted incomprehension descends on the disciples. Jesus struggles with their spiritual blindness and they finally succumb to fear.[3] As Jesus' tension with the religious authorities heightens in the Holy City (11:1–13:37), the reader senses the story's dénouement.[4] The disciples continue to struggle with his teaching and seem blind to the mounting opposition he faces. As the gospel climaxes in the passion story (14:1–16:8) culminating in his death and resurrection, the disciples flee. All the (male) disciples abandon him—one of them, naked—in the Gethsemane garden when Jesus faces a betraying disciple and guards sent by Jerusalem's religious leaders. The final scenes in Jerusalem where Jesus is in conflict with the religious authorities are set in the Temple. Here the religious authenticity of the conventional abode of God, the Temple, is critiqued. It throws into relief the nature of Jesus' household. For Mark's audience an authentic dwelling of God can be found in the community of Jesus' disciples. This new household has already gathered with him for a final family meal in the upper room, been decimated in the face of his suffering and death, and is promised rehabilitation and reconciliation in the gospel's final scene (16:7).

---

[3] J. D. Kingsbury, *Conflict in Mark: Jesus, Authorities, Disciples* (Minneapolis: Fortress Press, 1989) 89–103.

[4] On Mark's presentation of Jesus' conflict with the religious and civil authorities, see Kingsbury, *Conflict*, 63–88.

This brief overview now allows us to fill out more explicitly the way Mark unfolds the development of Jesus' household in 1:14–15:20 using the simple literary structure above. Remaining chapters will unpack this structure in greater detail.

Opening Verse (1:1)—*"A beginning . . ."*

The Wilderness (1:2-13)—Place of Homelessness

Jesus' Proclamation of the "Good News" (1:14-15)
The Gathering of the New Household (1:16–3:35)
Strengthening the Household (4:1–6:6)
The Missionary Household (6:7–8:26)

Transition: Healing the Blind person (8:22-26)

The Suffering Household (8:27–10:52)
The Household and the Temple (11:1–13:37)
The Passion (14:1–15:32)

The Cross (15:33-39)—Ultimate Experience of Homelessness

Concluding Verse (16:8)—*". . . they say nothing to anyone . . ."*

7

The Homeless Wilderness—Mk 1:1-15

The gospel's opening verses are crucial (1:1-15). They are a prologue to the whole gospel and present a framework for interpreting Mark's story of Jesus. The central issue for Mark concerns the identity of Jesus, a primary motif which will preoccupy the characters in the gospel. "Who is Jesus?" is the question which the following teaching and miracles raise for the audience. The correct perspective about Jesus' true identity is offered to the reader in these opening verses.

These verses are also important for a perspective of household, even though Mark's household theme is not explicit. In essence, these scenes identify the nature of the one who seeks to form a household of disciples. They demonstrate why Jesus needs a household. Jesus' ministry begins in the experience of solitude and domestic isolation. As we shall see, the desert or wilderness imagery grounds Mark's Jesus in the experience of homelessness. It is out of this context—and one which Mark's audience could easily identify given their historical and political circumstances—that Jesus' desire to establish a community or household of disciples is derived. Mark will return to this theme and experience of homelessness at the end of the gospel. I consider that what follows establishes the foundation for a prominent Markan theme that will emerge more explicitly in the subsequent pericopes of these early chapters.

The First Verse—Mk 1:1

The first verse is the gospel's introduction and summary.[1] It introduces the whole gospel story, links to the prologue which follows (1:2-15), and

---

[1] In dialogue with R. Guelich (" 'The Beginning of the Gospel'—Mark 1:1-15," *BR* 27 [1982] 6–8) M. A. Tolbert, *Sowing the Gospel: Mark's World in Literary-Historical*

connects with the final verse in 16:8 which, as we shall see, frames the gospel. The verse summarizes both the content and style of the gospel. Mark's deceptively simple literary approach, evident throughout the gospel and witnessed in this opening verse, conveys a most profound truth which could be easily overlooked in a casual reading:

> The beginning of the good news of Jesus Christ, the Son of God (1:1).

Mark's gospel is described in three ways by this first verse: It is "the beginning"; it is "of Jesus" characterized by the two titles "Christ" and "Son of God"; it is called "the good news."[2] An appreciation of these opening words is critical for what follows in the rest of the gospel. They offer an overview of the gospel, introduce the major aspects of Mark's portrait of Jesus and announce the story which is about to unfold as good news to a community experiencing struggle and division. Despite its apparent simplicity, this verse is a digest of what the reader is to expect and previews the response that the reader will be expected to offer through this encounter with Mark's Jesus. This verse also offers encouragement to an audience conscious of fragility, failure, compromise, and household discord.

There are three senses in which Mark's writing might be understood as "the beginning":

- To an audience attuned to Jewish biblical literature, what follows is reminiscent of the beginning of God's creative activity described in the first words of the Jewish Scriptures in Genesis: "In the beginning when God created the heavens and the earth" (Gen 1:1).[3] The readers' encounter with Jesus through Mark's story will be like a fresh experience of God's action at the very dawn of creation. It will renew them, opening them up to new possibilities. Through engaging Jesus in Mark's gospel, each reader will begin again along the path of discipleship.

- The gospel is also the beginning in the sense that it presents the reader with the beginning or the foundation for the Christian community. It offers the fundamental story about Jesus upon which the

---

Perspective (Minneapolis: Fortress Press, 1989) 111–12, argues that Mk 1:1-3 is a whole but also demonstrates rhetorically that 1:1 and 1:2-3 are a sequence and that 1:1 could stand on its own.

[2] The argument for the textual inclusion of the title "Son of God" is found in B. M. Metzger, *A Textual Commentary on the Greek New Testament* (London: United Bible Societies, 1975) 73.

[3] On the Genesis connection of "beginning" from Mark's opening verse, see D. O. Via, *The Ethics of Mark's Gospel in the Middle of Time* (Philadelphia: Fortress Press, 1985) 45; Myers, *Binding*, 122–23.

community's faith is established and depends. What will emerge is that Jesus' household was an inclusive one. This is the beginning or foundational spirit of Mark's household. To this spirit it must constantly return.

- Mark identifies what follows as "the beginning." If the next sixteen chapters are regarded as the beginning of the gospel, this has important implications for those followers of Jesus who are members of the disciple household in history. The gospel is continued in time through these disciples. Jesus' story is connected with and relative to their story. Their lives and experiences continue in history and make the story about Jesus tangible in their own world. No matter how disappointing, frustrating, or painful their lives, or how chronologically separated they are from the historical events recounted by the evangelist, or how fragmented the experience of their household, the present Christian believers are the extension of the gospel. The gospel begun by Mark is continued in its audience.

This third nuance of beginning will be especially helpful for understanding the function that the house will play in the gospel and the enigmatic conclusion in Mk 16:8, the gospel's original ending.

- The opening verse is connected to the gospel's final verse. In 16:7 the women are entrusted with the Easter message to announce to the disciples that the risen Jesus will meet them in Galilee where they will see him. In 16:8 they run terrified from the tomb and say nothing to anyone about what they have been told. Despite the apparent failure of the women, the reader knows that the gospel message was proclaimed. Somehow failure led to the proclamation of the gospel and the reader's faith in Jesus. The gospel continued to be told. The opening and closing verses frame the rest of the gospel.

- With regard to households, what is begun in Mark's household is not concluded but continued in every subsequent generation of discipled households. Mark's household mirrors what is to take place in subsequent households. In this sense it is the beginning. But the household in Mark's gospel also acts as a foil to highlight the key issues upon which future households will need to reflect deeply.

From the opening verse the reader is already confronted with a statement about Jesus' identity. He is "the Christ" and "the Son of God." The identity of Jesus is a key issue on which Mark wants the reader to reflect. It surfaces at important moments throughout the narrative and especially in Mk 8, the heart of the story. The first half of the gospel seeks to understand

Jesus as the Christ. The Greek word *Christos* means "anointed one." Jesus is God's anointed one. The reason for this is evident from his baptism and the wilderness temptation scene which follows the baptism. These scenes reveal Jesus as God's beloved one even in the desert experience. How this affects his ministry will also be revealed in the first half of the gospel. Jesus is also the "Son of God." This means he is God's human representative who sums up both God's response to the world and the appropriate human response to God. Mark will make clear that Jesus is the suffering one who reverses social and political acceptability. Readers are invited to focus on and reconsider their perception of Jesus. As God's anointed one (Christ) he will reveal God's solidarity with humanity. As Son of God he will reveal humanity's desire to be united with God. In other words, Jesus reveals a God who seeks to make a home among human beings and expresses the human quest for home with God.

Mark's writing is also described as "good news."[4] The Greek word for "good news" occurs here and twice more in the final and transitional scene of Jesus' inaugural proclamation (Mk 1:14-15). Good news is an overarching theme for this section and the whole of Mark's writing.

Euangelion originally had political and military connotations. The birth of a king or a military victory was considered "gospel." Mark's unique use of the word in identification with Jesus does not remove this original political nuance. For Mark the Gospel is primarily Jesus and the story about Jesus. This is the good news and the central preoccupation of the Gospel. The way Mark has constructed this opening section of the gospel highlights the importance of this announcement of the good news (in verses 1 and 14) and its connection to the wilderness.[5] The centerpiece of this section is Jesus' baptism.

A—*Overture:* The *good news* begins   (1:1)

   B—John the Baptist in the *wilderness*   (1:2-8)

      C—The Baptism of Jesus   (1:9-11)

   B[1]—Jesus in the *wilderness*   (1:12-13)

A[1]—*Proclamation:* Jesus announces the *good news*   (1:14-15)

---

[4] On "Gospel," see Taylor, *The Gospel According to St. Mark* (London: Macmillan, 1966) 152; E. Schweizer, *The Good News According to Mark* (Atlanta: John Knox Press, 1970) 30–31; E. Best, *Mark—The Gospel as Story* (Edinburgh: T.&T. Clark, 1987) 37–43; Myers, *Binding,* 122–23.

[5] The division of the prologue offered here is an extension of Tolbert's outline (*Sowing,* 108–13).

John the Baptist in "The Wilderness"—Mk 1:2-8

After the opening verse, the reader's attention is immediately directed to the "wilderness" or "desert" (*eremos,* in Greek).[6] John the Baptist is introduced as the one who "appeared in the wilderness, proclaiming a baptism of repentance for the forgiveness of sins" (Mk 1:4). The gospel begins in the wilderness, the inhospitable abode of evil and wild beasts, the place of Israel's testing and encounter with God. Here there were no distractions, only memories of the past and fear of the unknown lurking in this desolate space. The desert was far away from civilization and other human beings. It was the primordial place of solitude over which a person had little power.

Of all narrative symbols, the desert is a powerful representation of homelessness. It stands in contrast to the home and provides the perspective from which the rest of the gospel is read. This forsaken place found in the gospel's opening scene will connect to the end of Mark's story and the place of Jesus' abandonment—the cross, the ultimate symbol of homelessness. Between this opening desert scene and the gospel's concluding climatic scene of desertion, the drama about community and Jesus' household unfolds. This drama is the quest for home.

Jesus' Baptism—Mk 1:9-11

John ushers Jesus on to the Markan stage which prepares for the central scene of this gospel overture, his baptism. The evangelist surprisingly understates Jesus' first appearance in the story. He appears as one of the crowd coming to John for baptism. There is nothing of the miraculous or heroic in his introduction:

> In those days Jesus came from Nazareth of Galilee and was baptized by John in [literally, *into*] the Jordan (Mk 1:9).

Jesus comes from an unexceptional village of Galilee, unremarkable except that it belongs to a part of Northern Israel known for its peasant resistance to the political and religious authorities of Jerusalem. Already a contentious note is sounded: those who come to John seem to be from Jerusalem, its environs, and the surrounding countryside of Judea. Jesus is the only one mentioned who comes from the northern and most subversive part of Israel.

---

[6] A helpful overview of the function of the wilderness in Mark's narrative is found in U. W. Mauser, *Christ in the Wilderness: The Wilderness Theme in the Second Gospel and its Basis in the Biblical Tradition* (Naperville, Ill.: Allenson, 1963).

There is a second aspect about this verse that emphasizes Jesus' uniqueness. While everyone else is baptized in the Jordan, Jesus is baptized *into* the Jordan—a point missed by most translations. If baptism is a sign of openness to God, then Jesus' total immersion in the Jordan is a symbol of his absolute receptivity to God's action in his being and distinguishes him from the others who are baptized. Jesus is completely submerged and given over to God's way of thinking and acting. What follows from this is God's response to Jesus' total act of dedication:

> And just as he was coming up out of the water, he saw the heavens torn apart and the Spirit descending like a dove on him. And a voice came from heaven, "You are my Son, the Beloved; with you I am well pleased" (Mk 1:10-11).

Significantly, Mark makes Jesus' baptism the central scene of this opening section of the gospel. Here Jesus' identity and God's intention to communicate with humanity in a unique way through Jesus are clearly spelled out. Jesus' complete union with God is disclosed by the Spirit which alights on him, authorizes his ministry and introduces him to an encounter that will prepare him for his ministry. Jesus witnesses the rending of the heavens, the descent of God's dove-like spirit, and the heavenly voice. All three phenomena highlight this as a special moment of divine communication when Jesus' true identity is pronounced. The heavens are "torn apart." The presence of Jesus and his commitment to God reveal that God's traditional abode or realm can no longer be considered exclusively in the heavens. The heavens have been torn apart and expanded to include the human community. It is within the community, or house, formed by Jesus that God's presence can now be experienced.

The only other time that the verb "to rend" or "tear apart" is used in Mk is in 15:38 when "the curtain of the Temple was torn in two, from top to bottom." This occurs at the end of the gospel, at the death of Jesus. The Temple curtain preserved the sacredness of the inner sanctuary where the Holy of Holies was kept. This sanctuary was the place *par excellence* of divine communion. The curtain prevented unauthorized access to the inner sanctuary and provided a visible barrier to the Holy of Holies. Its symbolic rending on the death of Jesus meant that the communion between God and humanity was now a reality. Because of Jesus, those who are members of his household have unrestricted access to God.

Jesus in "The Wilderness"—Mk 1:12-13

After John's preaching (1:4-8) and Jesus' baptism (9-11), the Spirit drives Jesus into the wilderness. In the Greek, the word for "drive" *(ek-ballô)* is emphatic. It is as though the Spirit hurls Jesus into the wilderness, into life's desert and the experience of homelessness. There Jesus encounters Satan and, like the homeless wandering Israelites of the First Testament, is tempted. In this setting Jesus is "with the wild beasts" and the heavenly court of angels minister to him. In this scene, the eventual victory of the gospel in Jesus is anticipated. This will not occur without Jesus' battle with the evil that pervades his world. While victory and God's reign are guaranteed, suffering and the cross precede them. This again reveals Mk's narrative plot.

In his testing by Satan, Jesus is accompanied by wild beasts, possible reminders of the mythic wild beasts of apocalyptic literature (see Daniel 7 and Rev 11:7; 13:1f.) that symbolize images of political authorities.[7] If this is the case, then Jesus' struggle is not only personal but also against the seductive nature of authority, power, and popularity. His future ministry will confront evil in its social manifestations. Mark's Jesus will not encourage gospel readers to a privatized spirituality but insert them into the pragmatic domain of politics and economics reflected in their domestic worlds. It is here that the real struggle between evil and God's presence will be experienced.

Jesus' First Preaching—Mk 1:14-15

Only after this initial experience of homelessness and testing can Jesus announce the first words of good news about the nearness of God's kingdom ("reign" or *basileia*)[8]:

> Jesus came into Galilee preaching the good news of God, "The time is fulfilled, and the kingdom *(basileia)* of God has come near; repent, and believe in the good news" (Mk 1:14-15).

Jesus announces that the "time" *(kairos)* has arrived. This is the divine moment of God's beneficent action of grace on behalf of humanity; it is about to erupt onto the human stage through Jesus.[9] Like Mark's writing, Jesus' preaching is described as good news in two senses—good news about God and/or from God. It is a proclamation of the nearness of God's *basileia* and a call to conversion. This "good news" that is linked to the nearness of the *basileia* connects again to the political appreciation of the gospel already mentioned. For the evangelist and gospel reader cannot lose sight of the political and social dimensions of Jesus' ministry. God's *basileia* is present in the ministry of Jesus which is its concrete, local manifestation. The tangible

---

[7] Myers, *Binding*, 130.

[8] Helpful for understanding *basileia* is E. S. Fiorenza, *Jesus: Miriam's Child, Sophia's Prophet* (New York: Continuum, 1994) 93–95; E. Luz, "Βασιλεία," *EDNT* I, 201–5; C. Spicq, "Βασιλεία," *TLNT* I, 256–71.

[9] G. Delling, "καιρος" *TDNT* III, 459–62.

experience of God's *basileia* will be in Jesus' community, the household of disciples, which he begins to form in the next scene.

In this household human beings will experience divine intimacy and a style of living essentially inclusive of all human beings, irrespective of their cultural or social background. By inference Mark is suggesting that the *basileia* of God will be realized in the Greco-Roman household of the gospel audience. The stage is now set for God's *basileia* to break forth into the lives of those called to become members of Jesus' household. The closing words of Jesus in this prologue prepare for these new household-ers. They model for Mark's audience the radical openness, named "conversion," needed to form a household focused on Jesus, God's agent.

Summary

These opening scenes of Mark's Gospel present Jesus as the beloved one of God, the principal actor in the divine drama that is about to unfold through his career. His ministry is empowered by God's spirit. This spirit leads him to confront evil and announce the good news. It is this proclamation which completes this opening section and inaugurates his Galilean ministry, Mark's focus in the first half of the gospel. As will become obvious, the gospel's characters do not share the reader's privileged insight about Jesus. He remains an enigma to his protagonists, neighbors, hometown associates, family, and even his disciples. All this serves to reveal, even obliquely, Mark's theme of household and the possibility of domestic intimacy that Jesus seeks.

While the prologue explicitly raises the question "Who is Jesus?" it indirectly poses a second: "Who is with Jesus?" This creates another angle for reading Mark's prologue and exploring the theme of household. Mark reveals Jesus as God's beloved emissary in solidarity with human beings constantly confronted with their own loneliness or wilderness. From the perspective of the ancient worldview of the cosmic hierarchy, Jesus is a human being who is connected to the three spheres of existence: the human, supra-human, and sub-human.[10] His connection with these spheres indicates the kind of mission which follows. It is one that will continuously move between the human and non-human world. Jesus lives in solidarity with humans while protecting them from the evil that seeks their annihilation.

---

[10] On the cosmic social hierarchy as understood in the ancient Mediterranean world and presumed by Mark, see B. Malina and R. L. Rohrbaugh, *Social-Science Commentary on the Synoptic Gospels* (Minneapolis: Fortress Press, 1992) 182–83.

His communion with people announced in the prologue by his baptism prepares for his ministry that will gather together those who feel exclusion or oppression from each of the three spheres. This will become explicit as the excluded and socially unacceptable become invited and welcomed into a new community that Jesus forms. These are the ones who will be with him. In the wilderness—what I have been identifying as the narrative symbol for homelessness—Jesus seeks kinship. Instead he finds "wild beasts" from the sub-human realm, possible symbols of politically oppressive powers. This search for companions, his quest for home, continues in the next scene with the call of his first disciples (1:16-20).

8

The Gathering of the New Household—
Mk 1:16–3:35

Overview of Mk 1:16–3:35

After the gospel's introduction and prologue (1:1-15), the next several scenes establish more clearly Jesus' identity as God's agent and the healing nature of Jesus' ministry. Further, the concrete implications of his deeds and words are reflected in the calling together of those who will become the first members of his community and form his household of disciples. The nature of Jesus' household and its membership is distinctly spelled out in these first three chapters. This is particularly evident in the way that Mark juxtaposes Jesus' household gathering with the conventional religious gathering place, the synagogue, which needs healing and exorcism. The tension which Jesus and his household members will experience in the latter part of the gospel is prefigured in this early juxtaposition of these two spaces.[1]

Two blocks of material delineate this section. These are identified by what happens at the seaside.[2] In the first seaside setting Jesus calls the inaugural members of his household (1:16-20); in the second (2:13-14), Levi is called from his tax-gathering occupation; a third becomes the setting where a universal multitude gather to Jesus (3:7-9). This third seaside scene leads to a centerpiece in the first half of the gospel: Jesus' appointment of the Twelve (3:13-19) and, in a household setting, a definitive restatement of the true nature and membership of Jesus' household. The Twelve will represent the renewed household and its leadership, mirroring those who hold authority in Mark's Greco-Roman household.

[1] Struthers Malbon, *Narrative Space,* 113–20.
[2] Tolbert, *Sowing,* 132.

Seaside: Householders Called—Simon and Andrew,
James and John (1:16-20)

   Synagogue: An Exorcism (1:21-28)
   House: Healing and Exorcism (1:29-34)

Wilderness: Jesus Prays and Is Pursued (1:35-38)

   Synagogues: Exorcisms and Healing (1:39-45)
   House: Healing and Controversy (2:1-12)

Seaside: Householder Called—Levi (2:13-14)

   House: Controversy and Teaching (2:15-22)

Grainfields: About 'David's House' (2:23-28)

   Synagogue: Healing (3:1-6)

Seaside: Universal Multitude with the Disciples (3:7-12)

1

2

▼

Mountain: Appointment of Twelve (3:13-19a)
House: Nature and Membership of Jesus' Household (3:19b-34)

Householders Called

Jesus' call to "repent" from the gospel prologue is dramatically illustrated and modelled in the call of his first disciples (1:16-20). They are the prototypes of discipleship and household membership:

> As he passed by the Sea of Galilee, Jesus saw Simon and his brother Andrew casting a net into the sea—for they were fishermen. And Jesus said to them, "Follow me and I will make you become fishers of people." And immediately they left their nets and followed him. As he went a little farther, he saw James son of Zebedee and his brother John, who were in the boat mending the nets. Immediately he called them; and they left their father Zebedee in the boat with the hired men, and followed him (1:16-20).

In this carefully constructed scene, Mark telescopes into a single moment an event which Luke will later expand over several.[3] Mark is keen to

---

[3] D. R. A. Hare, *Mark* (Louisville: Westminster John Knox Press, 1996) 22–24.

emphasize the urgency and authority of Jesus' message that prompts an immediate radical response from those called. His power and authority will become the cause of dissension in the next few chapters. The call of the first disciples is narrated with brevity. Their response is immediate and total. This is the writer's way of involving gospel readers in a story in which they could identify themselves in a similar situation as these first-called disciples. Their response and radical attachment to Jesus parallels that of the disciples. In their conversion to the Christian movement, they would have had to break with the domestic, economic, and social securities.[4] The response by these first disciples would have fostered in the Greco-Roman reader a keen sense of loyalty and dedication to Jesus, before whom every other value or family relationship is relativized.

Mark's call story highlights the quality of those who respond to Jesus with such radical conversion. Their call is twofold—to "follow" Jesus and "become fishers of people," metaphorical language drawn from Near Eastern, extra-biblical, and pre-Christian traditions symbolizing the gathering together of people to experience God's salvific intent for them.[5] The first leads to the second; companionship with Jesus precedes and leads to the task of gathering others into Jesus' community of disciples. Companionship with Jesus is important for reordering one's values and socio-economic relationships.

When this dynamic is couched in domestic terms, the disciples are being invited into a new household formed by Jesus. Their membership in this household will require letting go of the *paterfamilias,* the conventional authority figurehead in the Roman *domus.* This is symbolized in Mk when those called leave their occupations (their nets and boats) and break their ties with the *paterfamilias* (their father Zebedee). In case the reader forgets this new household configuration, as the cross starts to loom large in the latter part of the gospel story, Jesus will remind his disciples about the authority structure and nature of his household (10:29-31).

This call story of the first disciples offers Mark a way of establishing the kind of *domus* that is well known to gospel's readers, yet culturally challenging and questioning of authority. It is this critical challenge that will bring some of its members into tension with Roman civil authorities and religious leadership. It is in this kind of *domus* that some of its members will experience doubts, compromise, and betrayal. Nevertheless, Jesus' proclamation of the Gospel and his declaration that God's presence is tangible wins immediate sympathizers in the disciples. Their attachment

---

[4] Myers, *Binding,* 132–33.
[5] W. H. Wuellner, *The Meaning of "Fishers of Men"* (Philadelphia: Westminster Press, 1967).

to Jesus in his new household ensures the final positive outcome of the gospel, despite the conflict and rejection it meets in the interim.

The exorcisms and healings that follow from the call of the first house-holders confirm the ultimate success of the good news lived out in Jesus' household. These scenes present a typical "day-in-the-life-of" Jesus during which he confronts and overcomes evil in healing the sick in and around Ca-pernaum. Although this confrontation with evil focusses on the afflicted in-dividual, the encounter also has far-reaching social consequences. Mark does not want to present Jesus as one who treats only physical disease or sickness. Jesus is portrayed as a healer of the deeper socio-political maladies symbolized by the infirmity. Jesus is concerned about the total well being of people and the social structures that create dis-ease in the human commu-nity. The gospel must be read at this deeper "political" level.[6] It prepares for 3:19-34 and Mark's restatement of the genuine social structure in which healing and divine communion can occur.

Healing in a Synagogue

It would be easy to read the first miracle story (1:21-28) with a clini-cal mindset: Jesus heals someone who is possessed. On another level the story is concerned with the nature of community and the renewal of the conventional religious setting as a place of healing. As we shall see, the re-newal of this setting in the earlier part of the gospel finds its parallel in the latter part of the gospel when the very household of Jesus will need heal-ing and purification. Mark notes,

> And immediately there was in their synagogue a human being with an un-clean spirit and cried out . . . (1:23).

The synagogue is identified with the people who are astonished by Jesus' teaching (1:22). This becomes the setting in which a "human being" (*anthrôpos,* in Greek) who is possessed cries out. There is no request for healing but a statement of identity about Jesus as "God's Holy One" (1:24). In other words, the story confirms an identity that the reader already knows.[7] His exorcism of the "unclean spirit" that follows reminds the reader that this religious setting and its leaders are not exempt from renewal and conversion. The place is not able to bring about human wholeness; its leaders lack au-thority. This is clear from the way the exorcism is framed by comments about the authority and power of Jesus' teaching (1:21-22, 27).

---

[6] Myers, *Binding,* 135.

[7] Kingsbury, *Conflict,* 38; J. D. Kingsbury, *Jesus Christ in Matthew, Mark, and Luke* (Philadelphia: Fortress Press, 1981) 33–34; J. D. Kingsbury, *The Christology of Mark's Gospel* (Philadelphia: Fortress Press, 1983) 86–99.

While the story is concerned about Jesus' deed of healing it is shaped by his word of teaching. This context offers the main clue to the story's meaning. Evil resides in individuals (and is in need of exorcism) because of religious institutions (synagogue) and their functionaries (the scribes) which keep people bound up and possessed. Such a religious system is in need of exorcism. With this second level of reading, the story signals a major controversy that will occur in the gospel—Jesus' confrontation with the religious and political leaders and the kind of structures they maintain that keep people oppressed.

Healing in a Household

If the synagogue is the place where unclean spirits can roam, the next scene and its domestic setting (1:29-31) provide a dramatic contrast where healing is sought, the resurrection anticipated, and ministry endorsed. The story is set in the house of the first-called disciples. Jesus responds to a request to heal the mother-in-law of Simon who is in bed with a fever,

> and coming, he lifted her up, taking her by the hand; and the fever left her, and she served them (1:31).

Jesus breaks through the social taboos that keep the marginalized—the sick and women—confined and out of public gaze.[8] Mark's Greek sentence is carefully constructed around three key verbs "lifted up," "left," and "serve." Jesus' touch liberates her: he "lifted her up," the fever is healed and the woman is free to "serve."[9]

There are several features of what happens here in Simon's house that need to be noted. The place where this deed occurs is in the house of Simon and Andrew. It also becomes the gathering place of the other first-called disciples. This, then, is the household of the disciples. Unlike the synagogue setting in the previous scene, this house becomes the environment where Jesus is requested to heal.[10] In the synagogue there was no such request.

Here the central action of Jesus is the "lifting up." Mark will use this same verb "lift up" in a couple of scenes later (2:1-12) and especially in the resurrection of Jesus (16:6). If the language is deliberate and the link to the resurrection intentional, then this first domestic story reveals the

---

[8] J. Dewey, "The Gospel of Mark," *Searching the Scriptures, Vol. 2, A Feminist Commentary,* ed. E. S. Fiorenza, (New York: Crossroad, 1994) 477. Behind the story lies an appreciation of the Mediterranean understanding of possession and illness. For a discussion of the causes of the fever of Peter's mother-in-law, see J. G. Cook, "In Defence of Ambiguity: Is There a Hidden Demon in Mark 1.29-31?" *NTS* 43 (1997) 184–208.

[9] Tolbert, "Mark," 267.

[10] Struthers Malbon, *Narrative,* 118–19.

household of the disciples as the setting in which the resurrection is anticipated and experienced. It anticipates and echoes Jesus' resurrection. The
household becomes the environment in which Jesus' resurrection is concretely experienced in history.

Simon's mother-in-law experiences the effects of the resurrection
through Jesus. He lifts her up by "taking her by the hand." He initiates the
deed through his touch; she cooperates. She is finally described as "serving them." The casual reader might be mistaken in thinking that, typically,
the sick woman after being healed returns to her domestic duties of wait-
ing on the men! The verb "to serve" *(diakonein)* indicates that more is
happening here than simply food preparation or servile performance. The
verb has a specific meaning in the ancient world.[11] It is generally associated with one who is called to represent and speak on behalf of another.
Simon's mother-in-law who is called to represent and act on behalf of
Jesus in Simon's discipled household carries out this ambassadorial function. "Serving them" could imply not only table service which, in Mark's
Christian household might be associated with eucharistic leadership, but a
ministry of the word.

If this is the case, then this healed woman has been released by Jesus
to engage in a ministry within the household of disciples. She is called to
minister to the community that gathers in this household renewed by
Jesus, liberated and realizing the resurrection in its midst. The ministering
woman becomes a tangible sign to this community of the power of the resurrection. The Greek tense of the verb further suggests that the action of
the woman is ongoing. It is not confined to one moment in history but is
a function that continues into Mark's day.

In terms of the domestic configuration, an extended household is envisaged in this scene. Mark presumes the *domus* of the gospel's Greco-
Roman audience. It is the dwelling place of two brothers with, at least, the
extended family of one of them. The Greco-Roman household was "patrilocal." This meant that the household's membership was centered on the
domus in which the sons and their wives and children could be accommodated. A married couple would be expected to live with the groom's parents. Only a large structured house, bigger than a simple or courtyard style
house, could accommodate the extended family of the married son. For the
purposes of the gospel narrative, Mark could be imagining that the *paterfamilias* of Simon and Andrew is still living, or, more likely that the *paterfamilias* has already died, and Simon has begun to assume the duties of

---

[11] For a fine treatment on the use of *diakonein* consult J. N. Collins, *Diakonia: Re-
interpreting the Ancient Sources* (Oxford: Oxford University Press, 1990) and its popular
edition, *Are all Christians Ministers?* (Collegeville: The Liturgical Press, 1992) esp. 86–108.

household head. It is his wife's mother who is sick in their house and the household large enough to extend hospitality to her family.

To understand how the mother-in-law comes to be resident in Simon's house invites us to consider further the kinship structure and the dynamic of Mediterranean marriages. This also warns us against hearing the story with modern, Western ears. In our experience of the nuclear (dual generational) Western family structure marriages occur by free choice of a couple who are unrelated to each other ("exogamous"). In the Mediterranean world marriages occurred within kinship or household groups between a couple selected by the family, especially the household head. The multigenerational nature of Mediterranean communities (called "endogamous") demanded that marriages occurred between close relatives. In other words, the ideal marriage partner for the groom was a first cousin. Such close relationships between the couple helped to cement family bonds and strengthen household ties.[12]

If this were Simon's situation envisaged by the gospel writer, then his mother-in-law would also have been his aunt.[13] She might have already been part of Simon's wider kinship or family group. His accommodation of her could have represented his fulfillment of a familial obligation expected of the *paterfamilias*.

Two other aspects about Simon's mother-in-law need consideration. She is either widowed or divorced. First, it is possible that besides his wife, Simon's mother-in-law is the only surviving member of the original household that belonged to Simon's father-in-law, possibly his uncle. His father's brother could have been already deceased, otherwise she would have remained in his house; she also has no sons to whom the immediate responsibility of care would have fallen in their mother's widowhood.

A second possibility is that the woman is divorced and her father's household, to which the divorced woman would return, no longer exists (for whatever reason). If this is the situation, then she would have found herself socially unsupported and destitute. Perhaps Simon's wife is her only family and it is into this household that she is invited to live. Though a member of the wider family group, her presence in Simon's household represents an invitation to join more intimately into the household in which Jesus' first disciples gather. The sense of caring for the woman is maintained or exercised by the male member (Simon) of her daughter's new household.

---

[12] K. C. Hanson offers a helpful discussion on kinship relationships and Mediterranean marriage practice in "Kinship," *The Social Sciences and New Testament Interpretation*, ed. R. Rohrbaugh, (Peabody, Mass.: Hendrickson Publishers, 1996) 62–79.

[13] J. J. Pilch, *The Cultural World of Jesus* (Collegeville, Minn.: The Liturgical Press, 1995) 160–61.

The nature of the above reconstruction is speculative, though not improbable. It is also in harmony with the direction in which the evangelist moves the narrative and reveals the gradual evolution of the household of Jesus' disciples. In such a household, its leader exercises faithful responsibility and care, and the healing for someone sick is sought. The request to Jesus for the woman's healing is immediate (1:30) and comes from a group of people in the household, presumably those four disciples mentioned in the preceding verse (1:29):

> And immediately leaving the synagogue he entered the house of Simon and Andrew with James and John. The mother-in-law of Simon lay in bed with a fever and they immediately told him about her (1:29-30).

Read from Mark's cultural perspective, this short scene in the opening chapter suggests interesting insights into the gospel audience. If there is any truth in the hypothesis that I have proposed then what is happening in Simon's *domus* is important for the residents in the house-churches of the late first century. Simon's household could well be a microcosm of the Markan community that has extended its welcome to those who were socially alone and destitute. These could conceivably include the widowed, singled, and divorced. For Mark the Christian household becomes the place of healing, where an alternative model of social equality and freedom is evident. It presents another way of exercising household leadership and authority that brings attention first to those in need. This is seen in the way Simon and his three companions act to bring Jesus' healing to the woman.

The Attraction of Jesus' Household

The attraction of this kind of healing household is seen in the next few verses (1:32-34): the household becomes the center of healing for the whole city (1:32-34). This is an urban household and, typical of the Greco-Roman *domus* of the first century, a place into which guests were invited. Its public function evident in the structure of the *domus* and especially in the space provided by the conjunction of the *atrium* to the door. This could well be the meaning of,

> and the whole city was gathered right up against the door (1:33).

Most commentators read the Greek from the viewpoint that the crowd are outside the door of the house ("And the whole city was gathered together about the door"—RSV). But from Mark's domestic perspective it might arguably be describing the public gathering inside the *domus,* an understanding presumed and reinforced in the people-packed house of

2:1-2. If this is the case here, then Mark is indicating the growing attraction of Jesus' household in which the disciples are gathered, healed, called to ministry, and into which the socially rejected gather. The popularity of this house is emphasized. It is packed with people; those who congregate in it represent the whole city. This emphasizes the universal effect of Jesus' deeds that bring "the whole city" into the *domus* and reinforces the wider social implications of his mission. Simon's house is a mirror of Mark's Roman household community.

After these domestic healings Jesus withdraws again into the wilderness for prayer (1:35). Here he is pursued by Simon and companions and he reminds them of his preaching mission to the neighboring villages (1:38). The next verse (1:39) takes the reader on a preaching and exorcising tour into synagogues throughout Galilee. It is in this context of a village synagogue mission that Jesus heals a leper (1:40-45). The figure of the pleading leper to be "made clean" (1:40) is a further poignant reminder to Mark's audience of the difficulty of finding a place of healing and community. Jesus' touching of the leper breaks through the isolation and barriers imposed by the religious elite. He destroys the religious taboos manufactured by the religious authorities. His touch of the afflicted person means that he himself now is regarded as leprous, contagious, and outcast. He deliberately defies those who uphold a system that makes people outsiders and isolated. This defiance is evident in his injunction to the healed leper to report to the priests as legislated "for a witness to them" (1:44). The healed leper will witness to the Torah officials that an alternative community is possible through Jesus. Through this healing Jesus confronts the total religio-political system that keeps people isolated from full community.

Household Healing of One Paralyzed

In the next healing scene (2:1-11) Mark again juxtaposes the oppression evident in the establishment constructed by public officials with the liberation attained in Jesus' household. Here Jesus has returned to Capernaum and it is reported that he is "in a house" (2:1). The only house mentioned to date that Jesus has been at in Capernaum is the one belonging to Simon and Andrew,

> and so many gathered together that there was no longer any room not even to the door, and he spoke to them the word (1:2).

As in the earlier house scene, the crowds gather into and fill the house. The good news that he has preached from the beginning of his public ministry continues to draw adherents. If Mark is envisioning the Roman *domus* then the *atrium* is again filled and the crowd is pushed right to the door. Into the midst of this crowded house a paralytic is let down after an opening has been made through that section of roofing above Jesus. Again, if the Roman *domus* is intended, then the place where all this action is taking place is the *cubiculum,* that part of the house connected to the *atrium* where the household head receives guests. It is here that Mark has the scribes "sitting" (2:6).

Jesus responds immediately to the request to heal the paralytic. But Jesus addresses the real source of human distress. Rather than dealing with the handicap itself—the incapacity to walk—he heals at the deeper level, the level of relationship and structures that keep a person economically and emotionally disabled. Throughout the story the disabled person is always identified as the "paralytic." This is the central focus of the story: the paralysis that can only be overcome through the healing word of Jesus in his household. Jesus also proclaims the person free of "sin." While the tendency has been to read this declaration from a moral perspective, as Jesus forgiving any moral guilt for which the man is responsible, the healing is more profoundly social.

To some interpreters of the Torah, sickness, handicap, or barrenness were signs of God's disfavor and punishment due to sin. Jesus overrules this interpretation and declares the person forgiven (literally, "released") of sin. The traditional interpreters of the Torah, the sitting scribes, consider Jesus' declaration a violation of God's evaluation that only they are qualified to discern. In their eyes his pronouncement is tantamount to blasphemy because he presumes to understand the mind of God. Jesus ratifies the paralyzed person's freedom to live as one blessed by God and to worship again with his own household. The authority of Jesus' word is born out in the healing of the paralysis. The outward healing confirms the inner healing of the person's total well-being.

There are two details about this healing story of the paralytic which are important to note. The first concerns what the healed person is called to do. As Jesus heals he says:

> "I say to you: Rise, take your pallet and go to your own house." And he rose and immediately taking up the pallet he went out before them all (2:11).

The paralytic is told to "rise" and does so. What is translated as "he rose" is actually "he was raised." The raising is not something that the paralytic does; it is something done to the person by Jesus. The same resurrectional language evident in the healing of Simon's mother-in-law is again here. The person is also told to "go home." As with Simon's mother-in-law, the healed person's ongoing life is focused back in the household. This becomes the setting in which what has been done by Jesus is witnessed by the one healed. The gesture of faith of the four who let the paralytic into the midst of Jesus' crowded house to be healed is now repeated in a similar gesture with the healed person returning back to the family household.

The second detail concerns those who are present at the healing. As the man walks the reaction of the people, presumably those gathered in the house, is that "we have never seen anything like this!" (2:12). Their reaction is more than a note of wonder about Jesus' power to heal. It is also about the kind of people who are healed and called back into community. This is the reason that Mark notes that they "glorified God" (2:12). Jesus' ministry attracts a wide range of people. The non-elite, the ordinary people of the land, the *ʿam haʾaretz* (2:13); the socially rejected and unclean (the sick, possessed, and handicapped), the artisans and retainers (as evident in the next story of Levi—2:13f.). All are present in Jesus' household. They mirror the mixture of peoples and backgrounds in Mark's community. Rather than excluding people from membership because of their religious pedigree or economic and social status, Jesus' household (continued in Mark's own community) is primarily inclusive of all. It represents an alternative social system based on equality. This comes from Jesus' experience of a God who seeks out the socially homeless: the oppressed, poor, destitute, sick, and handicapped.

The religious elite, the scribes, are also present in Jesus' household. These are noted as sitting and some of them start to question Jesus' boldness in forgiving sin. They are signaled out for their unwillingness to allow Jesus to heal the person totally. This group is present in the household of Jesus. They, like the rest, will be called to conversion and to see the possibilities of God's renewed household with new eyes. They could well represent those in Mark's community who are religiously scrupulous or unwilling to embrace the rejected and unworthy. Mark will develop the character of this group as the gospel unfolds.

The Members of Jesus' Household

The membership of Jesus' household and its implications for the Torah holiness code is spelled out in the next scene with the call of the tax-collector Levi and the household meal that follows (2:13-22). This third domestic scene highlights even more strongly the kind of community that gathers in Jesus' household. Its membership is the reason for the strong opposition from the official religious leadership ("the scribes of the Pharisees"):

> [15]And as he reclined [for dining] in his house, many tax collectors and sinners were also reclining with Jesus and his disciples, for there were many and they followed him. [16]And the scribes of the Pharisees seeing that he was eating with sinners and tax collectors, said to his disciples, "Why does he eat

with tax-collectors and sinners?" [17]And when Jesus heard this, he said to them, "Those who are well have no need of a physician, but those who are sick; I have not come to call the righteous but sinners" (2:15-17).

Verse 15 sets the scene. It is "in his house." The Greek text is ambiguous as to whose house is being referred. Most English translations resolve the ambiguity in favor of Levi and make the house Levi's house.[14] There is no explicit mention of Levi dining with Jesus or that it is his house. The scene occurs straight after the calling of Levi to discipleship and it is this closeness which has made some commentators associate the house with Levi. All we know of those who gather in the house are the tax-collectors (and presumably this would include Levi), sinners, the disciples, and group called "the scribes of the Pharisees" who are distinguishable from the scribes in the previous scene. The "his" could be equally read as Jesus' house. This is not to say that Jesus actually owned a house, but it is the house that is identified with Jesus. It is this house that becomes the subject of a religious argument.

The specific location in the house is the dining room. In Mark's world of the Roman *domus,* this would have been the *triclinium,* the place into which guests would have been invited by the household head. In the Greco-Roman world guests were reclined on three benches as they shared their meal. Into this room Mark has crowded the invited guests of Jesus: tax-collectors, retainers who acted on behalf of the elite and were regarded with disdain by the poorer majority, "sinners" who were non-observant in their religious duties, and the disciples, followers of Jesus.

Mark notes that the tax-collectors and sinners were "many" and "they followed him." This is discipleship language and suggests that the number of Jesus' community has grown to include the socially undesirable. They are also described "sitting with Jesus and his disciples." Mark emphasizes the meal setting in this domestic scene in which table communion is stressed. These social rejects are in the same posture of dining in the Roman *domus* as Jesus and his disciples. The dining posture underscores the social communion shared by all.

Read with Mark's Greco-Roman domestic sensitivity, membership to Jesus' house is not exclusive. It is a house of communion or *koinonia,* where healing takes place, forgiveness experienced, and the socially excluded find welcome, hospitality, and nurture. This is the point emphasized in Jesus' response to his questioners' interrogation of the disciples

---

[14] But see J. Painter's argument for the household belonging to Levi in "When is a House not a Home?" 498–500. My argument moves towards a more symbolic or metaphorical interpretation of the household language.

about his dining habits with those prejudged as unholy: "I have not come to call the righteous but sinners" (2:17). All the dimensions of Jesus' household evident in this scene are similar to the elements of the ideal Roman household and realized in Mark's community. There was a further insight into the Greco-Roman household that came through the Greek philosophers and Roman writers. This concerned the house as the place of happiness and the foundational unit of the city-state where people found happiness.

Jesus' Disciples Interrogated

After interrogating Jesus' disciples, the religious elite next question Jesus about his disciples (2:18-22). They appear joyful and do not fast because, as the reader knows, the very source of their joy, Jesus, is with them (2:19). Throughout this section of the gospel as Mark has been presenting the nature of Jesus' household, emphasis has also been given to the spirit that typifies its household members. Mark presents Jesus as God's parable of enacted joy who comes to celebrate those regarded as sinners. Jesus calls them to become members of God's household. God's delight in human beings evident in Jesus' household is reflected in the story of Levi (2:13-14).

Here the house guests dine with Jesus and his disciples (2:15-17). They are like wedding guests happy to celebrate the presence of the bridegroom (2:18-20). But Mark's Jesus also realizes that the presence of the bridegroom will not last, just as those who form his household will not be free from tension and struggle. In a veiled reference to his death, Jesus recognizes that there will be struggle because of the incompatibility between what Jesus has come to do ("new wine") and the past structures ("wineskins"):

> "And no one puts new wine into old wineskins; otherwise, the wine will burst the skins, and the wine is lost as well as the skins; but new wine is for fresh skins" (2:21-22).

Jesus will go to his death in Mark's gospel because he dares to presume a divine authority that redefines the boundaries of God's chosen people. He also offers with his alternative domestic structure a serious critique of the socially acceptable economic structure maintained by the wealthy minority. This theme is carried over into the next scenario that moves outside the house to grainfields (2:23-28). In a continuing controversy with the religious interpreters, Jesus' disciples are again attacked for working on the Sabbath as they pluck grain. His defense of his disciples becomes Jesus' reinterpretation of the meaning of the Torah and its religious institutions. Using language that is evocative of the Eucharist, Jesus describes how David and his companions went into the house of God when they were hungry and ate the bread of the Presence. The place and bread was sacred, but it was for the benefit of people. This leads Jesus to proclaim:

> "The Sabbath was made for humankind, and not humankind for the Sabbath so that the Son of Man is lord even of the Sabbath" (1:27-28).

Mark presents Jesus as one who liberates people. His ministry addresses the ills that keep people spiritually, socially, and economically disabled. His good news is that all religious institutions, the Temple and Sabbath included, are intended to assist the growth in the total well being of all. Jesus' controversial interpretation of one of Israel's sacred institutions upsets its guardians. The next scene (3:1-6) shifts back again to the synagogue and further reinforces the contrast between the conventional religious setting and the place in which Jesus gathers his disciples, between the "wineskins" and the "new wine." The scene spells out the implications of his teaching about the Sabbath as he publicly heals a man with the withered hand in the synagogue on the holy day. To his antagonists, Jesus says:

> "Is it lawful to do good or to do harm on the Sabbath, to save life or to kill?" They were silent. He looked around at them with anger; he was grieved at their hardness of heart and said to the person, "Stretch out your hand." He stretched it out, and his hand was restored. The Pharisees went out and immediately conspired with the Herodians against him, how to destroy him (3:4-6).

The inability of the religious leaders to see clearly the theological appropriateness and justice of Jesus' challenge comes from "their hardness of heart." This is the fundamental cause of the conflict that will eventually lead to his death. It is a form of ruthless stubbornness unwilling to be open to change, *metanoia* and, ultimately, the God of Jesus. The seriousness and pervasiveness of this attitudinal malady is not confined to the religious authorities. It will eventually affect Jesus' own disciples (6:52; 8:17). As the Pharisees and Herodians historically, unlikely bedmates, conspire to kill Jesus (3:6) the cross begins to cast its shadow over his ministry.

The mention of Jesus' destruction now plotted by the authorities for the first time enunciates explicitly a narrative theme to which everything else in Mark's story will be directed. The tension builds in these opening chapters, as those who seek membership in Jesus' household are more clearly identified. Their characters come under close scrutiny. The scenes that remain before the teaching of the parables in chapter 4 are occupied with clarifying the nature of Jesus' community and the potential hostility that its members will experience from the religious authorities. The antagonism experienced by the disciples outside their household will also have its counterpart within. This internal discord will be further identified as Mark's Jesus broaches the subject of household division in 3:20-27. It has already been flagged by the questioning scribal figures seated in Jesus' house in 2:6-7. Jesus will become a cause of division.

Jesus' Disciples and Antagonists

The line separating Jesus' true disciples from those who reject him now becomes more clearly drawn by the evangelist. In the first part of Mk 3, after the Sabbath healing and Jesus' confrontation with Israel's religious legislators, Mark describes the positive responses which Jesus receives.

First, in a summary of his healing activity in Mk 3:7-12, the crowds who are the *ʿam haʾaretz* again seek Jesus after he withdraws with his disciples to the Sea of Galilee.

> Jesus departed with his disciples to the sea, and a great multitude from Galilee followed him; hearing all that he was doing, they came to him in great numbers from Judea, Jerusalem, Idumea, beyond the Jordan, and the region around Tyre and Sidon (3:7-8).

Mark notes how Jesus withdraws from potentially overwhelming situations to the companionship of his disciples. This movement of conflict-withdrawal will continue and become more pronounced in the latter part of the gospel where Jesus concentrates on the instruction of his disciples in the light of his impending death. Jesus withdraws with them to the house. The conflict-withdrawal motif is more than a means of moving Jesus from one scene to another. Jesus must withdraw away from the scene of mission for a short time to reflect on the meaning of his ministry, discern its direction, and situate the conflict experienced within the framework of God's plan. The narrative device of conflict-withdrawal represents an important dynamic essential to ministry: the necessity of reflection in the midst of pastoral action. It also allows the gospel's narrative space to move back to the household of Jesus' community.

The evangelist notes how those attracted to Jesus are drawn from city and country, Northern and Southern Israel, Jewish and non-Jewish territories. In other words, the barriers separating people from each other are being broken down. The new household formed around Jesus transcends political, economic, social, and cultural differences. As we have already seen, it is a household in which healing and release from the demonic are sought:

> Whenever the unclean spirits saw him, they fell down before him and shouted, "You are the Son of God!" But he sternly ordered them not to make him known (3:11-12).

Jesus continues to confront and overwhelm the power of Satan. Unclean spirits "fall down" before him and remind the reader again about Jesus' true identity: He is so close to God that he can be called God's Son. Until that moment when human and divine reckoning about Jesus coalesce in his passion and death, clues from the demonic are silenced.

The second positive response to the Gospel proclaimed in Jesus' ministry is found in the appointment of the Twelve, the principal leadership group of his household (3:13-19). The scene begins the formalization of Jesus' household community:

> He went up the mountain and called to him those whom he wanted and they came to him. And he appointed twelve, whom he also named apostles, to be with him, and to be sent out to proclaim the message, and to have authority to cast out demons. So he appointed the Twelve: Simon (to whom he gave the name Peter) . . . and Judas Iscariot, who betrayed him (3:13-16, 19).

This theologically charged passage presents us with some of the key ingredients for a community focused on Jesus and a microcosm of Mark's house churches. Jesus goes up the mountain, like the other great founder of the Israelite community, Moses. Those whom he appoints are drawn from the wider circle of disciples. They are "called" like Simon, Andrew, James, and John in Mk 1, and Levi in Mk 2. The initiative for what happens comes from Jesus—not those called. The center of the assembled community is Jesus. He is the reason for its life and the focus of its attention.

The Twelve

Jesus "appoints" twelve. The list of names that Mark gives generally corresponds to the list in Mt, Lk, and Acts, though there are minor differences. For subsequent generations of Christians the memory of the number of disciples appointed was more important than the specific memory of their names. The function of the Twelve more than the details of its composition was remembered. The number recalls the tribes of Israel. In Mark's judgment, Jesus' Twelve functions as the renewal of these tribes; the Twelve are symbolic of the kind of authority and leadership necessary for a renewed Greco-Roman *domus*.

The mission of the first four disciples called in Mk 1 is repeated here with the Twelve. The order of what they are appointed to do is deliberate. They are commissioned to be with Jesus, preach, and have authority to cast out demons. Their primary function is to be companions of Jesus and form the nucleus of the discipled household. Their communion with him becomes the ultimate touchstone of authentic discipleship. Because of this intimacy they share with Jesus they are able to be his representatives. They can preach the Gospel and exorcise. Through their ministry the *basileia* of God is continued and Satan's power vanquished. Their ministry is shaped by and parallels that of Jesus'.

The list of the Twelve ends with the mention of "Judas Iscariot, who betrayed him." The note of betrayal introduces the theme of discipleship failure, a central concern in the second half of the gospel, and again reminds the reader of the narrative direction of the gospel which will culminate on the cross. The mention of the betraying Judas also repeats a motif that has started to merge in Mark's presentation of Jesus' household in Mark's opening chapters and will now preoccupy the final two scenes of chapter 3, internal discord and dissension.

After Jesus appoints the Twelve, the scene immediately shifts from a mountain to a house (3:20). In this domestic setting where Jesus gathers with his disciples, the crowds again assemble,

> so that they were unable even to eat a meal (literally, "bread"), and those who were from his family group came to seize him for they said that he was out of his senses (3:20-21).

The enthusiasm of those who gather with Jesus in his house contrasts to the rejection and embarrassment of his kinship group who are convinced that he is mad. They come to seize him for they consider he is "out of his senses." Their use of this expression reveals that they fundamentally believe he is possessed by a demon. This contrast between the members of Jesus' household and his natural family, between insiders and outsiders, will be explored further in the final scene of this chapter. At the beginning and end of this section, his family show that they do not really know him; they are outside his house.

The inference from Jesus' natural kin that he is possessed is taken up explicitly by "the scribes who had come down from Jerusalem" (3:22). These scribes are distinguished from those who earlier were inside Jesus' house. These are outsiders who represent the official Jerusalem religious leadership. They attack Jesus as one possessed by the prince of demons, "Beelzebul." This can be translated from the Hebrew *(ba'al z'bul)* as the "Lord of the house." In other words, Jesus is attacked for his household leadership that is regarded as demonic. His reply to his accusers takes the form of a "parable," the first time one is named in Mark's gospel and alerts the reader to how Jesus will use parables in the next chapter. Here the parable or riddle draws out for his antagonists the impossibility of the prince of demons casting out demons.

If Jesus were Satan, then he could not overthrow himself. His deeds of power clearly witness to the demise of Satan and the division of his house. That house is more than the symbolic house of evil; it is the abuse of legitimate religious institutions, like the Temple, by authorities who have little concern for the poor of the land. Mark affirms Jesus as the one who has entered into Satan's house and plundered it (3:26-27). Through his ministry and the growing membership of his household, Satan's house is divided and will collapse. For Mark, Jesus is ironically "Lord of the house." Those who reject him by describing him possessed are ultimately rejecting God's spirit working through him. They are exposing themselves to what Mark calls the unforgivable "eternal sin" (3:28-30).

Jesus' Natural Family and Genuine Household

The final concluding scene (3:31-35) is a summary of Mark's opening chapters. It establishes definitively the nature of membership in Jesus' household. It reasserts the distinction between his natural kin and those who really belong to his household, between family members who presume membership in his household and the disciples:

> And his mother and his brothers came; and standing outside, they sent for him calling him. And a crowd sat around him and said to him, "Your mother and your brothers and sisters are outside asking for you." And he replied to them, "Who are my mother and my brothers?" And looking at those who sat around him he said, "Here are my mother and my brothers! For whoever does the will of God is my brother and sister and mother" (3:31-35).

The distinction between the family and the crowd is intentional. It continues the contrast between "outsiders" and "insiders," one of the narrative riddles of the gospel. The physical location of the characters which make up this scene illustrate the insider/outsider tension: Those considered outsiders by the religious and political authorities are insiders in Jesus' community. They sit around Jesus and are physically closest to him. They constitute his household. Those who presume themselves to be insiders because of kinship connection are, in Mark's gospel, outsiders.

The contrast between kinship group and household community is further highlighted by the posture of the two groups. The family is standing; the crowd is sitting around him as disciples around the teacher. Only the crowd is able to speak to him directly; the family must communicate via the crowd who is in the discipleship position. Jesus finally praises those sitting around him as his genuine household. True kinship in the community of disciples rests not on natural relationship or blood ties but on the practice of God's will. In this one saying Jesus refashions household relationships and traditional lines of kinship and obligation, revered since the time of Abraham and Sarah.

Summary

The gospel's first three chapters after the prologue herald key themes which will develop as the gospel story continues. They confirm that Jesus is God's agent through a healing ministry that makes tangible God's *basileia;* they prepare for Jesus' passion as the cross' silhouette is subtly revealed; they introduce the antagonists who are hostile to Jesus and his disciples. Most importantly, these chapters establish who constitutes Jesus' household, its distinguishing features and how power will be exercised in it. Finally, Mark offers various contrasts in these chapters: the house and synagogue, the insider and outsider, the natural family and genuine household. These contrasts allow the gospel writer to explore a variety of reactions to Jesus which will flow over into the parable teaching in Mk 4 which expose the reader to another way of perceiving reality.

Read through Mark's domestic lens, these chapters also reveal the kind of household encountered by the gospel audience. If my way of viewing Mark's Roman urban world is correct and if Mark is writing the Gospel to allow the story of Jesus and his community of disciples to address a domestic-familiar audience in a relevant way, then it is conceivable that this has implications for the narrative description of Jesus' household. It is a *domus* typical of the Greco-Roman world, large enough to embrace a huge city population. In it the socially reprobate find a home. It becomes the place of healing, teaching, ministry and is an urban center in which the resurrection is tangibly experienced.

Mark's *domus* modeled on Jesus' household of disciples offers an alternative domestic structure. In this new household status, power, security and family connections are no longer the values that will determine its membership or structure its lines of authority. It is a renewed Roman *domus* in which the typical *paterfamilias* is absent. The authority of Jesus acting through the household's leadership replaces him. Because Mark presents this household as an alternative religious, economic, and political system that will challenge the status quo of the Roman Empire, it will become the center of a conflict from which neither the household nor its members will be immune. This conflict will come from outside the household. Unfortunately, it will also emerge from within.

9

Strengthening the Household—
Mk 4:1–6:6

Overview of Mk 4:1–6:6

The first three chapters of the gospel establish Jesus' credentials and the membership for his household. Now Mark further explores the nature of the household of disciples. The focus shifts to the tensions that this household will experience. The section is prepared for by the scene in which Jesus' natural family seeks him out in his crowded house (3:31-35). This provides the opportunity to identify unambiguously the members of Jesus' household. Similarly, the section concludes with the rejection of Jesus in his hometown, the questioning of his family connections, and their disbelief (6:1-11).

Between these two framing scenes, Mark presents Jesus' ministry in two blocks clearly defined by a boat/house setting. Mark does not contrast these two spatial settings through their juxtaposition as happens in previous chapters with the house-synagogue. Rather the evangelist aligns them. One ("the boat") speaks to and elucidates the other ("the house"). What is taught (in the first block) or done (in the second block) in the boat setting has implications for how the reader is to better appreciate or understand Jesus' household. The boat acts as a spatial symbol for and an extension of Jesus' household. For this reason, what occurs in the boat is important for instructing Mark's householders.[1]

---

[1] E. Best interprets the boat stories as reflective of Mark's community in *The Temptation and the Passion: The Markan Soteriology* (Cambridge: Cambridge University Press, 1990) 181–83. See also T. Woodroof, "The Church as Boat in Mark: Building a Seaworthy Church," *RestorQuart* 39 (1997) 231–49.

— *About Jesus' household:* affirmation of genuine kin (3:31-35)

Boat setting: The *meta*-parable: the sowing seed (4:1-9)

House setting:
    Commentary on Parables (4:10-12)
        • Allegory of the sowing seed (4:13-20)
        • Other parables (4:21-32)
    Final commentary on Jesus' parable ministry
        (4:33-34)

1

Boat context:
        • Storm on the lake (4:35-41)
        • Healing the Gerasene demoniac (5:1-20)

House context:
        • Healing of synagogue-official's daughter
            (5:21-24, 35-43)
        • Healing of hemorrhaging woman (5:25-34)

2

— *About Jesus' household:* rejection by kin (6:1-6)

The first section of boat/house material focuses on Jesus' teaching (4:1-34); the second explicates this teaching through his miraculous deeds (4:35–5:34). In the first, the opening presentation of the sowing seed is central (4:1-9). It indicates the opposition that Jesus and his household will suffer, though ultimately God's *basileia* will be fruitful. The remainder of this first block (4:10-12) also presents how parables are to be interpreted and forecasts the enigmatic reaction to Jesus' ministry. A commentary on how parables are to be interpreted (4:10-12, 33-34) frames the allegory of the sowing seed (4:13-20) and other parables (4:21-32). The frame identifies a private (household) space for Jesus' instruction of his disciples.

In the scenes which make up the second block of boat/house material, the implications of the parable teaching for the disciples and Mark's community are teased out. The first two stories are set within the context of a boat. The storm on the lake (4:35-41) identifies the faith problems that dog this household. The exorcism of the Gerasene demonic (5:1-20) dramatically illustrates the power of the household to nurture and be evangelized.

Finally the two scenes of female healing that intercalate each other (5:21-24, 35-43 and 5:25-34) remind the reader how Jesus' household of disciples is the place of healing and receptive of the socially excluded (a hemorrhaging woman and sick child).[2] Both healings occur in relationship to a household, either as Jesus journeys towards the house or is inside it.

Mark's Parables

The gospel's parables in chapter 4 reveal in a different form the mysterious and surprising nature of Jesus' ministry already evident from his healing actions in the previous chapters. The parables confirm Jesus' actions. Like these deeds of healing, they reveal the in-breaking of God's presence into lives subject to oppression and disorder.[3]

Parables can be stories, sayings, or surprising riddles. The listener who is open to the parable maker and to the parable is first attracted by its images. These can be understood simply on a literal level, but when put together with the other images in the parable they tease the mind on to a second, deeper, unexpected level of meaning that surprises or "catches out" the listener. The unexpected in the riddle traps the listener, upsets the assumed ending, and lays open an alternative vision of human existence. In the actual recognition of new possibilities, seeds of conversion are sown. At the moment of recognition, the parable itself becomes a vehicle of the *basileia* of God. The parable proposes a new way of seeing reality; it challenges the dominant social and political consciousness; it proposes a new vision of life free of the conventions that oppress and victimize. If the disciple accepts this, God's perspective bears fruit.

The imagery which Mark uses to set the scene for the parables is significant:

> And again he began to teach beside the sea and such a huge crowd gathered around him that he got into a boat to sit on the sea, and the whole crowd was beside the sea on the land, and he taught them many things in parables (4:1-2).

---

[2] This insight into the approach used by Mark regarding healings is supported by the ancient Mediterranean appreciation of illness. On this, see J. Pilch, "Healing in Mark: A Social Science Analysis," *BTB* 15 (1985) 142–50; J. Pilch, "Sickness and Healing in Luke-Acts" in *The Social World of Luke-Acts,* ed. J. H. Neyrey (Peabody, Hendrickson, 1991) 181–210; Malina and Rohrbaugh, *Social-Science Commentary,* 210–11.

[3] D. Juel, *A Master of Surprise: Mark Interpreted* (Philadelphia: Fortress Press, 1994) ch. 4.

The literalness of the Greek sentence as it is translated above reveals several things. The way the evangelist places the geographical images of land and sea side-by-side is deliberate; so too is the unusual expression of Jesus "sitting on the sea." For the Mediterraneans the sea was a barrier that divided one part of the world from another; it needed to be crossed. Its other side represented the unfamiliar; it was a place of chaos, the abode of evil and was fraught with danger for those that traveled across it. The "other side" represented for Mark's community the focus of Christian mission or evangelization. This meant moving from the secure to the insecure and unknown. Mark will explore all these images about the sea more fully in the first event which follows on from this section on the parables, the storm on the lake (4:35-41). Prior to that event, Jesus first teaches the crowd from a boat on the sea.

The boat is more than simply a convenient pulpit from which Jesus teaches. It offers Jesus a way of being with a large crowd gathered around him. It functions as the discipleship house in earlier scenes; where a large crowd gathers, evil is overcome and the sick healed, and people taught. The boat could be symbolic of Mark's household communities. Mark's house churches offer the environment for potential disciples to be strengthened before life's mayhem. Within these house churches Jesus' teaching provides a backdrop against which their experience of chaos and potential disaster in their mission can be interpreted.

The "Metaparable"

The first parable of Mk 4 is the most important. It is the parable by which all other parables are interpreted.[4] This is confirmed by the way Mark's Jesus addresses his disciples about the "Do you not understand this parable? Then how will you understand all the parables?" (4:13).[5] In fact, this initial parable becomes the interpretative meta-parable of Jesus' total ministry. How potential disciples respond to it shapes their membership in Jesus' household. In this opening parable about the sowing seed, the seed experiences several difficulties which prevent its fruitfulness. However, despite set backs:

> "Other seeds fell into the good earth and brought forth grain, growing up and increasing and producing thirty and sixty and a hundredfold." And he said, "Whoever has ears to hear listen!" (4:8-9).

[4] Tolbert, *Sowing,* 148–64.

[5] For a helpful overview of Mark's use of parables, see B. L. Mack, *A Myth of Innocence: Mark and Christian Origins* (Philadelphia: Fortress Press, 1988) 135–71.

The surprise for a peasant farmer, Jesus' chief original audience, was the superabundance of the harvest regardless of the seed's initial frustrations. For a Palestinian farmer, seed would be equivalent to money. In a normal harvest season first-century farmers would expect a sevenfold return on planted seed; a tenfold return was considered a very good harvest. Jesus' parable presents a harvest return of between three to ten times better than the very best crop. This indeed would be beyond the wildest dreams of peasant farmers. Such surplus would not only help them to pay their taxes but also to pay off their debts to the landowners, to purchase land and become forever independent.[6] There are obvious spiritual or religious associations with the parable in the fruitfulness of God's word proclaimed through Jesus. God's *basileia* will be abundantly enjoyed even despite apparent setbacks.[7]

For Mark's later Greco-Roman urban audience, the parable's original message addressed to a Galilean rural community retains its force. Mark's Jesus is concerned about the physical aspects of human living that prevent people from enjoying the kind of life God intended for them. The harvest's size and quality, a continual preoccupation of peasant farmers, can become a metaphor for the fruitfulness of God's *basileia* in Mark's later Roman household. Jesus' original intention for the parable could envision God's *basileia* in which the vassal relationship between peasant farmer and wealthy landlord were destroyed.

Mark translates this teaching into a vision about the ultimate fruitfulness of the Christian message in the Greco-Roman world. This is apparent in the allegory of the parable with its explanation by Jesus in 4:13-20. The allegory is a historical overview of Mark's household community. The original enthusiasm of some disciples has waned (4:15); others have broken their fidelity to the household through persecution (4:16-17) or have been lured away for social reasons (4:18-19). Despite failure, membership in Mark's discipleship household is strong and fruitful (4:20). It is from this positive and rich perspective that the remaining parables must be interpreted. All are essentially concerned about the humble and frustrating origins of a community in which surprising results unfold.

The three parables, of the lamp, the scattered seed and the mustard seed, explore further the manifestation of God's reign in Jesus. The parable of the lamp on its stand (4:21-25) calls for confidence on the part of the disciple. God's *basileia* will win out; the vision for inclusive community already evidenced in the household of disciples assembled with Jesus

---

[6] Myers, *Binding*, 174–77.

[7] R. H. Gundry, *Mark: A Commentary on his Apology for the Cross* (Grand Rapids, Mich.: Eerdmans, 1993) 192–95.

and, in later history, in Mark's house churches, will become reality. It will be inevitable. However, its realization will take time; it will not be instantaneous. The parable about the scattered seed (4:26-29) that grows imperceptibly and finally bears fruit without the farmer's knowledge confirms the need for patience and commitment. The disciple is to be committed to the task of seed scattering; the eventual harvest is the work of God. Change will eventually come about. The last parable of the mustard seed (4:30-32) offers hope to fragile disciples. It emphasizes how God's *basileia* can be experienced in the most unspectacular, commonplace, or "shrub-like" events. It is located in the ordinary.

This final parable draws together several themes already stressed in the other parables. The work of Jesus brings about the presence of a God who is as much concerned about the political and social situation of the gospel's audience as about their religious disposition. The parables are means for further communicating Jesus' conviction of a God passionately involved in the lives of Galilean peasant farmers or Greco-Roman families. The kind of community envisioned by Jesus is one in which kinship is not limited by blood ties, but is inclusive of all irrespective of economic position, harvest success, or social background. Mark writes to a beleaguered community with a conviction that Jesus' vision is already bearing fruit in Christian house churches. They must remain patient. Social change will eventually come about, but it requires courage, hope, and commitment.

Domestic Themes of Mk 4

Before concluding this overview of Mk 4, it would be important to note the way this chapter builds upon the domestic themes evident in the preceding chapters. Mark's Jesus presents the parable as the key for understanding and interpreting his ministry. The manner and place of the parable's hearing, however, determines the hearers' comprehension. Inside Jesus' community household, the parable deepens instruction and understanding. Outside this house, the parable remains enigmatic and divisive. It identifies insiders from outsiders. There are two indications for this division that identifies the members of Jesus' household who are able to interpret the parables. Both indications are in the form of a commentary on the nature of the parables.

The first occurs between the introductory parable of the sowing of the seed (4:3-9) and its allegorical explanation (4:13-20). Mark inserts an important comment that determines the nature of parables as enigmatic sayings that the hardened are unable to penetrate. When Jesus is asked by the Twelve and those about him concerning not just the parable of the sowing seed but the parables in general, he replies:

"To you the mystery of the *basileia* of God is given, but for those outside, everything comes in parables; in order that

> looking they may see, but not perceive, and
> listening they may hear, but not understand;
> so that they may not turn again and be forgiven" (4:11-12).

The scene of this commentary has shifted from the public setting of a boat. The saying now occurs in a situation of intimacy. Mark notes that it happens when Jesus is alone with "those who were about him with the Twelve" (4:10). The only other place so far where Jesus has been alone with the Twelve and the wider group of disciples is in the house. This becomes the backdrop for the explanation of the parables and the place of private instruction of the disciples. In the second half of the gospel, Jesus' solitude with his disciples in the teaching environment of the household will be explored further. This domestic location helps to explain the distinction between the insiders and outsiders. Those who are "inside" are the members of Jesus' household. They have an inside appreciation of Jesus.[8] They readily resonate with the parables and their presentation of God's *basileia*. For them the parables do not remain as parables that can be penetrated to their intended deeper level of meaning. Jesus' disciples are able to appreciate the "mystery" of God's abiding presence in the ordinary, unexpected, and frustrating.

Those outside this household remain outside the parable that stays a mystery. For them the parables are perplexing riddles that offer no insight. This is because as outsiders they do not have the kind of intimacy with Jesus which characterizes the members of the teaching household. They lack a fundamental openness to deeply see and hear. When they see Jesus' deeds, they see physical actions; when they hear him speak they hear only sounds. They are closed to the possibility of Jesus' words and deeds moving them to conversion, the fundamental disposition for members of Jesus' household.

The second commentary that reinforces the distinction between the members of Jesus' household and those outside comes at the end of the parables. This final explanation bolsters the parabolic nature of Jesus' teaching and the private clarification which the disciples are privileged to receive:

> And with many such parables he spoke the word to them as they were able to hear it; he did not speak to them without parables; privately he explained everything to his disciples (4:33-34).

---

[8] On Mark's "insiders" and "outsiders," see A. Stock, *Call to Discipleship: A Literary Study of Mark's Gospel* (Wilmington, Del.: Michael Glazier, 1982) 96–104.

The Greek sentence translated as "he did not speak to them without parables" is ambiguous. It could be understood that Jesus' teaching included parables (which is the sense taken above) or that his teaching was of its very nature parabolic. In this second sense, the Greek could be translated as "he did not speak to them except in parables." Whatever way the verse is understood, it underscores the manner of Jesus' teaching. Parables were central to his teaching. Their interpretation depended on the listeners' openness to hear deeply. Mark's final point that completes the first clearly defined block of teaching material reinforces the private nature of their explanation. The setting for this elucidation would have been the household, the place of discipleship instruction that the reader already knows from earlier in the gospel.[9]

The Disciples in a Storm

In the second segment of material of this section, the evangelist continues to focus on the in-breaking of God's surprising reign taught in Jesus' parables. Now it is realized through his miraculous deeds. What happens in the boat has implications for Mark's household. This link is further reinforced by the time reference that begins this new section. It explicitly links what is to happen with what has just been taught in private to the disciples:

> And he said to them on that day, when evening had come . . . (4:35).

The "that day" is the day of Jesus parabolic teaching. What is about to happen links with what he has just said. Jesus miraculous deeds and his parabolic teaching are two aspects of the one mission: to renew God's community in the households of the gospel's readers. As they will learn, the story of the storm on the lake is charged with symbolic imagery that would not be lost on Mark's anguished audience threatened with imminent annihilation from Rome's political powers:

> [35]. . . "Let us go across to the other side." [36]And leaving the crowd, they took him as he was in the boat and other boats were with him. [37]And there arose a great windstorm, and the waves beat into the boat, so that the boat was already filling. [38]And he was in the stern sleeping on the cushion; and they woke him and said to him, "Teacher, do you not care that we are perishing?" [39]And waking up he rebuked the wind and said to the sea, "Be silent! Be calm!" And the wind dropped, and there was a great calm. [40]And he said to them, "Why are you cowardly? Have you still no faith?" [41]And they were filled with great fear and said to one another, "Who then is this, that both the wind and the sea obey him?" (4:35-41).

[9] Myers, *Binding,* 151.

The setting is evening; a time of darkness, aloneness, and isolation. The focus is on Jesus and his relationship with a specific group of people whom Mark calls "they," a deliberately vague and unspecified naming of Jesus' companions. For the evangelist the incident is about any potential disciples who claim membership in Jesus' household. While the story concerns an actual event set within the historical ministry of Jesus, specifically it is about Mark's own house churches.

Jesus initiates the call to "go across to the other side" of the Sea of Galilee. As already mentioned, this invitation is one of mission; "the other side" is Gentile and unfamiliar. It is challenging to a community like Mark's now experiencing a new moment in its history as, through persecution, it is being forced into a new stage of growth. This is the first of several times that Mark mentions the movement of Jesus and his disciples across the lake "to the other side" and, later on, back again (5:1, 21; 6:45-53; 8:13, 22). The evangelist will use the geography of Jesus' travels to emphasize central theological points for the gospel's portrait of Jesus.[10]

The sea is a barrier that needs transgressing. It separates East from West and is symbolic of the great divide between Jew and Gentile. In the deliberate meanderings across the lake to the far side where Gentiles live, and back again, Mark portrays Jesus as one who seeks to bring into unity people from different cultural backgrounds. He overcomes the barriers of separation, removes the purity regulations that prevent Jewish and Gentile Christians from eucharistic Communion and reinterprets the Torah to highlight its original liberating potential for human beings. Through this portrait of Jesus, Mark encourages the gospel's Greco-Roman readers to realize Jesus' inclusive household in their own.

The "they" take Jesus in their boat, a traditional symbol for the Christian community. There is immediately the suggestion that Mark's community is not the only one in existence, for "other boats were with him" (v. 36c). We already know that to be "with Jesus" is the first quality asked of the disciple and apostle. These boats represent other faithful communities of disciples. The writer's focus is the particular boat into which Jesus is taken. The Greek is unclear about whether Jesus is already on Mark's boat or if it is the disciples who initiate boarding Jesus.

As the tiny craft sets out on its journey, it is beset by a huge windstorm and swamped by waves (v. 37). Those in the boat are terrified. They are distressed by the calamity that threatens to destroy them. In the midst of this potential crisis, Jesus is asleep. He is neither threatened nor overwhelmed

---

[10] On the importance of the sea crossing and Mark's Gentile mission, see Gundry, *Mark,* 237–47; Myers, *Binding,* 187–97; W. H. Kelber, *Mark's Story of Jesus* (Philadelphia: Fortress Press, 1979) 30–35.

by the evil that looms. Those in the boat wake him in what seems almost a prayerful plead. Their cry to Jesus, "Teacher, do you not care that we are perishing?" is the cry of the gospel household and voices two concerns of Mark's own readers: they fear extinction and suspect that Jesus does not really care about them. God's agent seems silent to their situation.

The word for "perishing" in the Greek text *(apóllumi)* conveys the sense of annihilation; they are deeply fearful that they will be physically and spiritually lost.[11] What intimidates them is a crisis that threatens their total being, not just their physical well-being. For Mark, the impending disaster symbolized through the strong wind and crashing waves, in falling light (for it is evening), is a mirror of what is happening in Rome's Christian households.

The disciples' pleading receives an immediate response. Jesus wakes and "rebukes" the wind. As already noted, Mark often uses the word "rebuking" when Jesus confronts evil.[12] In this story he confronts and defeats the evil that threatens to destroy the little community. He addresses the calamity and his word is immediately effective. The "great calm" that results cancels out the "great windstorm" at the beginning of the story. The question which Jesus directs to those in the boat is intended also for Mark's householders and to all disciples in history who feel swamped or overwhelmed by their situation: "Why are you cowardly? Have you still no faith?" (4:40).

Jesus' question is a reminder of a discipleship theme that the gospel will continue to pursue: the faithfulness of the disciples in the face of crisis. It should not surprise us to see the disciples' fidelity tested and found wanting in Jesus' passion. In the storm on the lake, the central issue is not Jesus' care about their perishing; it is the disciples' cowardice and faithlessness before the evil that threatens them. The evangelist's chief pastoral concern for the gospel's audience, experiencing oppression from Roman power, is the household's faith. When Matthew and Luke later edit Mark's story, they tone down the negative portrait of the disciples. Matthew's Jesus asks "Why are you afraid, you of little faith?" (Mt 8:26) and in Lk 8:25 the question is simply, "Where is your faith?" Matthew and Luke presume faith in the disciples; their concern is about the level of faith; Mark's is about its absence.

The story concludes appropriately with the question of Jesus' identity (4:41). Those in the boat thought they knew Jesus. But this event has raised the question about him with greater intensity as they realize he is

---

[11] Taylor, *Mark*, 275.

[12] D. E. Nineham, *Saint Mark* (London: Penguin Books, 1963) 148; Taylor, *Mark*, 275.

someone who can subdue the power of evil represented in the wind and sea. Mark's householders can look to Jesus with confidence. The first boat story offers powerful insight into Mark's domestic community. The next story continues to build on these insights on the power of community and the effectiveness of the household.

The Gerasene Demoniac

The disciples' question about Jesus' identity in this boat story of the second block of material provides the context for a further story featuring a boat; Jesus' healing the Gerasene demoniac (5:1-20). While the story is set on land on the other side, it occurs with Jesus' boat in the background. The healing begins as he disembarks from the boat (5:2) and is fully effected as he gets back into the boat (5:18). The boat is integral to the story.

Mark heightens the dramatic intensity of the story. The person is chronically possessed, unable to be restrained by chains and shackles, howls and bruises himself. The possessed person is the gospel's most powerful depiction of the homeless. He lives without community, is forced through the unclean spirit to house himself in the place of the unclean by living among tombs generally located outside the town or city. He runs to meet Jesus as he steps ashore from the boat and worships him (5:6), already hinting at the healing and household inclusion that awaits. In typical Markan fashion, the demoniac proclaims Jesus' identity:

> "What have you to do with me, Jesus, Son of the Most High God? I adjure you by God, do not torture me." For he had said to him, "Come out of the man, you unclean spirit!" And Jesus asked him, "What is your name?" And he replied, "Legion is my name; for we are many" (5:7-9).

The demoniac's name is perhaps an allusion to Rome's military might familiar to Mark's audience.[13] Jesus' power to deal with the evil of Rome's civil power is further emphasized through the continued use of military vocabulary and imagery: Legion seeks permission; permission is granted; Legion becomes a "herd" *(agélê)* of swine, the name for a group of army recruits; the swine "rushed down the steep bank into the sea" (5:13), as though heading into battle. Jesus heals the possessed man by drowning Legion in the sea, echoing the drowning of Pharaoh's army in the Sea of Reeds in Exod 15:4.

The effects of healing and liberation are powerfully described. The man is clothed, sane, and sitting before Jesus (5:15). Those who see this

---

[13] J.D.M. Derrett, "Contributions to the Study of the Gerasene Demoniac," *JSNT* 3 (1979) 2–17; Myers, *Binding,* 190–91; Dewey, "The Gospel of Mark," 481.

are frightened and beg Jesus to leave their district. As he gets back into the boat the healed man seeks to be with him, to be a member of his household of disciples. Jesus allows him to be a member of the gospel household, but not in the way he imagined. Instead of joining Jesus' original household of disciples he is commissioned to proclaim the healing action and mercy of God that he has experienced in his own household:

> "Return to your home to your family, and tell them how much the Lord has done for you, and has shown you mercy." And he went away and began to proclaim in the Decapolis what Jesus had done for him; and all were amazed (5:19-20).

Jesus' injunction to the healed person is very significant. It confirms his social and domestic healing. It represents the history of Mark's householders—a second generation of Christians. They are members of Jesus' household but not of the original household of disciples. Mark's Roman householders, like the healed demoniac, proclaim the Gospel in their own urban context. Rather than fantasizing about the possibilities of belonging to Jesus' original community as a way of distracting from the real business at hand, Mark's audience is encouraged to live in the present. This becomes the setting of the Gospel's proclamation and the fruit of their experience of God. The households of Mark's readers are the location of this proclamation.[14]

Jesus' power to heal households and make their members agents of the Gospel is exercised on foreign soil. Now it is repeated on Israelite land. Jesus crosses over "to the other side" (5:21) into the familiarity of the Jewish world. Again, Mark notes in words almost repetitive of the introduction to the parables in Mk 4 how a great crowd gathers around him beside the sea. Like the exorcism of a chronic demoniac, Jesus heals two others desperately sick. Both healings have a domestic context and implications for Mark's household. They are connected to and illuminated by the previous exorcism. All of these healing events are statements about the importance and function of the household in the growth of the Gospel.

The Healing in a Jewish Official's House

The first domestic healing concerns the critically ill family member of a synagogue official's household. Jairus pleads to Jesus for his daughter:

> "My little girl is at the point of death. Come and lay your hands on her, so that she may be saved and live" (5:23).

---

[14] For a different interpretation of Jesus' injunction to the healed person to return to his home, see Tolbert, *Sowing,* 168.

It is the clear that the girl's sickness is fatal. This is a condition for which no healing seems possible. As the story unfolds the illness eventually leads to the girl's death. However, despite the indications of death and the ridicule that Jesus receives (5:39), he raises the girl to life. Mark uses the resurrection language for the healing already familiar to the reader from earlier domestic healings.[15] The power exercised by Jesus here is from the same source which will eventually raise him from death; it is the power of God. What is also unique to this story is that this experience of the resurrection occurs in the private recesses of the *domus*. Mark presumes the large Roman house that is appropriately owned by a public religious figure. In it are gathered the traditional death mourners. These are put "outside" (5:40) because they do not belong to Jesus' household.

There are four other noteworthy details to this story. First, those who accompany Jesus to the house are the gospel's first called disciples. Their presence reminds the reader of the original domestic healing in the house of Simon and Andrew, the healing of a woman, the resurrection action that brought about her healing, and the resulting household ministry. Here the same pattern repeats itself, including the act of household ministry with Jesus instructing the parents to feed the child.

Second, the story continues to highlight indirectly the inability of the accredited official religious institutions to bring total healing to people. The death-dealing sickness occurs in the very household of a religious official. Four times Mark identifies the person requesting his daughter's healing as a "synagogue official" (*archisunágôgos*—5:22, 35, 36, 38). It is this religious leader who turns to Jesus.

Third, it is only when Jesus and his four disciples come into the official's house and those inside the house who laugh at Jesus are turned out side, that household relationships are restored. When the insiders become outsiders and the outsiders insiders, Mark identifies for the first time the official and his wife in their relationship to the little girl. They are called "the father of the child and the mother" (5:40). No longer is the father identified by an honorific religious title. Jesus' presence brings about a household of warm familiarity and nurturing relationships, the Roman domestic ideal not lost on Mark's readers.

Finally, the story concludes with the mention of the girl's age. Mark links this to her rising and walking ("and immediately the little girl arose and walked for she was twelve years old" 5:42). Twelve years is the age when a female ceased being a girl and became a marriageable woman who could become linked to a new household through a spouse. At this age she

---

[15] Hooker, *The Gospel*, 147–48.

was socially free to leave her paternal household. At a deeper level of hearing, this story about the healing of the synagogue official's daughter is one of overcoming the social restraints that keep people confined and of restoring the household as a place of healing and liberation.[16] It is a renewed household in which titles and religious status are inappropriate. The woman now is free to move from the synagogue household to a new one in which different relationships operate. She is a symbol of the freedom which Mark's audience feels in their Roman world as they establish an alternative style of household relationships not based on paternal structures.

The Public Healing of One Unclean

Mark intersperses the story of the healing of Jairus' daughter with that of the woman with the flow of blood (5:24b-34)—a sandwiching technique frequently used by the writer (1:21-28; 2:1-12; 6:7-30; 11:12-21.) This narrative device connects the central story to the domestic allusions found in the adjoining synagogue official's household healing. It also links similar themes (the suffering of two women, the role of touch in healing, the number twelve, and the importance of faith). In one respect, the bleeding of the hemorrhaging woman is more serious than the imminent death of the little girl. Her poor condition, spiritual and physical, assumes a priority over the request from a wealthier religious official seeking the healing of his daughter. Unlike Jairus, the woman is unnamed, ostracized because of her unclean condition, cut off from the life and support of a household, and economically destitute, having unsuccessfully wasted her resources on healers.[17]

Here is Mark's female counterpart to the leprous and paralytic sufferers seen in earlier scenes of domestic exclusion. What is even more pronounced is the public setting of her encounter with Jesus. In Mark's world the public world was that of men; the house was the conventional place of women. Here the setting is reversed. So too the way she is healed. She becomes a public agent who initiates her own healing from Jesus. She touches him, an action forbidden by Leviticus 15. By this gesture she upsets the barriers of ritual purity and makes Jesus unclean.[18]

Before Mark returns the reader's gaze to Jairus' daughter, the story concludes with Jesus' declaration of peace and well being to the woman. This is more than a recognition that healing has taken place. It is a confir-

---

[16] Dewey, "The Gospel of Mark," 481.

[17] Tolbert, "Mark," 267.

[18] Ibid., 268. On the purity implications behind this story see H. Kinukawa, *Women and Jesus in Mark: A Japanese Feminist Perspective* (New York: Orbis, 1994) 29–50.

mation that the conventional rules that govern purity conduct and honor no longer apply:

> He said to her, "Daughter your faith has made you well; go in peace, and be healed of your disease" (5:34).

The woman becomes a model of discipleship.[19] Her recognition of Jesus' true identity causes her to approach him. In her touch of him, she risks further domestic exclusion and breaks through the traditional structures of honor-shame that keep women separated from men, the domestic scene from the public, the sick from the healthy, the poor from the rich.[20] Her faith in Jesus contrasts with the absent faith of the disciples revealed in the boat in 4:40. She takes the initiative for her own liberation, trusts in Jesus, and receives the gift of healing and wholeness—the gift of Shalom. This story will have its parallel later in the healing of the daughter of the Syro-Phoenician woman (7:24-29).

Jesus' Kinship Connections Questioned

This section of the gospel concludes as it began, with a final scene that raises again the central theme of these chapters of the gospel—the nature of Jesus' household and its authentic membership. The faith exercised by the impoverished woman and Jairus in two healing stories filled with domestic inferences is starkly contrasted to the impoverished faith of Jesus' hometown associates (6:1-5). As he preaches in their local synagogue, his listeners are surprised at his wisdom. They had already determined what he was like from an analysis of the members of his family household. They had decided his limited status from his manual profession and family connections:

> "From where did this fellow get all this? What kind of wisdom has been given to him? What deeds of power are being done by his hand! Is not this the carpenter, the son of Mary and brother of James and Joses and Judas and Simon, and are not his sisters here with us?" And they were scandalized by him (6:2-3).

These words of surprise identify Jesus' ministry of wisdom and power, emphasize the growing hostility that surrounds him and list the members of his family household. The reader is already alert to the difficulties that Jesus has with his natural family members who do not constitute his true household. The questions voiced above are ironically appropriate. They identify

---

[19] The woman is also an exemplar of faith (Tolbert, *Sowing,* 168–69).

[20] ". . . her timorous deference reflects her renewed conventional status as a woman in a male world of honor and shame" (Tolbert, "Mark," 268).

Jesus as bearer of a wisdom that has "been given to him," speculate about the relationship of this wisdom to his earthly origins and inquire into the members of his household: his mother, brothers, and sisters. At the end of the gospel, we will discover a "Mary" present at the death, burial, and Easter proclamation of Jesus, who is called the "mother of James and Joses" (15:40; 16:1). One wonders if this Mary is also the mother of Jesus. If she is, then while she is portrayed negatively in Mk 6, she is present throughout the career of Jesus, remains with him in his final moments and is finally portrayed as a faithful disciple. Here, together with Jesus' siblings, she makes up his natural household. His disciples constitute his authentic household. If this interpretation about Mary's presence in the final scenes of the gospel is correct, then eventually she also would be included as a member of this household.

The reader is also familiar with the tension that comes from Mark's juxtaposition of synagogue and Jesus' household. A similar note of tension occurs here. The synagogue setting provides the opportunity for Jesus' antagonists to question his household origins. Jesus is paradoxically recognized as a person of power because of his deeds of healing. Earlier misunderstanding changes to animosity. His interrogators are scandalized by him. He upsets the self-opinionated (6:3). This rejection from his townspeople and those who comprise his wider kinship grouping heralds the definitive split between the natural, local family household and Jesus' genuine community of disciples:

> . . . and he was unable to do there any deed of power, except laying his hands on a few sick people he cured them. And he was amazed at their faithlessness (6:5-6).

Summary

This note of unbelief, a fundamental unwillingness to be "surprised" by God's *basileia* manifest in Jesus' deeds, concludes this section of the gospel in which two themes dominate. One of them concerns faith. The absence of faith at the beginning by the disciples in the boat and at the end by the townspeople surrounds and contrasts fine examples of faith: the request of the healed demoniac to be with Jesus (5:18), the courage of the hemorrhaging woman (5:34), and Jairus' pleading for the restoration of his sick daughter (5:23). The unbelief of the religious authorities from earlier chapters has now spread to the townspeople and is starting to show up in the disciples. Mark's exploration of the role of faith in discipleship is a timely reminder to a Greco-Roman Christian household overwhelmed by the political forces arraigned against it and tempted to return to exclusive and domineering power structures.

The second theme concerns Jesus' household. Who constitutes membership in this household is the subject of each vignette. It is obvious in the opening and closing scenes which affirm or question Jesus' kin. It is prepared for by the meta-parable of the sowing seed (4:1-9) and its accompanying commentary about parables in Jesus' discipled household (4:10-34). The qualities necessary in this household are dramatically illustrated by the fierce storm on the lake that finds the disciples wanting (4:35-41). The final three healings illustrate the power of an authentic household to exorcize, commission, liberate, and nurture.

From the perspective of the domestic world of Mark's Roman readers, this section of the gospel confirms and expands on the presentation of the ideal Christian household presented in earlier chapters. The opening and closing scenes (3:31-35; 6:1-11) and the healing of Jairus' daughter (5:21-24, 35-43) are the most instructive. In each the gathering around Jesus presumes a physically large household setting. Jesus is surrounded by a crowd of disciples that keeps his natural family outside and makes it impossible for them to get to him; Jairus' household is filled with mourners who laugh at Jesus. The physical size of the households presumed by Mark could approximate to the *domus* familiar to the gospel readers.

Besides presuming certain physical characteristics of the household, Mark is more concerned in describing its nature. Uncharacteristically, the *paterfamilias'* domination is absent or, at least, curtailed. Jairus is described no longer as the synagogue official when Jesus and his disciples enter his house. Mark deliberately names him and his wife as the father and mother of the sick child. Their roles are described with reference to the sick person—and not independently of the child. She is the focus of the event and what is to occur in this household. Jesus' action in this important and elite household renews its relationships and moves them away from the status expectations of the Roman urban domestic world.

With the presence of Jesus and the first-called disciples, the household begins to function as a discipled household. The owner ceases to officiate as a religious leader to whom deference is paid, but as a sick child's parent whose only preoccupation becomes the health of his child. Rather than being ordered through hierarchy and status, this household, now modeled on Jesus' household, is characterized by the nurture of its members.

10

The Missionary Household— Mk 6:7–8:26

Overview of Mk 6:7–8:26

The principal focus of the gospel up until this point has been to establish Mark's portrait of Jesus and the kind of people who gather around him. Mark's christology and the gospel's clear definition of the nature and membership of the disciples' household allow for a new moment in the gospel story. This is the gospel's "turn" to the other.[1] Mk 6:7–8:26 shows how those who lack the correct or socially defined purity, gender, and ethnic credentials are invited to become members of Jesus' household.[2] The section is framed by stories concerned about household instruction or mission. The opening scene has Jesus instruct the Twelve for their mission to new households (6:7-13). The final moment of the section's concluding healing of a blind person (8:21-26) has Jesus instruct the healed disciple to return to his household. As we shall see, this healing is paradigmatic of the ongoing healing required in Jesus' disciples and in their house-centered mission.

---

[1] On the boundary crossing theme behind Mark's geography and healing stories, see W. Loader, "Challenged at the Boundaries: A Conservative Jesus in Mark's Tradition," *JSNT* 63 (1996) 45–61.

[2] V. K. Robbins in *Jesus the Teacher: A Socio-Rhetorical Interpretation of Mark* (Minneapolis: Fortress Press, 1992) 125–69, inserts this section of Mk into a broader narrative framework of the gospel that runs 3:7–12:44 and represents an "intermediate phase" in a teacher/disciple cycle. This intermediate phase is preceded by an initial phase in which a relationship is established between teacher and disciple and leads to a final phase in which teacher and disciples become separated. The intermediate phase is further divided into two stages: the first (3:7–5:3) focuses on Jesus teaching the basis of his ministry; the second (6:1–8:26) focuses on the disciples' activity on behalf of Jesus but a fundamental incomprehension about the purpose of his ministry.

Between the two framing stories there are three blocks of material (6:30-44; 7:1-37; 8:1-21). The first and third are concerned with feeding and feasting. Jesus twice feeds a huge number of people in a desert place (6:30-44; 8:1-10a). The first occurs on Jewish territory, the second on Gentile land. A water crossing fraught with danger, misunderstanding and fear for the disciples follows each feeding story (6:45-56; 8:10b-21). The first story of Jesus' feeding the desert household is prepared for by and contrasted to the lavish feast that Herod throws in his palatial household (6:14-29). Herod's party concludes with the martyrdom of John the Baptist, prefiguring what awaits Jesus. The second and central block of material (7:1-37) is concerned with refashioning the purity regulations which determine who belongs to God's sanctified household. Jesus' controversy with Torah interpreters leads to two healing events (7:24-30, 31-37) that put into practice Jesus' renewed Torah vision of household purity and inclusion.

The mission of the Twelve: *Household Instruction* (6:7-13)

Herod's palace celebration (6:14-29)

Feeding of multitude (6:30-44)

Boat crossing (6:45-56)
- Jesus walks on the sea (6:45-52)
- Healings at Genessaret (6:53-56)

A

Household purity: Instruction and Practice (7:1-37)

- Legislated purity and household instruction (7:1-23)
- Healing of the Syro-Phoenician's daughter (7:24-30)
- Healing of the deaf and dumb (7:31-37)

B

Feeding of multitude (8:1-10a)

Boat crossing (8:10b-21)
- Jesus' testing (8:11-12)
- Disciples' lack of bread (8:13-21)

A¹

The healing of a blind person: *Household Mission* (8:22-26)

Over these chapters Mark shows how Jesus' household needs to be concerned about mission and evangelization. This challenging task moves the household beyond a form of self absorption or preoccupation to a new stage. This comes not without its difficulties, confusion, and tensions. The water crossings are symbolic of the new missionary endeavors that must preoccupy the discipleship community. The feeding stories allude to the way the household is to be sustained in its missionary activity. Finally, the centerpiece of the section—the concern over household purity—reminds Mark's audience about the call to a household lifestyle that is essentially inclusive.

Jesus' Instruction to the Twelve

The missionary thrust of Jesus' community is first prepared for by his instructions to the Twelve (6:8-11). The reader already knows that they are his companions who are now to be sent on mission, to be his representatives, to preach, heal, and exorcize.[3] For the first time in Mark's story, they carry out their original commission. For Mark, the Twelve are more than representatives of Jesus' household. They form the inner circle of leadership, like the leaders of Mark's Greco-Roman households. Jesus instructs them to take nothing for their journey; no bread, money, or extra clothing. He wants the Twelve to rely solely on the hospitality of the households they visit and for their words and deeds to conform to his. This missionary activity of itinerant preachers reflects a scene well known in Mark's house churches, founded by traveling preachers authorized by Jesus himself.

Before returning to the Twelve to learn how they went on their mission, Mark inserts the story of the beheading of John the Baptist (6:14-29). In Mark's frequent "sandwich" technique, the middle story contrasts with and expands on the stories that frame it. In this case the episode of John the Baptist also suggests what will await all those who follow Jesus (including the community leaders of Mark's house churches as symbolized by the Twelve). Authentic discipleship can never be divorced from suffering.

The story of John the Baptist is domestically and politically charged.[4] It is set within the palatial household of Herod. His sumptuous birthday feast will contrast with the miraculous desert feast in the next scene. Politically, the marriage between Herod and Herodias and his rejection of his first wife, the daughter of Aretas IV, king of Nabatea, a powerful kingdom

---

[3] The emphasis is on the authority of Jesus exercised through the Twelve; they are to be received as Jesus would be. Hence their lack of need for provisions. See Gundry, *Mark*, 301.

[4] For a gender critique and reader-response approach to this story see J. C. Anderson, "Feminist Criticism: The Dancing Daughter," *Mark and Method: New Approaches in Biblical Studies*, eds. J. C. Anderson and M. Moore (Philadelphia: Fortress Press, 1992) 103–34.

to the east of Israel, had made relationships between Israel and Nabatea politically unstable.[5] Herod would have been sensitive to any criticism of his repudiation of the Nabatean princess. John's judgment on this second marriage would have been received with severe displeasure from Herod which resulted in Herodias' contrived strategy for John's execution.

The decision for John's death is an arbitrary one based on a promise to a dancer. Herod's decision makes a parody of legitimate decision-making by government, military, and business representatives assembled at his birthday party. After John's death, "his disciples came and took his body and laid it in a tomb" (6:29). This same deed will be repeated by Joseph of Arimathea in the burial of Jesus (15:46), thus confirming the connection between the fateful ministry of John the Baptist, and Jesus and his disciples.

It is appropriate at this point that Mark returns to the story of the Twelve who are now named "the apostles" (6:30), a reminder of their missionary household activity. Two incidents continue to explore the implications of discipleship and their faith in Jesus: the miraculous feeding of five thousand (6:30-44) and a second boat story (6:45-52). The two stories are concluded with a summary of Jesus' healing ministry in Gentile territory (6:53-56). Together, these stories make up a block of material that leads to this section's central focus: Jesus' public confrontation with the Jerusalem authorities concerned about his interpretation of the Mosaic tradition and its application to purity laws. The focus concerns, again, the membership of the genuine household of Jesus.

Jesus Feeds the Household

In the feeding story Jesus and the apostles are in a "deserted place," a point Mark makes three times (6:31, 32, 35). Already noted from the prologue, the desert is a place of homelessness. It will be such for the disciples and will recall for Mark's readers the testing of Israel in the desert as it cried out to Moses (and God) for food and drink. Curiously, Jesus and the disciples travel into this deserted place by boat! The narrative connection that Mark makes between boat and desert-homelessness hints further at the domestic instruction that awaits Mark's readers in this scene.

As Jesus and the disciples disembark, "a great crowd" throngs around them. These *ʿam haʾaretz* have accompanied Jesus from the first stages of his ministry. Jesus' immediate reaction to the Jewish crowd is one of "compassion" (6:35)—an attitude that reveals the deep feeling that he has

---

[5] R. A. Horsley and J. S. Hanson, *Bandits, Prophets and Messiahs: Popular Movements in the Time of Jesus* (Minneapolis: Winston, 1985) 180–82.

for them as they look for leadership and direction. The disciples become aware of the crowd that is with them and the lateness of the hour:

> and as it was already late, his disciples came to him and said, "This is a desert place, and it is already late; send them away so that they may go into the surrounding country and villages and buy for themselves something to eat." He answered them, "You yourselves give them something to eat." And they said to him, "Are we to go and buy two hundred denarii worth of bread, and give it to them to eat?" (6:35-37).

What purports to be the disciples' concern for the hungry is, in fact, their self-protection. The disciples overturn the roles of the taught and teacher. They instruct Jesus to do something about the situation. They abrogate responsibility for this difficult pastoral situation, misunderstand who Jesus is, and negate their relationship with him. The solution they propose is based on conventional economics: the hungry could individually purchase food for themselves.

Jesus suggests an alternative which conflicts with the economic solution proposed by his disciples, "You yourselves give them something to eat." Jesus' proposal is personal, not economic; it is based on the disciples' giving. In the Greek text the word "give" is emphatic. According to Jesus, the disciples have the resources within themselves to address the situation. However, the disciples are blind to his proposal. They miss entirely the point of his suggestion and return to the economic approach, "Are we to go and buy two hundred *denarii* worth of bread, and give it to them to eat?" With a *denarius* being equivalent to a day's wage, all the disciples could see was about six months of someone's well-earned pay being eaten up by this crowd![6]

Jesus returns to the point he made earlier: the disciples have resources within to satisfy the ancient hungers of the Jewish people:

> [38] And he said to them, "How many loaves have you? Go and see." When they had found out, they said, "Five, and two fish." [39]And he ordered them to recline in drinking/eating parties on the green grass. [40]So they sat down in groups of hundreds and fifties. [41]Taking the five loaves and the two fish, he looked up to heaven, and blessed and broke the loaves, and gave them to his disciples to set before the people; and he divided the two fish among them all. [42]And all ate and were filled; [43]and they took up twelve baskets full of broken pieces and of the fish. [44]Those who had eaten the loaves numbered five thousand men (6:38-44).

---

[6] On the economics of this scene, see Malina and Rohrbaugh, *Social-Science Commentary*, 218–19.

Jesus calls forth the disciples' resources. Everything that now happens in the story originates from Jesus and concerns his direct contact with the people or with the people through the disciples; they become the mediators of his action. When he directs them, they respond; their proper relationship to him is restored. Retaining a more literal reading of the Greek text at verse 39 reveals two features about the event. First, Jesus instructs the crowd to "recline" (the position at the Passover banquet). Here is a Passover banquet that promises life in the wilderness. The "green grass" is a fine touch from Mark which echoes Psalm 23 and alludes to the messianic banquet God promises the desert wandering Israelites in Exodus. Second, what I have translated as "drinking/eating parties" is the repeated Greek word *sumpósion*.[7] It is the mealtime gathering of the household. In other words, the sustenance of a large hungry group of potential disciples occurs through their establishment of household groups or communities. Here, in the wilderness, the deepest hunger of those who seek Jesus is met through the household of disciples which Jesus asks them to form.

The crowds respond to Jesus' instruction and order themselves into "groups" or, as the Greek text literally reads, into "flower beds" of hundreds and fifties. The color, conviviality and order of the scene intended by Mark is lost in most English translations and offers a surprising contrast to an event that began with a depressed and hungry crowd. Through Jesus the crowd is ordered and gathered into households small enough to know each other and to celebrate. Their size would reflect that of Mark's house churches and Jesus' actions that follow would be deliberately reminiscent of their eucharistic celebration. Through the eucharistic action performed in collaboration with the disciples, the hungry crowd is satisfied.

This first feeding story illustrates that conventional economic thinking is unable to really address profound human need. The issue at stake for Mark is not the feeding of a physically hungry crowd; it is the search for a pastoral approach that satiates the deepest longings of human beings. The story is intimately linked to an appreciation of the role that Jesus' household must continue to play. The household of disciples that gathers around Jesus and is taught by him, and that is continued in Mark's house churches, has within itself the capacity to satisfy that for which people are truly searching. Mark is convinced, from reflecting on the ministry of Jesus, that people can only be adequately satisfied within households committed to sharing their own resources. The Eucharist they share in these households reflects this commitment. Such a sharing mirrors the desire of God to feed Israel in the wilderness. The presence of Israel's God is con-

---

[7] M. Zerwick and M. Grosvenor, *A Grammatical Analysis of the Greek New Testament,* vol. 1 (Rome: Biblical Institute Press, 1974) 124.

tinued through Jesus and his disciples through the eucharistic sharing in Mark's Greco-Roman households.

The Disciples' Crossing to "the Other Side"

The feeding story reveals the disciples' propensity to offer quick, efficient, and pragmatic answers to situations that require compassion. The story also reveals their inadequate faith that becomes the focus of the next scene (6:47-52). Jesus makes the disciples get into a boat a second time (6:45) to cross to the "other side" to Bethsaida as he leaves them and prays on a mountain. The reader remembers the earlier connection between Jesus' instruction to the household of disciples and the boat event that followed. The two were connected and illuminated Mark's exposition of the nature of this household. Now, a few chapters on, the evangelist again explores the link between the preceding household feeding and what takes place in the boat. Noteworthy are those narrative features that prepare for a difficult situation among the disciples.

The disciples are heading a second time for the other side, into Gentile territory; they have been forced again into a situation that is unfamiliar. As the story unfolds, the dramatic tension is heightened: it is evening (6:47); they have to cross the lake, the abode of evil; they are on their own without Jesus. When Jesus notices their plight in struggling against the wind, he responds immediately (6:48). Then, as Mark cryptically notes, it is morning—"the fourth watch of the night." With the presence of Jesus, the evil and gloom associated with evening passes; it is early in the morning. The breaking of dawn represents the dawning of divine presence in Jesus "walking on the water"—an action attributed to God who rescues the distressed (in Job 9:8 and 38:16).

Jesus' greeting further reveals the presence of God acting in him: "Take heart, it is I; do not be afraid." "It is I" literally means "I am," God's name in the Hebrew Scriptures. In Jesus' response to his distressed disciples, the God of Israel is acting. For this reason, when he immediately gets into the boat with the disciples, the wind that was so troublesome, drops. As in the previous scene of the miraculous sharing, the meaning of the event is lost on the disciples. They fail to recognize God's self-revelation in Jesus. Mark poignantly concludes:

> And they were utterly astounded, for they did not understand about the loaves, but their hearts were hardened (6:51c-52).

Tragically, the disciples themselves are becoming victims to a form of chronic obstinacy characteristic of Jesus' detractors. Despite their experience of Jesus in the wilderness and on their boat, the disciples are unable to penetrate the meaning of the events. The initial words of Jesus in the gospel about *metanoia* as a primordial quality in the household of disciples and reception of the good news is now being frustrated in these very examples of faith.

This first feeding of multitude—boat crossing segment closes with a final summary set at Gennesaret. Back on land, Jesus is surrounded again by the faithful crowds drawn from every social setting. They seek him out and search for healing. The crowds show the same kind of faith as the unnamed woman healed of her bleeding. The crowd's faith in Jesus contrasts to the hardening of the disciples. Their crossing to the other side was unsuccessful; they never arrive at Bethsaida but are back at Gennesaret, their mission failed.[8] This summary and the two immediately preceding scenes stress the disciples' failure in relationship with Jesus. They need conversion and healing to recognize who Jesus truly is and what his mission is all about. The reader awaits to see the disciples' response to Jesus in the face of mounting rejection and suffering.

This segment allows Mark's audience to recognize the problems that are beginning to develop in Jesus' household. Its members are prone to some of the theological and religious problems that have plagued Jesus' opponents. The failure to see and deeply understand is what ultimately prevents the members of this household to succeed in mission. The multitude feeding (6:30-44) demonstrated the disciples' inability to recognize the nurturing potential of Jesus' community. This has been reinforced in the episode on the boat. The fissures that are beginning to appear in the household of the disciples will be found more explicitly in the second segment concerned with feeding of multitude—boat crossing (8:1-21). Between these two segments the gospel becomes preoccupied with household purity (7:1-30).

Jesus' Conflict with Religious Leaders—Table Communion

Mark's Jesus is now in public dispute with the official religious leaders. This controversy underlines the conflict escalating against Jesus from the authorities and parallels the growing failure of the disciples. The dispute in Mk 7 is more than an argument over hygiene. The controversy is two fold: it concerns the authentic interpretation of the Torah and the practice of ritual purity. While this dispute is set within the historical career of Jesus, read through the lens of a later Roman Christian community in the 70s, Mark's concern about the issue has important implications. The issue

---

[8] Myers (*Binding*, 194–97) sees behind the unsuccessful water crossing a deeper symbolic and theological meaning filling out the portrait of the faithless disciples.

touches on table-communion between Jewish and Gentile Christians celebrating Eucharist in their house churches. Jesus' redefinition of the function of purity laws through his interpretation of the biblical tradition has important implications for Jews and Gentiles eating together. That the controversy can be read at this secondary symbolic level concerned with table-communion is reflected in the accusing language leveled at the disciples by Jesus' antagonists:

> ²and seeing that some of his disciples were eating the bread with defiled hands, that is without washing them. ⁵And the Pharisees and the scribes asked him, "Why do your disciples not live according to the tradition of the elders, but eat bread with defiled hands?" ⁶He said to them, "Rightly Isaiah prophesied about you hypocrites, as it is written, "This people honors me with their lips, while their hearts are far from me; ⁷in vain do they worship me, teaching human precepts as doctrines." ⁸You abandon the commandment of God and hold to human tradition" (7:2, 5-8).

The disciples are observed "eating the bread with defiled hands" in verse 2 and are accused in verse 5 of not abiding by the interpreted tradition of Moses. The accusation is over the eating of bread and reminds the reader about what has preceded—the miraculous household sharing among the five thousand (6:30-44) with its eucharistic allusion and the failure of the disciples to recognize its meaning, confirmed in the incident in the boat in 6:47-52. There Mark explicitly mentions that the disciples "did not understand about the loaves" (6:52).

The authorities complain that the disciples were not keeping the regulations of purity when they broke bread. The debate about the disciples' ritual cleanliness impinges on Mark's later situation in Christian house churches in which Jews and Gentiles gather together to break the bread or loaves of the Eucharist. Mark considers that the validity for these eucharistic gatherings, in which purity divisions separating Jews from Gentiles are removed, rests on Jesus' own reinterpretation and abrogation of traditional purity laws. His conduct brings into being a renewed religious household that lives out the true purpose of the Torah and does the will of God. This community is from God and not merely a human construct. Jesus' criticism of his adversaries is that they seek to construct a household essentially divorced from God and the Torah (7:8).

This statement of the commandment leads Jesus to continue his interpretation of the Torah's real injunctions. This is finally framed in the form of a parable, "There is nothing outside a person which can make one unclean; but the things which come out of one make a person unclean" (7:15). In his explanation to the disciples back in the household (7:17), Jesus identifies the true center of impurity—the heart. In this setting of the household of disciples, Jesus explicitly declares all food clean and thus paves the way for table-communion between Jews and Gentiles in Mark's Roman households. Mark's readers, predominantly Gentile but conscious of their Jewish origins, would have read this controversy between Jesus and the official interpreters of the Torah as a confirmation of their own eucharistic practice. They would have also been challenged by Jesus' argument over purity laws that would have made them reconsider their genuine welcome of others from the wider Roman society seeking initiation into the Christian household.[9]

This becomes further spelled out in the two healing stories which follow (7:24-30, 31-37). Both are concerned about the welcome which this household offers to others, especially foreigners (in the healing of the Syro-Phoenician's daughter in 7:24-30). The second (7:31-37) is particularly concerned about the way the discipled household assists its members to articulate their experience of God. In both, Jesus' teaching about clean and unclean, and its radical implications for the eucharistic table, is confirmed in action. God's saving power is extended to the Gentiles beyond Jewish nationalistic ties.

An Inclusive Household for Gentiles

Jesus moves from one household—that of his disciples in which he explains the riddle about what makes one defiled—to another. He enters a household located away from Israel, in Tyre and Sidon for "he did not want anyone to know that he was there" (7:24). A Gentile woman, a Syrophoenician, comes to Jesus and begs him to exorcize her little daughter who is possessed. It is not clear where the woman comes from physically. She is not described as coming into the house and it could be that she is already in the house. This is further suggested by the discussion between Jesus and the woman which follows. To her request for help, Jesus says:

> "First let the children be fed, for it is not fair to take the children's bread and throw it to the dogs." She answered him, "Sir, even the dogs under the table eat the children's crumbs." Then he said to her, "For saying that, you may go—the demon has left your daughter" (7:27-29).

Jesus initially rejects the woman's request and reminds her of his Jewish understanding that Israel's salvation takes priority over Gentiles. The Jewish people (the "children") are to be fed first from God's table before others ("the dogs"). The woman respects Jesus' Jewish position, but

---

[9] That purity issues were important for Mark's Mediterranean audience is obvious from Malina and Rohrbaugh, *Social-Science Commentary*, 221–24.

she is not deterred from her request and matches wits with him. She suggests that while salvation can have an order of historical or chronological priority it is not exclusive; it can include even non-Jews! By her carefully crafted argument the woman indirectly critiques Jesus' Jewish provincialism. By challenging him and expanding his limited understanding of salvation, her request is granted.[10] The daughter is healed.

The references to "bread," "food," "table," and "crumbs" are allusions to the Eucharist and suggest another way of hearing the story. Gentiles cannot be excluded from the eucharistic table first set solely for Jewish Christians.[11] For Mark's readers the story is a reminder that their households are to be inclusive of all, especially those from cultural, political, and economic minorities. This teaching will be repeated in the third miracle story in which Jesus feeds four thousand Gentiles (8:1-10).

The second healing story in this double literary cycle touches on an important issue emerging for Jesus' disciples. This is the first of three perception miracles and is instructive of the disciples' need for healing as their relationship with Jesus deteriorates. Mark's geographical note of Jesus' roundabout route from Tyre sets the stage for the healing:

> And again returning from the region of Tyre, and went by way of Sidon towards the Sea of Galilee, in the region of Decapolis (7:31).

Jesus begins near Tyre, the scene of his encounter with the Gentile woman, travels north for about thirty-two kilometers (twenty miles) and then heads southeast for the Sea of Galilee, some ninety-six kilometers (sixty miles) away. The awkwardness of this itinerary might indicate the evangelist's lack of familiarity with the geography of Israel and thus a place of gospel composition some distance from Palestine. The route is more symbolic of the difficulty experienced in the early Christian missionary program and countenances the Gentile mission which Jewish Christians will later undertake.

---

[10] J. Perkinson, in "A Canaanitic Word in the Logos of Christ; or The Difference the Syro-Phoenician Woman makes to Jesus," *Semeia* 75 (1996) 61–85, argues that the woman's word opens Jesus to the possibility of salvation coming from "the other." A similar reading is proposed by Tolbert ("Mark," 269) and Dewey ("The Gospel of Mark," 484–85). Kinukawa (*Women and Jesus*, 51–61) focuses on the "mutual transformation" that occurs in the scene: She enables Jesus to see who he must be; Jesus enables her to transgress the bounds of purity restrictions.

[11] Tolbert (*Sowing*, 185–86) also sees eucharistic allusions in the language of the story and its invitation to reconsider table communion and those who are able to share the "children's bread."

The Healing of the Inarticulate and Blind

The healing that is about to take place is in the Decapolis, non-Jewish territory. The healing has implications for Mark's predominantly non-Jewish, Roman households and for all who seek to be disciples:

> ³²They brought to him a deaf person who had an impediment in speaking; and they begged him to lay his hand on him. ³³Taking him aside, away from the crowd in private, he put his fingers into his ears, and spitting touched his tongue. ³⁴Then looking up to heaven, he sighed and said to him, "Ephphatha," that is, "Be opened" (7:32-34).

The man in need of healing is described in verse 32 as having an "impediment in speaking." He can speak but only with difficulty. In other words, the ability of this non-Jew to proclaim and speak is handicapped and in need of release. The initiative of the healing comes from the "they" (Is this "the crowd" or the same "they" from the storm-swamped boat of 4:36?) who bring the deaf person to Jesus' attention. Their faith in Jesus is evident as they "beg" (v. 32) him to lay his hand on the person to cure him, an action synonymous with other healings in the gospel (5:23; 6:5; 8:23).

The healing occurs "away from the crowd" (v. 33). Mark intends to rivet the reader's gaze on Jesus and the one to be cured. Before Jesus heals the organ of speech, he heals the man's hearing. For Mark, all of Jesus' acts of healing are works of God liberating people from evil. This healing is no exception and occurs both in deed and word. Jesus' gesture to the heavens (v. 34) acknowledges this act as the work of God; the "sigh" comes from Jesus' acknowledgement that what he encounters in the handicap of the person is the manifestation of the reign of evil. Through a ritual of touching and spitting, the healing is finally effected. These rites will be repeated in Mk 8:23 in a second miracle story that involves healing of senses. Jesus' word and action are immediately effective:

> And immediately his ears were opened, his tongue was released, and he spoke clearly (7:35).

The man is able to hear and what is translated as "his tongue was released" literally reads from the Greek text "the chain of his tongue was freed." This evokes the memory of the exorcism of the chained demoniac, Legion, in 5:1-13. Mark's imagery underlines Jesus' confrontation with Satan in the healing of this inarticulate human being. With the demonic chains around his tongue snapped by the power of God, the man can speak "plainly."

The Greek word translated as "clearly" *(orthôs)* can also mean "rightly" or "truly." Jesus enables the man to speak truly. This hints at the deeper issue that the story addresses and explains why Mark inserts it at this point of the gospel. The story is concerned about a deep-rooted linguistic impediment that people have to speaking truthfully about Jesus. This healing occurs as arguments from the religious powers mount against him and not long before the disciples' ability to proclaim the good news about him is to be tested, with tragic results.

The story is as much concerned with Mark's readers as it is with Jesus' disciples. Mark is writing to besieged readers experiencing difficulty in remaining steadfast in the good news and proclaiming truthfully about Jesus. Mark's Jesus offers hope. He can heal their disability to speak truly. This can only happen in the private, not public, space of the household. This becomes the setting of healing for frightened disciples linguistically paralyzed by the events that confront them. The story concludes with the crowd, like a Greek chorus, proclaiming in words similar to Isa 35:5-6, of God's mighty salvific act revealed in the ministry of Jesus:

> And they were overwhelmed beyond measure, saying, "He has done everything well; he even makes the deaf hear and the mute speak" (7:37).

Jesus' healing which brings about correct and true speech in a Gentile concludes the section of material in which Mark is concerned about demonstrating the practical implications of a household that is inclusive and receptive of all. What began as Jesus' confrontation with the religious authorities and their exclusive interpretation of household purity becomes reinterpreted by Jesus (7:1-30) and applied to the household healing of foreign woman's daughter (7:24-30) and the private healing of a Gentile (7:31-37). This leads to the miraculous sharing of four thousand non-Jewish people (8:1-10) and begins the second block of multitude feeding—boat crossing material.

This second feeding story has obvious links with the exorcism of the Syrophoenician's daughter and its eucharistic language. There are also clear parallels with the earlier feeding of the five thousand (6:30-44): both emphasize the messianic banquet set by Jesus for the hungry crowds in a desert setting; Jesus feeds the crowds from the bread which the disciples offer; the disciples act as mediators to the crowd; a large amount of scraps are left over; the crowd is satisfied. In feeding the four thousand the seven baskets filled with scraps and the geographical setting underscore the Gentile context of this messianic banquet.

A Second, Eucharistic Feeding

The second feeding story continues a theme already noted in preceding episodes—Jesus' ministry is inclusive of Jews and Gentiles and is to be reflected in the eucharistic gatherings of Mark's households.[12] The story concludes significantly with another geographical note that moves the setting for the next event back on to Jewish soil in a context in which the boat figures prominently. What happens in the boat again testifies to themes and concerns in Mark's households:

> And immediately getting into the boat with his disciples he went to the district of Dalmanutha (8:10).

Although the exact location of Dalmanutha is unknown, most commentators site it somewhere near Tiberias on the western side of the Sea of Galilee in Jewish territory.[13] With his arrival back into Jewish territory, Jesus is confronted again with leaders who argue for a divine sign to prove his authority. Mark says that the purpose of their confrontation is "to test him" (Mk 8:11), a prerogative previously assumed only by Satan who tested Jesus in the desert in Mk 1.[14] Jesus rejects their request as he "sighed deeply in his spirit" (8:12), reminiscent of the sigh in confronting the evil responsible for the man's speech impediment (7:34).

As in the previous literary cycle (three miraculous deeds followed by the controversy with Israel's religious elite) in Mk 6:30–7:23, Jesus withdraws from his adversaries,

> And leaving them and getting into the boat again, he went across to the other side (8:13).

Jesus goes across "to the other side"—presumably back to Gentile territory and a place of welcome, in contrast to the inhospitable reception from the religious leaders. Though the next scene (Mk 8:14-21) presumes that others are with him in the boat, at this point there is no mention of any other companions. The gospel's exclusive concentration on Jesus and his missionary preference for the Gentiles signified by his crossing alone to the

---

[12] There are several differing features between the two feeding stories. One of the most frequently noted is the decline in numbers of people fed (from five thousand to four thousand) and fewer baskets of scraps (from twelve to seven). Some scholars have identified the number difference in terms of the audience: five and twelve are numbers reflecting a Jewish audience; four and seven, a Gentile audience. See D. Harrington, "Mark," *NJBC*, 613; Hooker, *The Gospel*, 187–88; E. K. Wefald, "The Separate Gentile Mission in Mark: A Narrative Explanation of Markan Geography, the Two Feeding Accounts and Exorcisms," *JSNT* 60 (1995) 3–26. Others have seen this decrease in numbers as symbolic of the hardening of hearts and gradual loss of faith in those following Jesus. See Tolbert, *Sowing*, 183; L. W. Countryman, "How Many Baskets Full? Mark 8:14-21: The Value of Miracles in Mark," *CBQ* 47 (1985) 643–55.

[13] Gundry, *Mark*, 403; C. S. Mann, *Mark: A New Translation with Introduction and Commentary* (New York: Doubleday, 1986) 327; Taylor, *The Gospel*, 360–61.

[14] For further on Jesus' testing in Mk, see Myers, *Binding*, 223–24.

other side, anticipates the "crossing over" of the Christian movement to the Gentiles reflected in Mark's missionary-oriented but struggling households.

The Disciples and Their "One Loaf"

The obvious split between Jesus and the religious leaders is analogous to the rift developing between Jesus and the disciples. This becomes amplified in the discussion over the one loaf that now takes place in the boat between Jesus and his disciples (8:13):

> [14]Now they had forgotten to take any bread; and except for one loaf they had nothing with them in the boat. [15]And he cautioned them, saying, "Watch out—beware of the yeast of the Pharisees and the yeast of Herod." [17]And they said to one another, "It is because we have no bread." And becoming aware of it Jesus said to them, "Why are you talking about having no bread? Do you still not perceive or understand? Are your hearts hardened? [18]Having eyes do you not see and having ears do you not hear? And do you not remember? . . . . [21]Do you not yet understand?" (8:14-18, 21).

Mark does not identify Jesus' boat companions in verse 14. While the presumption from the end of the feeding story in 8:10 is that those in the boat are the disciples, Mark has the story apply to all who consider themselves companions of Jesus. There is a twofold concern that the disciples raise: having enough food for the crossing and, specifically, possessing only "one loaf." The disciples' quandary identifies a crucial concern in Mark's household, spotlights a major theme that has surfaced in the gospel over the past two chapters, and brings to a climax the central issue confronting Jesus' disciples and, by inference, Mark's readers.

The disciples are concerned that they did not have enough bread for the crossing but only one loaf. The miraculous deeds that they saw working through Jesus is lost on them. Jesus' capacity to sustain people, Jews and Gentiles, in the wilderness through their sharing is forgotten; the disciples do not recognize who Jesus truly is; his identity is obscure; their discussion about bread on the physical plane camouflages the deeper "feeding" that they need and that can be satisfied only by Jesus. Mark's community seeking to cross over to the unknown and unfamiliar, like the disciples in the boat, does not need to be anxious about the source of nourishment for its missionary endeavors.

The disciples also miss the point about the one loaf. With the Gentiles affirmed by Jesus as legitimate participants in the community of disciples, there is no need for separate eucharistic gatherings or "loaves." The one eucharistic loaf is enough; it expresses the one household of disciples to which all are called, irrespective of cultural, social, and economic differences.

Jesus' renewed household subverts the conventional mindset perpetuated by a powerful elite. This mentality is like yeast which permeates the whole of society and of which Jesus warns his followers to be aware.[15]

The disciples fail miserably to understand the point of his words. This teaching moment in the gospel is crucial.[16] All is not perfect in Jesus' household of disciples. They are exposed as inexcusably flawed and failed. Their perception of Jesus is fundamentally defective and in need of a double healing.[17] This is the point of the final story (8:22-26) that concludes this section of the gospel concerned about the missionary thrust of Mark's household. The disciples are chronically blind. They have failed to perceive deeply the meaning of everything that has preceded. The healing of the blind person acts as a literary link between this present segment with the next major and central section of Mark's gospel outline. Its discussion and domestic implications will be taken up in the next chapter. Here it is worthwhile noting that the story ends with the healed person being sent back to his household. This household mission of the one healed balances Jesus' household instruction to the Twelve sent on mission in the opening scene in 6:7-13.

This section of Mark's narrative prepares for and leads to the gospel center and the focus of our attention in the next chapter. The evangelist's concern over these two chapters has been to spell out the implications of the household as a missionary and evangelizing agency. Mark raises the key concerns with which such a household must be concerned. These include its inclusivity of membership and its freedom from purity regulations that restrict its celebration of the Eucharist to certain cultural and gender groups. The two feeding stories (6:30-44; 8:1-10a) further underscore the household as an agency which offers unimaginable nurture in life's wilderness. These stories also invite the household's leaders to move away from conventional economic and practical strategies to resolve community concerns. They need to look with faith within the household for the "bread" that will satisfy the longings of its members.

This brings the reader to the brink of the central section of the gospel where a second perception healing (8:22-26) connects to the major christological question that Jesus asks his community of disciples, "Who do you say I am?" (8:29). Mark has deliberately placed this question at the

---

[15] On yeast as a corruptive influence see Gundry, *Mark*, 413–14; Harrington, "Mark," 613; Taylor, *The Gospel*, 365.

[16] For the educational import of Jesus' words at this moment in the gospel and its connection to other similar moments, see Robbins, *Jesus the Teacher*, 153–59.

[17] Harrington ("Mark," 614) also argues for a symbolic meaning underlying the healing story that connects directly to the disciples.

half-way point in the gospel. The disciples and the authorities are confronted with this question and wrestle with his identity in what now follows. This section (8:22-29) appropriately acts as a literary "hinge" that concludes the first half of the gospel and prepares for the second.

Summary

Along with clarification about the missionary nature of Jesus' household, Mark alerts the reader to central problems within the household. This is revealed also in the two feeding stories and the respective boat crossings that accompany and follow (6:45-52; 8:10b-21). The disciples, the members of Jesus' household and images of Mark's, are convicted by Jesus for having insensitive or "hardened hearts" (8:17). This echoes a verdict made back in 6:52 where they became terrified of Jesus walking on the water. They were beside themselves in amazement. There Mark explained the reason for their reaction as due to an incomprehension about the loaves and a hardening of their hearts (6:51, 52). Now, as we near the middle of the gospel, the disciples appear to be no better than the religious authorities first identified in 3:4 with "hardened hearts." This comes as a shock to Mark's householders who would have expected something more from Jesus' constant companions.

This shock might also reverberate within the readers themselves who, perhaps for the first time, recognize that the evangelist has accomplished a superb literary feat. The questions in 8:17-21 that Jesus directs to his disciples are also posed to each generation of readers. These become a self-scrutinizing inquiry for anyone who seeks to belong to Jesus' household of disciples:

- *Do you still not perceive or understand?*
- *Are your hearts hardened?*
- *Do you have eyes, and fail to see?*
- *Do you have ears, and fail to hear?*
- *Do you not remember?*
- *Do you not yet understand?*

Through these questions the evangelist, and Jesus, turns from his disciples and interrogates the gospel's audience that has sympathetically journeyed with the disciples, from the beginning empathetic to their struggle to understand Jesus. Mark's literary skill has "trapped" those who belong to a household of disciples in a later generation. It will do so again in the final verse of the gospel.

From the first chapter the members of Mark's *domus* have had the inside story. They know what God thinks about Jesus; they have been privileged insiders. Now as Mark's narrative nears the halfway point, at this central moment they find that they, too, are like the disciples, still not perceiving or understanding. Despite having the "inside" story, they find themselves to be outsiders. Mark has executed a masterly reversal. The gospel convicts both disciple and reader. There is no person or position in Mark's household that is exempt from suffering and incapable of a lack of real perception or hard heartedness. This is a sobering insight as the disciples are about to be plunged into Jesus' struggle, suffering, and death. What follows is of paramount importance for the disciples, Mark's community and us.

11

The Suffering Household—
Mk 8:27–10:52

Overview of Mk 8:27–10:52

The last chapter offered a way of reading Mark's presentation of Jesus. Jesus' deeds of power and healing reveal his true character more clearly. Accompanying this revelation was the deepening blindness of the disciples and the growing conflict with religious officialdom. As we near the halfway point in Mark's story, the lines on Jesus' portrait become more filled and the dominant issues emerge with crystal clarity: Jesus is more misunderstood and controversial; an unbridgeable rift has developed between himself and the religious officials; membership in his missionary household has been expanded to include the impure and foreign. This has occurred not without revealing serious problems within this household. Its leaders are blind to him and, like the authorities, their hearts dull.[1]

Mark's structure at this central portion of the gospel reflects these thematic undercurrents that look back to what has already been going on in the narrative and forward to what is about to unfold in the disciples. The section begins and ends with miracle stories in which Jesus heals blindness.[2] These symbolize the need in the disciples of Jesus' household for profound healing in their perception of Jesus. Both contain important instructions for the household of disciples. In the intervening story flanked by these two perception miracles, Jesus withdraws from his detractors and

[1] Kingsbury (*Conflict*, 95–103) explores the gradual incomprehension and dullness of Mark's disciples.

[2] The way this section begins and ends with two healing stories dealing with blindness suggests that it is an "inclusio" in which discipleship, christology, and community are explored. Hooker (*The Gospel*, 197–98) suggests that the two healing stories are "acted parables" about faith and truth.

the crowds and concentrates more on his disciples gathered in the household. As they draw closer to Jerusalem and the cross looms larger, he teaches them about his impending passion and the meaning of true discipleship. How well the disciples comprehend what is about to take place will be ultimately tested in Jesus' suffering and death. The reader suspects, however, that they will fail; already on the road to Jerusalem they show signs of misunderstanding.

Healing of a Blind Person: *Household Mission* (8:22-26)

    1. Jesus Teaches about his Passion (8:27–9:1)
- Misunderstanding by Peter
- *Instruction about Household Discipleship*

    The Transfiguration (9:2-13)
    Healing of a Boy (9:14-29)

    2. Jesus Teaches about his Passion (9:30-37)
- Misunderstanding of Teaching by Disciples
- *Instruction about Household Discipleship*

    Implications for Household (9:38–10:31)

    3. Jesus Teaches about His Passion (10:32-45)
- Misunderstanding of Teaching by Disciples
- *Instruction about Household Discipleship*

Healing of Blind Bartimaeus: *Household Instruction* (10:46-52)

In three powerful scenes Jesus speaks openly about his imminent suffering and death. The teaching that flows from these poignant moments are all directed to the household of disciples. Immediately there is evidence of rejection: Peter argues with him about his dying (Mk 8:32-33); the Twelve contest who is the greatest (Mk 9:33-37); they rail against James and John who seek leadership privilege in Jesus' household (Mk 10:35-45). Each dispute builds on its predecessor and reaches a crescendo as Jesus and the Twelve near the outskirts of Jerusalem. The rivalry among the Twelve shows how far they have moved from Jesus' original vision.

The gap between Jesus and the members of his household, especially its leaders, could not be more forcefully presented in this finely crafted section. This has important implications for Mark's Greco-Roman household and is evident by the frequency of reference to the "house" (9:28, 33; 10:10, 29, 30) as the preferred place in which Jesus instructs his disciples. Jesus' preoccupation with the household instruction of his disciples is not accidental for Mark. More importantly, in 10:29-45 Mark clearly articulates the characteristics of Jesus' household framed in explicit Greco-Roman terms that the gospel's audience could not fail to understand. In a sense, this could be regarded as an important point for Mark's domestic theme.

Healing a Doubly Blind Person

The healing of the blind person at Bethsaida (8:22-26), opens this section of the gospel. The initiative for the healing comes from those who bring the person to Jesus, While most English translations determine that these requesting the healing are "some people,"[3] the Greek text is left open. It is "they." These could well be the "they" of the previous scene, the blind disciples who do not understand about the miracle of the bread or the significance of the one loaf. This links the story to the previous section of Mark's gospel and to this centerpiece framed by stories in which blindness is healed. These disciples beg Jesus to touch the blind person.

Their request is more than an invitation to physically touch the person; it is to confront the evil that has brought about this disease and prevents the man from really gaining true insight into what is happening. Jesus responds to the disciples' request, but away from the village and, characteristically, away from the public gaze, in a private space. Through a ritual of anointing with saliva and a double laying-on of hands, the blind person is eventually healed.[4]

The blind person's response to Jesus' question whether he can see anything is intriguing, "I can see human beings, but I see them as walking trees" (8:23). For a blind person to mistake people for walking trees seems mysterious. The man's unusual statement offers a clue to the story's deeper meaning. The healing is not about restoring sight to one totally blind; it is about healing the sight that is already there.[5] When such healing occurs, it is the fruit of a double action by Jesus. The inability to see

---

[3] That it is "some people" who bring the blind person to Jesus is also presumed by several commentators. For example, Harrington, "Mark," 614; Gundry, *Mark*, 417.

[4] The purpose of Jesus' double healing action has been the subject of some scholarly discussion: Hooker (*The Gospel*, 198) sums up the various views: The miracle demonstrates Jesus' ability to overcome the most chronic malady; the story is symbolic of the disciples' inability to see or comprehend Jesus. Hooker favors a view that sees the event as symbolic of those who fully don't appreciate the Gospel and need a chronic cure. They live and are disciples with eyes only half open. My own emphasis is derived from seeing the story in the context of the portrait of struggling discipleship which Mark has been constructing carefully over these central chapters of the gospel. See also E. S. Johnson, "Mark viii:22-26. The Blind Man from Bethsaida," *NTS* 25 (1979) 370–83.

[5] Mann, *Mark*, 337; but contra Hooker, *Mark*, 199.

clearly is a more profound handicap than total blindness. Its healing is gradual and, at first, incomplete.

As a result of Jesus' action the person can see "clearly" (8:25). The word "clearly" (*têlaugôs*, in Greek) literally means "far-shining" or "glittering from afar."[6] The healing is so effective that everything the person looks upon sparkles with new brilliance. He has received a new ability to look deeply at everything. The story ends with Jesus' instruction to the one healed to stay away from the more public setting of the villages but to return to his own house. The healing results in a household mission. This becomes the site where the Gospel is proclaimed—a dynamic we have seen in earlier domestic healings.

Given the context in which this healing occurs, it has obvious reference to those who are members of the disciples' household. Their healing is not instantaneous and will be initially imperfect; they are in need of ongoing healing in order to see clearly; their spiritual vision is impaired; they still do not see Jesus clearly enough. Initial conversion and commitment to discipleship is not enough. Constant *metanoia* needs to be the hallmark of those who constitute Jesus' household.

The Gospel's Center and Pattern: Teaching and Misunderstanding

The disciples are, however, not totally blind about him, as the next episode will emphasize. In this scene we arrive at the gospel's center with Jesus' question to his disciples, "Who do you say I am?" (8:29). This is the central christological question of the gospel posed to all who declare solidarity with Jesus. The disciples' response through Peter, "You are the Christ," indicates that they do have sight, but it is still imperfect. Jesus' correction of Peter's declaration leads to the first of three teachings about his impending passion and death that dominate this section. Each teaching affirms that Jesus is the Human One, "the Son of Man," who will suffer, die, and rise (8:31; 9:31; 10:34).

An event, that signals the disciples' misunderstanding or subtle rejection of the passion and death that awaits the one they follow to Jerusalem, accompanies each teaching. In the first Peter rejects Jesus' teaching as of evil origin in his "rebuke" (the same word used in exorcising evil spirits) of Jesus (8:32-33).[7] In the second the disciples squabble about who is the greatest (9:35). The third teaching is followed by the request from

---

[6] Zerwick and Grosvenor, *Grammatical Analysis*, 133.

[7] The "demonic" connection with the play on the word "rebuke" is deliberate. First, Peter infers Jesus' self-declared prediction is demonic; then, Jesus in turn attributes the demonic to Peter (Gundry, *Mark*, 444–46).

James and John to Jesus that they be considered for prominence in the household of disciples (10:37). Each builds upon and adds to the disciples' misunderstanding. Collectively, they underscore the apprehension that the leaders of the household have as they follow one who will ultimately suffer and die. Each moment of incomprehension leads to a significant correction by Jesus addressed to the disciples and to the household they form. These three corrections become instructions on household discipleship important for Mark's audience confronting misunderstanding, apprehension, and rejection.

In the first correction, after being "rebuked" by Peter, Jesus turns, sees his disciples and "rebukes" Peter (8:33). What he is about to say is for their benefit as much as for Peter's, the one in most need of rebuking. Jesus' severe correction of Peter to align himself with God leads to further teaching about discipleship that has implications for the household of disciples. Those who follow Jesus must be prepared to take up suffering, "the cross," in discipleship (8:34-38). What awaits Jesus also awaits those who follow him. Discipleship and suffering with possible martyrdom go hand in hand. This is not without its transformation, the point of the next story, Jesus' transfiguration (9:2-8).

This event naturally follows on from Jesus' recognition of the disastrous inevitability of his mission. He seeks communion and transformation from God. Mark leaves the reader without doubt that the disciples are blind and inarticulate even in this experience of Jesus, "For they do not know what to say, for they were frightened" (9:6). They do not understand the meaning of what has happened. This becomes even clearer in the linking scene that follows, the healing of the spirit that causes deafness and speechlessness (9:14-29). This story further exposes the real problem among the disciples.

A Second Sensual Healing

This second healing of the senses symbolizes the spirit of deafness that infects the disciples and keeps them inarticulate about Jesus. Because they possess this same spirit they are ineffectual in exorcising it from the boy (9:18). The story, however, has powerful domestic implications for Mark's readers. The event is as much concerned about the disciples and the kind of household they form as it is about the healing and restoration of a boy to his parents. It is the *paterfamilias* of a household who again seeks help from Jesus. The father says to Jesus:

". . . if you can do anything, help us and have compassion on us." Jesus said to him, "If you are able! All things are possible for one who believes."

> Immediately the father of the child cried out, "I believe; help my unbelief!" (9:22-24).

The father's request is significant. It is further evidence for Mark's Greco-Roman household that the traditional power and authority of the *paterfamilias* is ineffectual against the malady of silence which afflicts the disciples.[8] Only by returning to the real source of authority in the household of Jesus can this affliction be overcome. The father seeks help for "us"—not just the boy. This acknowledges that the boy's demonic possession has social consequences for others and underscores the political implications of Jesus' power to heal. When Jesus addresses the evil which traps the boy it is from an unclean spirit, "which keeps the boy from speaking and hearing" (9:25). The boy's incapacity to speak and hear is a symbol of a more profound handicap that affects human beings—an inability to hear what is happening in society and to articulate the paths of social restoration.[9]

The profundity of the disability is indicated by the description that accompanies Jesus' exorcism of the lad. Mark describes Jesus' confrontation with evil as an encounter with death. The terrible convulsion, the corpse-like response in the boy, and the declaration by most that "he is dead" (9:26), suggest more than demonic possession. The potential evil present in a person's inability to hear deeply and announce God's activity in Jesus is symbolized in the boy's possession. It is so penetrating that it affects the core of human happiness. In actions reminiscent of the household healing of Simon's mother-in-law (1:31) and echoed in his own resurrection, Jesus raises the boy to full household participation:

> Jesus, taking him by the hand, lifted him up, and he stood up (9:27).

The scene concludes with Jesus' private domestic teaching of his disciples back in the house (9:28). What now emerges is instructive for every discipled household in history. Lack of prayer is identified as the principal reason the disciples could not cast out the demon. Their lack of communion with God and openness to their own ongoing conversion prevent them from really hearing and speaking about God, seeing God working in Jesus, recognizing the suffering in Jesus' mission, and appreciating the wide-

---

[8] That the disciples are the problem in the story because of their inability to exorcise is further emphasized in vv. 19-20. The text is intriguingly unspecific, but that the disciples are intended is clear from the context which surrounds the scene. Mark is deliberately contrasting the faith of the father with the growing faithlessness of the disciples (Harrington, "Mark," 615–16).

[9] Behind the story lies a Mediterranean perspective on demonic possession and chronic illness.

reaching social and political implications of his ministry. They have become impotent before the political powers they seek to overcome; they are unable to heal because they need to be cured of the same malady that afflicts the boy. They too are deaf and dumb; they are insensitive to what is happening around them.

Jesus' Domestic Instruction

Jesus' second correction of his disciples is again in the house (9:33) and represents the most explicit domestic instruction in this section of the gospel. Jesus' teaching concerns the exercise of authority and power that lies at the heart of household leadership. Between this correction and the final one, the house is prominent. Twice the evangelist has the house as the setting for Jesus' schooling of his disciples (9:33, 10:10); twice Jesus speaks to them about the role that the house plays in their discipleship (10:29, 30). Over these chapters, Mark gathers together the main domestic issues addressed by Jesus and about which the gospel's audience is concerned.[10]

The evangelist also makes use of the most inconsequential household figure, the child, as the model of instruction to the bickering disciples. Between the second and third passion "predictions" of 9:30-32 and 10:32-35, the evangelist constructs Jesus' teaching in a finely balanced way: Jesus' concern for the child (also called "the last," "little one," or "the least") is interleaved with teaching about true discipleship (9:38-41), divorce (10:1-12), and wealth (10:17-31).[11]

A: Second Teaching on the Passion	*(9:30-32)*	
B: About the Child	*(9:33-37)*	
C: Teaching on True Discipleship	*(9:38-41)*	
B¹: About the Little Ones	*(9:42-50)*	
C¹: Teaching on Divorce	*(10:1-12)*	
B²: About Children	*(10:13-16)*	
C²: Teaching on Wealth	*(10:17-31)*	
A¹: Third Teaching on the Passion	*(10:32-34)*	

---

[10] For a more expanded reflection of this section, particularly in its connection to a discussion on divorce and the divorced in Mark's community, see M. Trainor, "The Divorced and their Inclusion in Community (Mk 10:1-12)" *ACR* 72 (1995) 211–24.

[11] The literary pattern suggested here is similar to, though not derived from, Myer's structure centered around the key themes/words "on the way" in 9:33; 10:17, and 10:32 (*Binding,*

The evangelist's point is made clearer by the literary structure of this section. It argues for a subversion of the household relationships typified by the household codes of conduct and submission well-known in the Greco-Roman world. Mark's house churches must be characterized by inclusion and equality, not exclusion and superiority. Relationships between its members are not intended to be hierarchical or oppressive. Leaders are not to use their power for self-aggrandizement but for others; theirs is a servant form of leadership. This does not mean that they must become doormats but must reach out to those considered "last of all."

About "the Little Ones"

The implications of this for the household are explored in the scenes that interleave the material that deals with the "little ones" (9:38-41; 10:1-12, 17-31). Here Mark subverts the conventional understanding of the role which the child performed in the Roman household. In this view the child was the object of discipline. The child, whose attention was directed to the parents, needed to be trained or educated in a style of unquestioning obedience, especially towards the *paterfamilias*. Mark's vision of the Christian household expressed through Jesus' teaching is one in which the little one is a full member and the focus of nurture. In fact, the members' attitude towards the child becomes the touchstone of true household membership. The child as the least important and powerless household member, whose obedience to the *paterfamilias* was expected, becomes the symbol for leadership *metanoia*. Jesus' physical gesture of wrapping the child in his arms (9:36) symbolizes this attitude. It also reflects the kind of nurturing quality found in Roman households between father and child, praised by writers of the period and identified above.

Jesus' welcome of the child is illustrative of the kind of leadership expected of the Twelve (and in Mark's household). The capacity to receive the rejected and maltreated demonstrates an ability to use leadership as service, to be open to God and to be willing to be taught by Jesus. Such hospitable leadership also runs counter to the usual style exercised by the *paterfamilias* in the Roman *domus*.

The reconfiguration of household relationships evident in Jesus' teaching and gesture with the child is further reinforced in his teaching to his disciples indignant over two requesting preferential leadership as they bask in Jesus' glory (10:35-41). Jesus' instruction concerns the attitude of the slave in the household of disciples. Again, Mark offers through Jesus'

---

258). Both structures recognize the way in which the teaching on divorce is framed, and subsequently interpreted, by Mark's presentation on children in 9:36f. and 10:13-16.

teaching further insight into the kinds of relationships that should be typical in the Christian household. The one who seeks to be regarded as great in the household must in fact be the "servant," *diakonos* (10:43), in the community. This style of servant leadership, which is the "first" and most important function, can only be a reality if the one exercising it adopts the attitude of the "slave."

How well this message sinks in will become evident in the final chapters of the gospel as Jesus' servant leadership reveals itself in his passion and death, and his disciples abandon him. Here, in the middle of the gospel narrative, Mark presents a most radical and subversive vision of household relationships familiar in the Greco-Roman world: the first is the slave; the greatest, the child. It must also be noted, though, that the possibilities of exploring and presenting such a vision is not totally foreign in the Roman literature.

We have already seen among some writers the function of the household in nurturing its inhabitants, the affectionate relationship that could exist between parents and their children, and the bond between slave and master that was more than one of subservience. It might be argued that if these thoughts about household were known to Mark and the gospel's audience, then the evangelist is interpreting their meaning in the spirit of Jesus and applying this to Rome's Christian households.

From another perspective, each of the teaching segments that occur between Jesus' passion predictions encourages the disciples to be tolerant of others who seem to be open. The disciples are not to see other healers as competitors in power but must show welcome and openness. Read from the perspective of Mark's victimized householders exposed to public hostility, the gospel's readers might be closing ranks for their own self-protection. As a result of this natural reaction they might be forming an exclusive and sectarian Christian community. Jesus' attitude to children and to non-members would rail against such cliquishness. Mark's readers are being encouraged to open themselves up to the possibility of new membership from unforeseen and extraordinary quarters of the Roman population. They can't be stumbling blocks to those seeking membership in their house churches. These "little ones" need to be welcomed not hindered or rejected. As Jesus reminds his disciples:

> "If any of you put a stumbling block before one of these little ones who believe in me, it is better for you if a great millstone were hung around your neck and you were hurled into the sea" (9:42-43).

In Mk 9 the evangelist deals with the danger of scandal and apostasy, issues that relate to the internal life of house churches already hinted at in the explanation of the parable of the sowing seed in 4:14-20. At a time of tension, when everyone is being tested "by fire," household cohesion or "peace" is essential. Jesus' final words to his disciples are most pertinent to Mark's audience and summarize this chapter:

> "For everyone will be salted with fire. Salt is good; but if salt has lost its saltiness, how can you season it? Have salt in yourselves, and be at peace with one another" (9:49, 50).

Jesus' teaching on divorce (10:1-11) including his additional explanation to the disciples in the house (10:10) is strategically set in this context of the "little ones." The teaching is preceded by sayings about the "little ones" and followed by Jesus' teaching about the availability of the *basileia* to "children" (10:13-16). Jesus presents the child as the paradigm of the *basileia's* recipient. This further confirms the welcome of the divorced in Mark's household. Any consideration of the "little ones" of the household must be broadened to include those who are victims of divorce. No barriers are to be placed in their way for full household membership and welcome.

In the final block of household teaching (10:17-31) before the third and last statement of Jesus' impending passion and death (10:32-45), Mark's Jesus presents a surprising reversal of convention that considers wealth and possessions as tangible signs of God's blessing. This whole discussion about discipleship, the little ones, and wealth touches at the heart of the life of Mark's household. To be a member of the Christian house churches in Rome requires more than consensus about the kinds of values enshrined in the Torah and its stipulations. It requires a following of Jesus in a socially radical way: an openness to God reflected in the all-embracing welcome of society's rejected and victimized, and in membership of an inclusive community empowered not by a system of oppressive kinship based on patriarchy or economic privilege but by servant leadership. Economic security and privilege are ephemeral; salvation is ultimately God's gift.

Mark's Vision: a Renewed Household

This whole household teaching section concludes by a return to the themes of "the last" and "the least." It is here that we arrive at what I would consider Mark's most explicit and unambiguous articulation of the essence of the Christian household.

Mark's Jesus reemphasizes the divine value of the community that forms around him. To the question asked about how one can inherit life, he points to the household established on an equality of kinship that includes women, men and children.[12] This renewed kinship structure is to be encouraged in Mark's house churches. Their structure, though politically threatening and unfavorable in the eyes of the Roman civil elite, is a viable social alternative that is a concrete expression of God's presence or "eternal life":

> "Amen I say to you, there is no one who has left house or brothers or sisters or mother or father or children or fields, for my sake and for the sake of the gospel, who will not receive a hundredfold now in this age—houses, brothers and sisters, mothers and children, and fields with persecutions—and in the age to come eternal life. But many who are first will be last, and the last will be first" (10:29-31).

These final words offer a superb summary to the style of community and the fruits of authentic discipleship that Jesus has been at pains to inculcate in his own disciples. For Mark, the "hundredfold" is a present reality in the Christian households at Rome. They are tangible signs of the fruitfulness of the seed in the parable of the sower (4:8) as its members experience in their renewed kinship structure "houses, brothers and sisters, mothers and children and fields" (Mk 10:30). What is clearly absent in the redefinition of membership in Jesus' household is the *paterfamilias*. There will be no need for a father. This does not mean that male parents are absent from the community. On the contrary, through the restructure of power relationships with its focus on the least, servant and slave, the ultimate figure of power in the hierarchy of the Greco-Roman world, the *paterfamilias*, will have no part to play.

Mark's Jesus envisages a household where the exercise of a hierarchical and discriminatory use of power symbolized in the role of the *paterfamilias* is non existent. This is the theme of Jesus' third correction of his disciples after the final announcement about his impending passion (10:32-45). Jesus calls his bickering Twelve back to a form of household leadership that is characterized by service. It is in this atmosphere that Mark presents the final story of healing that concludes the journey of Jesus' household of disciples to Jerusalem, the healing of blind Bartimaeus (10:46-52).

Healing of a Blind Beggar

On the verge of entering Jerusalem, the city to which everything has been directed and the place of ultimate testing, the disciples' need for ongoing healing is graphically and symbolically portrayed in Bartimaeus'

---

[12] Dewey ("Mark," 492–93) interprets this section of Mk as a vision for an egalitarian, kinship community focussed on God's leadership.

healing. It is a story that reflects on the function of the household and the role played by its members in welcoming or rejecting others:

> [46]And they came to Jericho, and as he, his disciples and a large crowd were leaving Jericho, Bartimaeus son of Timaeus, a blind beggar, sat alongside the road. [47]And hearing that it was Jesus of Nazareth, he began to shout out and say, "Son of David, Jesus, have mercy on me!" [48]And many rebuked him to be quiet, and he cried out even more loudly, "Son of David, have mercy on me!" [49]Jesus stopping said, "Call him." And they called the blind man, saying to him, "Take heart; arise, he is calling you." [50]Throwing off his cloak, springing up, he came to Jesus. [51]Then Jesus said to him, "What do you want me to do for you?" The blind man said to him, "My teacher, let me see again." [52]And Jesus said to him, "Go; your faith has saved you." And immediately he regained his sight and followed him on the way (10:46-52).

The story opens with Jesus and his retinue passing through Jericho, the last town before Jerusalem and the final stage of their journey. The scene involves Jesus, his disciples, the crowd, and a blind beggar. It is a microcosm of the composition of the Markan household on its journey through history. At the beginning of the story Bartimaeus is found on the side of the road. The story ends with Bartimaeus following Jesus "on the way." The "road" or "way" is a symbolic term for the Christian path of discipleship. In other words, Bartimaeus becomes one of the accompanying group of disciples who follow Jesus to Jerusalem, suffering, and death. While the story is about discipleship, Mark's focus is particularly on how Bartimaeus becomes a disciple. Here the writer offers a lesson to leaders of Christian households about the function which their members play in enabling fringe and apostatized Christians return to full membership in the household.

To Mark's readers, the pathetic figure of the blind and begging Bartimaeus would be a reminder of the victims of injustices and oppression experienced in a society heavily controlled by a wealthy elite.[13] The evangelist is concerned with more than a healing of a blind person. The story is about the total liberation of the oppressed. In verse 47 Bartimaeus hears that Jesus of Nazareth is passing by. This prompts him to shout and cry out for mercy. He acknowledges that Jesus is the only one who can truly liberate him from his affliction. The reaction he encounters is significant. "Many" (v. 48) treat him in the manner that Jesus treated the demoniacs—they rebuke him to be quiet.[14]

---

[13] Myers, *Binding*, 281–82.

[14] Mark's use of "rebuke" clearly links this story with other uses of the term—all of them dealing with the removal of evil. The "many" recognize this loud blind beggar as more than an irritation. He is a social evil that needs exorcism more than being heard or healed.

Who this "many" is, is not clear. Besides the disciples, the only group we know of in the story so far is the crowd accompanying Jesus. Is this "many" (1) some of the disciples who react negatively to Bartimaeus' plea just as they reacted to the crowds seeking food in the desert (6:36) or the children who came to be blessed by Jesus (10:13)? Is the "many" (2) the crowd of potential disciples or (3) casual observers who, like Bartimaeus, are on the side of the road? Perhaps the lack of clarity is deliberate and is the evangelist's way of indicting all three groups that have their representatives in Mark's house churches.

Undaunted by the reaction of the "many," Bartimaeus persists in his appeal for mercy to Jesus who responds. Jesus stops and instructs the "many" to "call him" (v. 49). Those who had actively tried to silence the blind beggar are now made the means of his healing. This dynamic is also found in the feeding stories in 6:30-44 and 8:1-9 where Jesus turns complainants into messengers of the Gospel.

The call to Bartimaeus originates from Jesus but is directed via those who initially kept him oppressed. Their reversal of function brings about Bartimaeus' liberation. Those who acted as a defiant barrier to Bartimaeus become the instruments that release him from economic destitution; they become the active promoters and cause of his healing. Their words in verse 49 are encouraging ("Take heart") and bear resurrectional language ("arise"). At their call, he is released of his economic and spiritual handicap. He throws off his begging cloak, springs up, and comes to Jesus. The act of dispensing of the cloak is an economic statement. Bartimaeus has now no use for the cloak spread out before him into which the generous could throw their alms. Freedom from oppression is dependent on the action of householders called by Jesus who consciously seek to liberate the marginalized. Here, as in earlier scenes, the resurrection language is obvious and connected to the nature of the household.

Bartimaeus' desire for healing is confirmed in verse 51. In responding to Jesus' question about what he most desires, Bartimaeus reveals one the most chronic tensions in Mark's households:

"My teacher, let me see again" (10:51).

The accurately translated "see again" indicates that Bartimaeus could see once before. If the capacity to see, with which Jesus' present disciples are struggling, is a sign of genuine discipleship, and Bartimaeus' request to Jesus is to "see again," then we are dealing with a story about one who was once a true disciple, fell from the path of discipleship (apostasy), and seeks to return. The harsh treatment which Bartimaeus initially received is indicative of the reaction that former members of Mark's house churches are receiving as they seek full membership. There are "many" in Mark's community who are withholding reconciliation from former apostates. The evangelist's point is clear: These "many" hold the key for other Bartimaeuses returning to full, reconciled membership in the Christian household.

Given the size and number of Mark's Greco-Roman households and the high level of members' commitment, the pain of someone breaking faith would have gone deep. The difficulty, which "many" would have felt towards that same person wanting to be accepted back as a full member of the house church, is understandable. The evangelist is encouraging readers to be hospitable to those seeking reconciliation. The story is a remarkable and painful reminder of Jesus' teaching to his disciples: the need for households to be reconciling agents of God's love, inclusive of all, irrespective of their former lives.

Summary

The story completes the deliberate literary frame that surrounds this important section of the Gospel. The frame is represented by two stories of Jesus' healing blindness and indicates its central preoccupation for Mark. The healing of Bartimaeus is the final climactic story of Jesus' healing. It is paradigmatic of the healing needed by those who follow him and the deep need to truly "see"—an emphasis found throughout. The evangelist's viewpoint about the disciples over this section has been consistent: they, too, must have their eyes reopened as they struggle to follow Jesus on the path of suffering.

The figure of the healed and liberated Bartimaeus following Jesus on the road to Jerusalem is a living example of true *metanoia*. He reflects the kinds of qualities of which the Twelve and wider group of disciples are devoid. In Jesus, Mark's economically poor, politically oppressed, and socially rejected householders are empowered to confront the source of their oppression located in the political, economic, and religious leadership of their day. Bartimaeus' following Jesus on the road to Jerusalem is an image needed by Mark's Roman *domus* as it seeks to make its assault on power politics. As this section of the gospel has stressed, this household needs to keep purifying its vision of Jesus and the place which suffering plays in its life. Mark's household needs to keep widening its doors to welcome the marginalized, the little ones, the divorced and, finally, those seeing reconciliation and return.

12

The Household and the Temple—
Mk 11:1–13:37

Overview of Mk 11:1–13:37

Until this moment in Mark's story the nature, structure, and role of the household of disciples has been carefully outlined. The household has become the narrative site for the presentation of Mark's christology and discipleship. It is also the place around which conflict and hostility is increasingly experienced from those who are outside the household. The opposition to Jesus increases as he and his household of disciples near Jerusalem. The last few chapters have revealed the internal tensions, difficulties, growing faithlessness and incomprehension among the disciples. With Jesus' explicit instructions to his household concluded, Mark's narrative site changes to Jerusalem itself—the final anticipated destination of the gospel story.[1]

Jesus reclaims Jerusalem and the Temple (11:1–12:44)

- The Temple as God's "House of Prayer"
- Parable of the Vineyard
- The "Widow" Stories

Apocalyptic Teaching (13:1–37)

- What will take place
- The Division in the Patriarchal Household
- "Watching"

---

[1] Kingsbury (*Conflict*, 75–86) sees the heightened tension in this final section of the gospel dealing with the Temple structures and those who control them. This inevitably leads to Jesus' passion and death.

In the remaining chapters as the antagonism to Jesus reaches flash-point, the focus moves from the household to the Temple, from the disciples' instruction to the debate with the religious establishment. Everything that now unfolds in Jesus' deeds and teaching has one focus in mind—to confront the powerbrokers of the political and religious leadership and dismantle their machinery of oppression, symbolized in the Temple. This unwavering and uncompromising prophetic stance leads ultimately to his death. The "house" becomes the counter symbol of the religious institution, the Temple that, from Mark's perspective, needs renewal. This is enacted in the opening scenes of Mk 11, as Jesus rides into Jerusalem on a colt (11:1-10), and by his symbolic conduct in the Temple (11:11-19).

Jesus' Political Entry into the Temple

The political intent of one riding into a country's capital and being hailed by the crowds could not be more obvious. Mark's genius, though, lies in the manner in that Jesus rides into Jerusalem and its subversion of traditional messianic politics. This action precipitates the final conflict with Israel's leaders and remains until its denouement in the gospel's closing scenes. By these acts he reclaims Jerusalem for God's holy people. Significantly, the Temple is renewed and redefined by Jesus as God's house:

"My house will be called a house of prayer for all nations" (11:17).

This becomes the overarching image that shapes the rest of Jesus' Jerusalem ministry that concludes with his death and the Temple curtain tearing (15:38). This last act to the Temple, deliberately connected by Mark to Jesus' act of dying, is the final statement about the function of the Temple for Mark's audience. The Temple is considered now refashioned by Jesus through his Temple in the household that gathers about him.[2] Between this opening statement of the Temple as "God's house" and the concluding divine action to the Temple's curtain, the symbolic barrier between human beings and God, Jesus' opposition to the religious authorities deepens. These themes permeate Mk 11 and 12.

The Fig Tree

The incident with the fig tree (11:12-25) is typical of the redefinition that Jesus gives the Temple and those who profiteer from it. The incident

---

[2] Struthers Malbon clearly identifies the Temple vs. household motif in the final chapters of Mk (*Narrative Space*, 120–26) as a spatial alteration highlighting the prominence of the house and echoing the tension between house and synagogue from the gospel's earlier chapters.

at first reading seems strange and out of context, given the anticipated conflict about to erupt between Jesus and the authorities and the fact that it "was not the season for figs" (11:13). Mark comes back to the fig tree image after an intervening scene in which Jesus enters and confronts those who abuse the Temple's institutions (11:15-19). Mark's chiasmic structure is the best clue for understanding this section and the meaning of the fig tree. The centerpiece of the structure is an episode in the Temple.

A—Jesus enters into Jerusalem and withdraws   (11:11)

   B—Curse of the fig tree   (11:12-14)

   > C—*Confrontation in the Temple*   (11:15-19)

   B¹—The withering of the fig tree   (11:20-26)

A¹—Jesus enters Jerusalem
   and opposed by the Sanhedrin (11:27)

The incident with the fig tree revolves around Jesus' deeds and words in the Temple. This central episode amplifies the futility of the present religious institution and its inability to offer genuine liberation and equality. The fig tree speaks to what happens in the Temple.[3] Jesus reclaims this institution for God as a "house" of prayer. It is to this house that all people will come. In Jesus' prophetic action the universal inclusiveness of God's house, expressed in the household of disciples, is reinforced. In contrast to what happens in this household and the call of its members to servant leadership, Jesus attacks the commercial self-interest of the religious leaders of the Temple. As the Temple leadership sees its profitable industry potentially restricted through the act of a peasant rabbi from Galilee, it schemes to do away with him.

Jesus' challenge of the authority of the conventional religious leaders continues into Mk 12 in the parable of a vineyard leased to tenants who plot for its ownership (12:1-12). In its allegory the parable sketches the inevitable conflict that awaits Jesus and his household of disciples. As the story shifts back from parable to narrative, the reader is reminded of the mounting resistance to Jesus as Mark notes the machination between

---

[3] The fig-tree/Temple connection is argued by W. R. Telford, *The Barren Temple and the Withered Tree* (Sheffield: JSOT Press, 1980); Myers, *Binding*, 297–98. Taylor, who would represent the other end of the scholarly spectrum, allows the possibility of a symbolic inference of the cursing of the fig tree and its connection with Jerusalem and Judaism as a whole (*The Gospel*, 458). Taylor prefers to argue instead for the historicity of the event, despite his anti-Judaic interpretation.

Pharisees and Herodians to kill him (12:13-17). In Jesus' skillful avoidance of their attempt to entrap him about taxes and allegiance to Caesar (12:13-17), his response to the Sadducees' question of marriage in the afterlife (12:18-27) and a scribe's query about the first commandment (12:28-34), the procession of antagonists swells.

The staged concern from the Sadducees over the patriarchal descendants of seven married but childless brothers (12:18-27) provides Mark with an opportunity to remind the reader of the qualities that characterize Jesus' household: gender inclusiveness and nurture enunciated earlier in the gospel. This is not the point of view of Jesus' Temple questioners who see the hypothetical widow of the brothers as an object of male debate. Her plight finds an echo in the "widow" stories in the final scenes of 12:38-44. Jesus' inquisition and the widow stories serve to reinforce the gospel's deliberate distinction between the defenders of the religious institution and Jesus, between the Temple and Jesus' household.

The Temple and "the Widow"

In the final two episodes of Mk 12, Jesus' indictment of the Temple continues. The two scenes (12:38-40, 41-44) are linked together by the word "widow," explores the function of the Temple and incriminates its beneficiaries. In the first scene (12:38-40) Jesus berates the religious interpreters for their all-consuming quest for status and privilege in every social setting—in the marketplace, at the prayer center and during the exclusive banquet. Their attitude is confirmed in the way they "devour widows' houses" (12:40).

In Mark's world women were economically dependent on men. The household became the setting in which this dependency was reflected. Widows were doubly disadvantaged. Through the death of their spouse, they were deprived of their only means of ongoing financial support. Apart from an often meager inheritance, support from family, and the generosity of others, they had little else to live off. Second, they were usually deprived of managing their own household and were dependent on a male household administrator allotted to them by social convention and family.

Mark recognizes the way that religious officials were entrusted with the administration of the financial affairs of the poor, including widows. In contrast to the scribe who seeks to know from Jesus the greatest commandment (12:28-34), some preferred to use their position for public notoriety as a way of gaining access to the paltry financial resources of the disenfranchized.[4] They made a pretense of piety and trustworthiness, took over the financial administration of widows and exploited their inherit-

---

[4] Myers, *Binding*, 320–22.

ance. Their "house" becomes the symbolic location for economic opportunism by a privileged profession. This further reinforces the theme explored throughout this section of the gospel: the profiteering motivation of those who abuse the household and the dire consequences for those, like widows, who rely on belonging to a household which respects and includes them.

These widow scenes towards the end of the gospel are the very antithesis of the domestic healing and emancipation experienced by women in the earlier sections of the gospel. Jesus' household of disciples, continued in the household of Mark's readers, is the new site of religious worship. The Temple as a place of divine communion has been moved from Mt. Sion in Jerusalem to the hearts of people formed in prayer (11:24-26). Such a site is accessible to all irrespective of their gender and economic, religious or cultural status. The action of the Temple-giving widow with Jesus' commentary on it (12:41-44) incriminate those who have control of the Temple and make worship a source of oppression. This prepares for the prediction of the Temple's destruction in Mk 13, the gospel's great apocalyptic chapter that seeks to lance the boil of the pain that Mark's household bears as it deals with suffering and conflict within and without. All this steers the reader to the ultimate conflict that Jesus will have with the Temple authorities in the final two chapters.

The Household in an Apocalyptic Era

There are two points that emerge from Mk 13 that are relevant to a domestic reading of the gospel. The first has to do with the author's use of verbs. Throughout the gospel Mark reads the current experiences of the house churches into Jesus' teaching. This same feature is noticeable here. The future tense of the verbs throughout the chapter, "will hand you over . . . ," "will be beaten . . . ," "will stand before governors . . . ," (13:9) is designed to give confidence to the readers who will not be surprised by what is happening. They will continue to be the victims of civil prosecution and persecution. More than that, in the light of Mark's domestic interest, their following of Jesus will bring them into conflict in traditional patriarchal families:

> "and brother will deliver up brother to death, and father, his child. And children will rise up against parents and have them killed" (13:12).

Despite all this, Mark assures the suffering household that everything is under the control of God. The disciples' suffering is limited. It will be "cut short" and they can be confident that they will be delivered by God (13:20).

A second feature of this apocalyptic chapter is the way Jesus' teaching is surrounded and impregnated with the theme of attentiveness.[5] Commands to "watch" (13:5, 9, 23, 33), which is variously translated as "beware" or "be alert," and "see" or "keep awake" (13:34, 35, 37) remind Mark's householders to be forever vigilant to what is taking place in their present historical situation, rather than be caught up in idle speculation. The tendency to distance themselves from the present through flights of fantasy that had no grounding in the real world would have been very strong. Mark's Jesus encourages his followers to remain rooted in the present. It is here that salvation will ultimately come about. In the final verses of the chapter, Jesus urges:

> "Keep awake therefore—for you do not know when the master of the house comes, in the evening, or at midnight, or at cockcrow, or at dawn, or else coming suddenly he may find you sleeping. What I say to you I say to all, keep awake!" (13:35-37).

Jesus' final words are for the benefit of the members of Mark's house churches and all readers of the gospel. The verses are framed by Jesus' injunction to "keep awake." The chapter encourages disciples to stay awake and ready for the coming of the real *paterfamilias* of Mark's household, God, the "master of the house." Disciple watchfulness is not intended simply in the physical sense. The disciple needs an interior alertness by reflecting on what is happening.

Summary

The reader senses in chapters 11 and 13 of Mark's gospel that the story of Jesus is nearing its crescendo. Over these chapters the reader is prepared for the passion of Jesus and the ultimate struggle of Jesus' household of disciples. The tension with the authorities and their institutions is heightened. The Temple becomes the site of conflict, argument, and exorcism; the religious interpreters of the Torah find themselves unable to comprehend Jesus' action or prophetic teaching. His disciples appear as "flat" characters with little interaction or apparent connection to Jesus' mission. They continue to misunderstand and are unable to scrutinize clearly what is about to happen. To them the final words of this section are directed. They must "keep awake."

Still, behind this injunction to remain alert and reflective before the face of impending disaster, Mark's great apocalyptic chapter that concludes the section offers a faint note of hope. Suffering and persecution

---

[5] Robbins (*Jesus the Teacher*, 178–80) interprets Mk 13 as a typical farewell speech or testament designed to prepare the disciples for what is to come and to infuse them with the spirit of the teacher as they become the proclaimers of Jesus to others.

will have reign for a limited period only; afflicted householders can be confident that God is with them and that ultimate victory and salvation is inevitable. This is the hopeful apocalyptic message that Mark seeks to convey to despondent Christians living under the aegis of a Roman despot.

The closing words of Jesus' powerful message act as a bridge to the passion. He encourages the disciples to keep awake through each of the major divisions of Roman time (evening, midnight, cockcrow, and dawn). These divisions will reappear as explicit temporal markers in the passion narrative (14:17, 72; 15:25, 33, 42; 16:2). Mark uses them to identify significant moments in the unfolding of the passion's drama—namely, to reveal the disciples' lack of alertness in contrast to the spiritual wakefulness of Jesus engaged in intense cosmic battle. With the injunction to keep awake echoing in the readers' ears, thirteen chapters of gospel introduction conclude as the drama of the passion begins.

13

Homelessness—Mk 14:1–16:8

In the gospel's concluding chapters Mark returns to the narrative theme with which the gospel began—homelessness. Jesus' passion for human and divine intimacy, what I identify as the preeminent purpose behind the quest for a home, seems unrequited. Silence and loneliness dominate. But Mark's final story, the resurrection of Jesus, will offer a way of comprehending the tragic disappointment of all human beings in their quest for companionship and "home." The final words of Mk 13 speak to the gospel's actual audience as it reads itself in the events "predicted" by Jesus and filled with hope in God's ultimate victory over evil and suffering. This apocalyptic conviction is now transferred to the story of Jesus in the great climax of the gospel.

What is about to take place is not a dispassionate historical account of the events that led to Jesus' death. Mark is inviting the gospel's readers also to identify themselves in the passion. They are not mere spectators or casual readers; they become participants in what is about to unfold. They, too, are invited to remember their experiences of homelessness and to identify with those who are totally homeless. In this final story Mark will challenge the gospel's Greco-Roman householders to reflect on their current experiences of homelessness and sense of divine absence. These have the potential to be the sources of ultimate communion. In Jesus' story the definitive quest of Mark's audience for a home will be realized.

Overview of Mk 14:1–16:8

The story of Jesus' passion, death, and resurrection takes place over eight scenes. The first two (14:1-11, 12-31) are strategically centered on the household where Jesus gathers with his disciples. They reformulate in a fresh way domestic themes that have filtered through from earlier scenes.

The second scene (14:12-31) highlights the inadequacy of the household of disciples as they contest among themselves. The scene predicts their betrayal and abandonment of Jesus. This prepares for what will take place in the garden where Jesus is finally deserted (14:32-52). The contrast between the alleged loyalty from the household of disciples and their fleeing figures could not be stronger.

In the final house scene of the gospel (14:53-72) where the religious elite are gathered with the high priest, Mark's portrait of Jesus is reinforced. Here, too, Peter's professed loyalty from the earlier household supper is put to the test and found absent. The christological trial with the religious establishment is paralleled in Jesus' trial before Pilate (15:1-20). This leads to the gospel's climactic scene with Jesus' crucifixion and death in the midst of the pain of divine absence (15:21-39). Though God may be silent and Jesus abandoned, the final scenes (15:40–16:8) proclaim a different story as the reader is invited to ponder an enigmatic conclusion which overturns all expectations.

1. **Public Infidelity vs. Household Fidelity** (14:1-11)
2. **Final Household Meal and Instruction** (14:12-31)
3. Abandonment in the Garden (14:32-52)
4. **In the House of the High Priest** (14:53-72)
   • Jesus' Fidelity vs. Peter's Infidelity
5. Trial before Pilate (15:1-20)
6. Crucifixion and Divine Abandonment (15:21-39)
7. Burial (15:40-47)
8. Resurrection (16:1-8)

Public and Private Acts Towards Jesus

The passion opens with three carefully constructed stories (14:1-2, 3-9, 10-11). These contrast the deliberate act of public betrayal and scheming against Jesus by men, especially one of the Twelve, with the private, intimate, domestic act of authentic discipleship by a woman. The plotting frames the central domestic story, the anointing of Jesus.[1]

A—The **public plot** by the Sanhedrin (14:1-2)
   B—*The **household anointing** by an unnamed woman (14:3-9)*
A¹—The **public betrayal** by Judas commences (14:10-11)

---

[1] D. Senior, *The Passion of Jesus in the Gospel of Mark* (Wilmington, Del.: Michael Glazier, 1984) 42f.

The household anointing is significant. Until this point the household setting becomes the opportunity for teaching about discipleship. In the house Jesus offers a vision of what Mark's community could be. Now, in the context of Jesus' passion and death to which everything in the gospel has been directed, the household provides the setting in what it says about Jesus. Its focus has shifted from an emphasis on discipleship to christology.

As Mark's story nears its climax, the evangelist places side-by-side a story of betrayal by one of the male leaders of the household of disciples with ultimate discipleship and fidelity of an unnamed woman in a house owned by one socially rejected. Jesus gathers in the house of a leper.[2] This household, like many other previous ones in the gospel, becomes the setting for healing, welcome, and communion. The household meal that Jesus shares with Simon has eucharistic overtones and anticipates the final banquet he will shortly share with the disciples prior to his trial and death.

Within this setting a woman, possibly already in the room and perhaps a member of this household, comes to him. The woman models Mark's conviction that the household can also be the place in which its members come to know Jesus' true identity. The household of disciples has the potential to be the household of christological proclamation: The woman, like a prophet of ancient Israel who anoints the head of a designated king, anoints Jesus soon to be recognized ironically as "king." Her act of fidelity contrasts powerfully to Judas' act of betrayal that surrounds this scene. In his action the words from Jesus' apocalyptic discourse in the previous chapter are dramatically fulfilled: "brother will betray brother to death" (13:12). Internal betrayal from within the household of disciples and apostasy are high on the agenda in Mark's opening scenes of the passion. This is continued in the next scene, the final upper-room meal in the household of disciples (14:12-31).

The Final Meal and Ultimate Betrayal

The meal is set in a "large upper room." Mark's Greco-Roman audience could well have read their familiarity of the *domus* with its large upper-story dining room *(cenacula)* back into this scene. It is clear from the scene's structure—centered on the meal with its attendant focus on Jesus and the Twelve, the themes of betrayal and desertion—that Mark is not simply concerned about recalling a historical event, of letting the story become a "window" into the past. The evangelist's interest is in creating a

---

[2] Senior regards the anointing woman as a further example of an "outsider" showing the presumed "insiders" the kind of generosity and discipleship behavior directed to Jesus (ibid., 48–49).

mirror so that Christian householders of a later time and place could read themselves into the scene. Jesus' concern about his impending betrayal (14:19-20) from one of the disciples is particularly poignant for Mark's household. Betrayal was a real possibility if not an actual reality experienced by the gospel's audience. It could have tempted the presiders or hosts of eucharistic celebrations in Rome's house-churches. This perspective becomes strengthened by 14:26-31 where Jesus foretells the desertion of all the disciples, especially Peter, and indirectly addresses all who hold positions of eucharistic leadership in the Christian household.

These themes of betrayal and desertion that have arisen in the upper-room *domus* meal of the discipled household are continued and reinforced in the public setting of a garden. Here Mark carefully crafts a scene of profound pathos around the struggling figure of the lonely Jesus. Jesus is portrayed as deeply distressed and troubled (14:33). He seeks companionship with his disciples, but they fall asleep—a point noted by the evangelist three times (14:37, 40, 41). He cries out to his God, whom he addresses in the familial "Abba" (14:36) for relief from the struggle and impending disaster. His God seems comfortless. Now, as the events of the passion are about to unfold in hurried and predictable succession, Jesus reaches out for the kind of intimacy and friendship that was to typify his household of disciples. Yet he is denied solace and companionship. This only accentuates his sense of homelessness, the same experience with which the gospel began.

Even his betrayal into the hands of his executors will be brought about by one of his closest companions. Finally, the prophesied betrayal is enacted as Judas, pointedly identified as a member of the Twelve (14:43) and "betrayer" (14:44), arrives with a retinue from the religious elite. It is complete in the false gesture of intimacy and greeting, a kiss (14:44-45). As one of the household leaders betrays Jesus, the rest desert him. The household of disciples is completely decimated. Mark simply notes,

and deserting him, all fled (14:50).

Before the shift to a religious household and the first of Jesus' two trials (14:53-72) the evangelist leaves us with a final mysterious figure of a fleeing naked young man (14:51-52).[3] For Mark's readers, perhaps he is symbolic of those newly baptized members of their household who have deserted the path of discipleship metaphorically leaving behind them their baptismal robes.

---

[3] The scene of the fleeing naked figure reinforces the disciples' desertion of Jesus. See, H. M. Jackson, "Why the Youth shed his Cloak and fled Naked: The Meaning and Purpose of Mark 14:51-52," *JBL* 116 (1997) 273–89.

In the household of the high priest with all the religious leaders gathered, two trials take place: the trial of Jesus and that of Peter.[4] In the first Mark allows all the major insights into Jesus to emerge. He is declared ironically as prophet, Christ and Blessed One by his accusers (14:61). He identifies himself as the Human One (14:62). In the second trial, Peter's denial of Jesus is comprehensive. The principal leader of the household of disciples denies companionship with Jesus (14:67) and those who belong to the household in which he is prominent (14:69-70).

In the context of Peter's total denial and Jesus' complete solitude, the scene switches to a second trial before the political authority of Pilate (15:1-20). Throughout this trial Pilate pursues the accusation of Jesus as king. Again, in ironic fashion with Pilate's questioning of Jesus about his alleged kingship (15:3-15) and the mock coronation executed by Pilate's soldiers (15:16-20), Mark unequivocally announces to an audience familiar with the despotic pretensions of the Roman emperor: Jesus is the true king.[5]

This image of Jesus as king pervades the following scene of Jesus' crucifixion and death (15:21-39), described by the evangelist with an economy of language. The royal Jesus goes to the place of death accompanied by a rural attendant who carries his cross. He is finally crucified with his regal status declared above him and enthroned between two servants.

Divine Abandonment

The highpoint of the gospel arrives. The apocalyptic note of darkness (15:33) prepares the reader for the tragic death of one who epitomizes the homeless and rejected figures familiar to Mark's householders.[6] In his final death screams that echo from the cross, Jesus shouts out to Mark's audience his familiarity with the most painful and shattering experience of any human being, the experience of divine abandonment. This is the real and incontrovertible experience of absolute homelessness, of which the quest for home is its shadow:

> [34]And at the ninth hour Jesus cried out in a loud voice, "Eloi, Eloi, lema sebachthani?" which means, "My God, my God, why have you abandoned

---

[4] Struthers Malbon sees in these physical settings a "movement mediation" between room and courtyard, between the solemnity of what took place in the upper room and the hypocrisy of Jesus' trial (*Narrative Space*, 136–37).

[5] On the kingship theme which permeates Mark's passion narrative, see F. J. Matera, *The Kingship of Jesus: Composition and Theology in Mark 15* (Chico, Calif.: Scholars Press, 1982).

[6] The note about darkness draws on the imagery of Amos 8:9 (Hooker, *The Gospel*, 377; Harrington, Mark, 628; Senior, *Passion*, 122–23). This underscores the event as an

me?" [35]And when some of the bystanders heard this, they said, "Behold, he calls Elijah." [36]And someone ran, filled a sponge with sour wine, put it on a stick, and gave it to him to drink, saying, "Wait, let us see if Elijah will come to take him down." [37]Then Jesus giving a loud cry breathed his last. [38]And the curtain of the Temple was torn in two, from top to bottom. [39]Now the centurion, who stood facing him, saw that in this way he breathed his last, he said, "Truly this man was God's Son!" (15:33-39).

Rejection and misunderstanding that have dogged Jesus throughout the gospel pursue him to the bitter end. His dying words are the felt experience of solitude from God and utter homelessness. The baptism event (1:11) declared Jesus as God's son. From the earliest chapters the reader has known that Jesus belongs to God; in God Jesus finds security, a "place." Now in these final chapters it seems as though all this is reversed. Rather than discovering in God one who welcomes and comforts, Jesus encounters absolute solitude,[7]

"My God, my God, why have you abandoned me?" (15:34).

"My God" is Jesus' cry to God to answer his need for a home.[8] Though he knows abandonment he also seeks to reestablish the sense of belonging to God. From this experience of divine silence Mark's Jesus emits his final death scream searching for God. Despite feeling deserted, Jesus cries out, "My God." His fidelity remains.

On Jesus' expiration the Temple curtain is severed. Access to the inner sanctuary of holiness is now possible through Jesus' faithful death.[9] His death proclaims what has been flagged earlier in the gospel, out of

---

apocalyptic act of judgement. See R. E. Brown, *The Death of the Messiah: From Gethsemane to the Grave* (New York: Doubleday, 1994) 1034.

[7] Many commentators see the words of Jesus as the beginning of Psalm 22. Echoes of this psalm permeate the passion narrative. As Jesus dies, these are his final words in the gospel. The psalm ends on a note of confidence to God and thus points the reader to the tenacious faith of Jesus who continues in fidelity to his God despite abandonment. See Senior, *Passion,* 132–33 and 118, n. 85 and the relevant literature quoted there. For Brown (*Passion,* 1044–45) Jesus' words continue the apocalyptic imagery introduced at the beginning of the scene. Jesus' ultimate death cry, according to Brown, is symbolic of the eschatological victory over evil.

[8] Tolbert (*Sowing,* 287) understands that Jesus' experience of divine absence in his death cry may contain the seeds of its own resolution. It is this reversal which offers the answer to the human quest for home.

[9] Harrington ("Mark," 628) interprets the veil rending as the end of the old covenant. In a similar vein, Brown (*Passion,* 1102) considers the rending as a sign of irrevocable divine judgement and that the Temple sanctuary has now been replaced by Jesus. Taylor sees the event as a theological statement symbolizing "the opening of the way to God effected by the death of Christ" (*The Gospel,* 596). My own interpretation seeks to pursue Taylor's line of thought.

Jesus' total encounter with homelessness, here symbolized through his sense of utter desertion, comes the possibility for the fulfilment of the human quest for home. Communion with God through Jesus is now a reality. The Temple, Mark's "house of prayer" (11:17), is now the house of divine communion.

Jesus' Death: Moment of Faith or Mockery?

On Jesus' death the executing centurion declares that Jesus is "God's son" (15:39). Many commentators regard this an important climactic moment in the gospel. It is seen as the culmination of Mark's christological plot in which the gospel's narrative conclusion is explicitly stated: Jesus belongs to God and God's fidelity remains. Jesus is "God's son." What Jesus encountered as divine abandonment became instead the vehicle for divine encounter. For Mark's audience the death scene of Jesus affirms the myriad of human experiences of failure, rejection, misunderstanding, and ultimate loneliness as the path to divine communion.[10]

Given the important theology that impregnates this scene, it is noteworthy that the Greek text preserves a certain ambiguity in the centurion's statement. There is no definite article for "son" in the Greek text. In other words, rather than "Truly, this man was *the* son of God," the centurion's words can be literally translated, "Truly, this man was son of God" (Mk 15:39c).[11] The reader is left wondering why Jesus is not declared unambiguously as the son of God.

The lack of precision in the centurion's statement can only mean one thing. The ambiguity or obscurity of Jesus' identity throughout the gospel is maintained right to the end. It further affirms the struggle in Mark's readers as they wrestle with experiencing divine communion in their own encounter with suffering and death. But there is a further ambiguity in the centurion's statement that moves it beyond a declaration of faith, the general consensus among interpreters.[12]

Many have seen the centurion's statement as a declaration of faith: Jesus is the son of God. But it is not clear from the Greek whether what the centurion says is a statement or a question. If the first, then it is a faith

---

[10] This is supported by an appreciation of Greco-Roman tradition of the suffering teacher-king. See Robbins, *Jesus the Teacher,* 187–91.

[11] See Brown's discussion on the "son of God" without the use of the definite article (*Passion,* 1146–68).

[12] Most scholars presume a faith attestation by the centurion. For example, Taylor, *The Gospel,* 597; Best, *The Temptation,* 181; Senior, *Passion,* 129; Kingsbury, *Conflict,* 53–54; Brown, *Death,* 1143–44, 1146–52.

declaration.[13] If the second, then this is the ultimate act of irony that continues the suspense about Jesus for the reader. Even at the extreme moment of ministry, in death, Jesus is not recognized or acclaimed for what the reader has all along known. If this is the case, for Mark's faithful and searching household this means that the struggle for divine communion, the quest for home, will continue. This is the point of the last scene of the gospel, Mark's story of Jesus' resurrection (16:1-8).

The Tomb: from Homelessness to Home

After the burial of Jesus (15:40-47) the women who had witnessed his death and place of burial arrive at the tomb early in the morning after *Shabbat* to anoint his body (16:1). They are surprised to find the stone over the tomb's entrance already rolled back. On entering the tomb they encounter a white-clad young man who proclaims to them the Easter message and their mission:

> "Do not be afraid. You seek Jesus the Nazarene who was crucified. He has been raised; he is not here. See the place where they laid him. But go tell his disciples and Peter that he goes before you into Galilee. There you shall see him just as he told you" (16:6-7).

The most important statement of the young man is the Easter declaration "He has been raised" (16:6b). The resurrection is God's act to Jesus. What has been perceived as defeat has become victory. God has vindicated Jesus. Mark links the Easter message to the place of emptiness. The tomb's void is the proof of the message, "he is not here. See the place where they laid him . . . ." (16:6c). As in the death scene, the perception of abandonment, solitude, or absence becomes the means for divine encounter. Only through the engagement with failure, defeat, and misunderstanding can the disciple know the resurrection.[14] These negative experiences lie at the heart of the quest for a home and are the foundation for *metanoia*. They enable the householder to recognize Jesus' resurrection.

Through the story of Jesus' death and resurrection, Mark makes the experience of homelessness and the struggle to form a household of disciples focussed on Jesus—the actual situation of the gospel's householders—the authentic path to discipleship. Enigmatically, the disciples' desire

---

[13] For Kingsbury (*Conflict*, 54) this is the first time in the gospel that a human being unreservedly declares Jesus' identity in harmony with God's point of view revealed in Mk 1.

[14] Struthers Malbon puts this differently. She describes the tomb after the resurrection as a place which once enclosed the body of Jesus with its function destroyed, or at least reversed. The outside/inside distinction is overturned with the Easter injunction to the women (*Narrative Space*, 128–31).

for home created through the counter experiences of homelessness becomes the actual ground for the realization of the divine home. In gospel
language, this is the resurrection. Defeat becomes victory; death, resurrection; homelessness, home. This could well be the point of the gospel's
original final verse 16:8:

> And going out they fled from the tomb, for they were gripped with trembling
> and ecstasy and they said nothing to anyone for they were afraid.

On first reading this seems an unusual and baffling way to conclude
the gospel. Later writers added to the original manuscript endings more in
keeping with the other (later) gospels as a way of tidying up the conclusion. This betrays their perplexity over the first ending and their desire to
correct it. With the ending as it stands, it seems that the women failed in
the Easter mission entrusted to them.[15] However, in line with what has already emerged from our reflection on Mark's story of Jesus' death and the
words of the young man in the tomb, the ending is consistent.[16]

The final verse highlights the frustration experienced by disciples in
proclaiming the Gospel. Their "trembling and ecstasy" is not the terror of
fear but the overwhelming awe of the religious encounter. The only appropriate stance in Mark's gospel before such an encounter is silence. This
has been a constant theme throughout. Mark's householders know that the
Easter message has been proclaimed to them. They are the fruits of that
message.

Summary

Mark's final verse cautions contemporary householders against looking for the experience of the resurrection in the extraordinary, heavenly
arena of religious expectation. Instead they are encouraged to reflect on
their ordinary, domestic struggles and encounters as the place of the resurrection—an insight noted several times by Mark in the domestic healings
in the early part of the gospel. This domestic setting becomes the place of

---

[15] Certainly this is the sense that Kinukawa (*Women and Jesus*, 107–22), Dewey
("Mark," 506–7) have of the female disciples. The women have failed like their male coun-
terparts. P. Perkins, in *Resurrection: New Testament Witness and Contemporary Reflection*
(New York: Doubleday, 1984) 122, considers Mk 16:8 as the evangelist's way of indicating
the women's equality with Jesus' other disciples. For Tolbert (*Sowing*, 298–99) the enigmatic ending is a rhetorical device which deliberately ricochets back to Mark's readers
leaving them pondering their own response to proclaim the Easter message. Similarly, Robbins, *Jesus the Teacher*, 193.

[16] For different ways of reading Mark's final verse, see M. Trainor, "The Women, the
Empty Tomb, and *That* Final Verse," *The Bible Today* 34 (1996) 177–82.

divine encounter and mission, and the experience of the resurrection. Through this enigmatic ending, Mark unequivocally proclaims that in the gospel's Greco-Roman household of readers or auditors the Easter message is being enacted. In them the real quest for home is fulfilled.[17]

---

[17] Robbins (*Jesus the Teacher,* 193) interprets Mark's conclusion as a beginning.

Part Three

Summary

14

The Household in a Gospel Community

Since I began to write this book, a major event occurred in my family—the sudden decline in my mother's ability to walk. This physical handicap precipitated a number of other issues that all impinged on the way we perceived the family home. We needed to ensure that Mom had the right nursing care and attention that her declining condition warranted; we also needed to provide support for Dad who up until this time had been Mom's principal home carer.

As I drove away from the nursing home that finally accommodated her, I realized the reason for my preoccupation, almost obsession, with houses and households in archeology, ancient literature and Mark's gospel. Unwittingly, I had been searching for a way to understand the experiences that were dawning upon me through my aging parents. With Mom's accommodation in a nursing home, I realized how formative and influential my family household had been. Now this house was definitively changed and I was mourning its loss.

This experience of relocating one of my parents with its accompanying grieving underscores how deep is my own quest for home. This returns me to where I began in chapter 1. The human longing to belong and grow in a nurturing, welcoming environment is common and deep. It is expressed in all social and cultural contexts. For people of faith, it is particularly sought after in the Christian community and the movements concerned about basic ecclesial communities or house churches. Whether our experience is personal, social, or ecclesial, Mark's gospel can bring a fresh insight to this common quest for home.

Mark's Pro-Cultural and Counter-Cultural Stance

I have hypothesized that Mark's gospel written around 70 C.E. was addressed to a Greco-Roman urban community, possibly in Rome. While

I have read the gospel from a specific urban Roman setting, the conclusions I have drawn are not invalidated if another urban center was the actual historical location of Mark's audience. The domestic reading I offer can be extrapolated to any other city of the Roman world in which a few Christian households were clustered. Insights gleaned from a study of urban architecture of the period and the writings of ancient Greek and first-century C.E. Roman writers can further enhance this reading.

What emerges from this exploration of Mark's household theme that I have argued was deliberate and pervasive throughout the gospel narrative can be summed up simply: the evangelist was pro-cultural and counter-cultural. The writer presented insights into Jesus' household and the nature of discipleship that were judged as vital for the future of Mark's households and the survival of the Gospel into a new era. These insights had their parallel in the Greco-Roman world. From this perspective Mark's attitude was pro-cultural: the social and cultural context of the gospel's audience encouraged ways of living that were in harmony with the true spirit of Jesus and Mark wanted gospel readers to emulate them. At the same time there were other insights into Mark's portrayal of household life that critiqued some of the deeply held beliefs and conventions of the Greco-Roman world. From this point of view Mark was counter-cultural.

I would suggest, then, that Mark's task was more than writing a Greco-Roman update of the story of Jesus, originally set in a Jewish world. A cultural discernment and sensitivity also shaped Mark's spin on the story of Jesus. The evangelist regarded Greco-Roman society positively, but not uncritically. Mark saw the positive side of some of the social values that were held and known to the gospel's audience. Mark also recognized their limitations. The cutting-edge critique for this came from Jesus of Nazareth. Mark believed in the ongoing relevance of Jesus' life, death, and resurrection that was the climax of a ministry lived in commitment to society's powerless.

Urban Roman Architecture

I have been arguing that Mark presumes a specific architectural context in writing the gospel. This architecture is, in a sense, a "given" for Mark and culturally neutral in value. Mark's use of it though presumes a pro-cultural attitude: the writer does not seek to write the gospel using architectural styles that were unfamiliar to the audience, adapted from the peasant, Jewish world or the original architectural setting of the foundational story. However, Mark adopts a counter-cultural stance in critiquing the kinds of relationships typical of Roman households.

What is clear from the urban architecture of the Roman city is the prominence of the *tabernae* (shops with houses) and *insulae* (apartment-style blocks of residences) as the common residences of the poor, and the *domus* (mansion-style house) as the preferred dwelling of the elite. Mark's community members would have reflected a social cross-section of urban society— poor, artisans, city workers, merchants, and elite. When they gathered to hear and reflect on the story of Jesus, they would have gathered in their apartments. The possibility of the existence of a Christian gathering site in an apartment above the *Casa di Bicentenario* at Herculaneum in 79 C.E. is eloquent testimony to this apartment-style house church. However, for a meeting of the whole Markan community a larger dwelling was needed. Arguably this would have been the *domus* owned by one of the Christian elite. It is this kind of structure that is conceivably read back into Mark's gospel story of Jesus.

There are several features of the *domus* which allowed it to be appropriately used as a narrative space for the gathering of Jesus and his disciples and the exploration of the key themes of christology and discipleship:

- The *domus* was essentially public in nature. People could enter it easily and be received. Hospitality was inscribed into the architectural articulation of the house with its *atrium, tablinum* and peristyle courtyard. Mark's household of disciples is concerned about the welcome it offers, those who are included as members and the numbers who can gather within it.

- The *domus* was articulated to bring honor to the household's *paterfamilias*. It was designed for his public adulation. Throughout the gospel Mark invites a critique of the conventional way the *paterfamilias* is appropriated as the locus of authority and power. The gospel relocates this authority in God and in God's agent, Jesus.

- The *domus* provided especially easy access to invited guests and patrons of the *paterfamilias*. Mark's gospel invites its audience to reconsider the social convention and expectation of the invited and uninvited. The clear narrative discernment of the "insiders" from "outsiders" enhances this reconfiguration of those who can enter Jesus' household of disciples.

- Those who belonged to the family of the *domus* were those who lived under its roof. Family membership was larger than what we would call today the nuclear family. Membership of the household of disciples is an important issue. Surprisingly it does not (initially?) include the natural family of Jesus, but is expanded to embrace the most unlikely and socially reprehensible of people.

- The *domus* structure specifically and the Roman urban landscape generally point to the close-knit arrangement of the populace. The close proximity of the *domus* with the *insulae* and the *tabernae* enhanced the social cohesion of Mediterranean people reflected in their dyadic personality. Mark's gospel reveals a household of disciples that struggles with internal cohesion and unity. In the final chapters of the gospel, Jesus' desire for companionship is sadly unfulfilled as the household that once formed about him tragically fragments through betrayal and flight.

Greek-Roman Writers on the "House"

Designing a set of "domestic lenses" for reading Mark's gospel is further helped when this appreciation of first-century c.e. Roman urban architecture is enhanced through the contribution which Greek and Roman writers make to the appreciation that Mark's Greco-Roman audience has about houses. With such a study we are able to see a little more clearly Mark's pro-cultural and counter-cultural critique.

Pythagoras, Plato, and Aristotle reveal the pervasiveness of the understanding of the household's relationships in terms of domination-subordination and superiority-inferiority. These relational paradigms seem to define family relationships in the typical Greco-Roman house. Foundational for the Greek household was "orderliness" (Plato) or "partnership" (Aristotle). The Roman writers in the Republican Period also argued for ordered and stable domestic structures that would enhance a people's communion with each other. They adopted the Greek hierarchical spousal and parental model to bring about this desired order and stability.

In Mark's household of disciples partnership and communion are important discipleship themes. The disciples struggle with them as they accompany Jesus to Jerusalem and his death. While on this journey, Mark's Jesus firmly challenges his disciples against reverting to the domination—superiority model of household structure evident among these preeminent Greek philosophers and adopted into the Roman household. In fact, Mark appealed to other motifs that find their parallel in Greek and Roman literature. These present a more egalitarian, nurturing, and affective valuation of the Roman household.

Mark's description of Jesus' household was most culturally radical. It presented a household characterized by mutuality and partnership, not domination-subordination. Mark's alternative household pattern, though secondary to the predominant superiority-inferiority model of domestic relationships, was part of a Greek cultural heritage already evident in a philosophical tradition that stemmed from Pythagoras and Aristotle.

While Mark's audience also knew the cultural appreciation about houses and their management, the evangelist with a counter-cultural critique offered an alternative way of being "household" within the gospel audience's Greco-Roman environment. This alternative pattern had also been reinforced by the style of relationships adopted by the historical Jesus in his first community of disciples. This option was critical of some domestic conventions. It offered a different approach for exercising authority and determining membership in the Christian household. Authority was to be collaborative and membership inclusive irrespective of status, gender, and wealth.

In Mark's Roman world the household was structured along patriarchal authoritative lines. This is clear from Cicero's writings. Cicero, however, explored other themes important for the *domus:* the centrality of "communion," the domestic nurture of the pivotal social virtues ("solidarity," "partnership," "affection"), the nature of the authority exercised by the *paterfamilias,* and the importance and appropriateness of affection in the spousal relationship that spilled over to the children.

These themes might have also been available to Mark in shaping the story of Jesus and the setting of his teaching in the household of his disciples. If this is true, then we view most clearly Mark's pro-cultural stance. As we have seen, Mark's use of similar themes is evident in the gospel's portrait of Jesus, his welcome and respect of children, a non-patriarchal use of power and the inclusion of those marginally disregarded, including the divorced. Most significantly, the type of household envisaged by Mark's Jesus was one in which the human, male, household head, the *paterfamilias,* was absent. This absence would have had implications for the way power was to be exercised in this Markan household.

The male's use of *potestas* would be unknown. Instead, its exercise would have been through the leadership of the household, a leadership of female and male disciples, and would have honored the source of the *potestas,* God revealed through Jesus. Clearly, the *paterfamilias* of Mark's household was God. This alternative shape and ordering of the household, especially with its more egalitarian exercise of *potestas* and authority, would represent Mark's cultural critique. It would have been regarded by those with the conventional Roman mindset as radical and possibly threatening.

To reiterate, Jesus' sayings about the household, spouses, and children, although radical, would not have been received with total unfamiliarity. The gospel would have been regarded—perhaps by the majority—as an unpopular and sectarian voice. But it was not the only voice arguing an alternative position. It would have tapped into the vision of an ideal household argued by some writers and historians of the Republican Period. In this respect the Gospel was both counter-cultural and pro-cultural. It countered the dominant image of households and spousal relationships that permeated the republic. It also supported and explicated the presentation of a Roman household and marriage ideal. In this ideal, *potestas* was not exercised in a malevolent or dictatorial way, marriage not driven by the need for political or social alliances, divorce not determined by the whim of the male, and children not regarded as victims of unstable marriage alliances and insecure households.

If the provenance of Mark's gospel was a Roman situation as some have argued, then its presentation of the household was shaped by the spirit of Jesus of Nazareth and by what was judged as the cultural ideal. If the gospel's provenance was not a Roman setting, when it was received into a Roman Christian community it would have been seen as arguing for a household ideal parallel with the insights of some orators, historians, and philosophers of the republic. In this view the gospel would have been regarded as a document culturally relevant and socially radical.

This appreciation of first-century C.E. urban Roman design and Greek and Roman writers alerts us to the fact that in the ears of Mark's audience the house is more than simply an architectural space where Jesus and his disciples gather. It is a social symbol that connects to Mark's portrait of Jesus and the disciples. It is a narrative feature that provides the reader with a clue for knowing the ingredients required of a community of disciples who seek to follow Jesus. Just as the historical Jesus refashioned the Galilean household to address the powerlessness experienced by the debt-ridden peasant farmers affected by a specialized market economy, Mark refashions the house in the gospel to present an alternative way of being community in a Roman urban environment.

Mark's household of disciples becomes a narrative symbol of the possibility of social cohesion within the Christian community in a period of powerlessness and unrest, similar to the time of Jesus. What happens in Mark's households reveals much about discipleship. I have suggested that these households mirror issues with which Mark's audience is wrestling in its discipleship of Jesus: growing isolation, rejection, persecution, martyrdom, and factionalism.

Reading Mark's Gospel—A Recapitulation

There are several insights that a closer reading of Mark's gospel offers contemporary home searchers. The household of disciples envisaged in the gospel is one in which women and men collaborate in ministry, authority, and leadership. This reciprocal and mutual style of relationships builds a community in which people experience welcome, hospitality, and nurture. This is the kind of environment in which people are healed at the deepest levels of their being. Such healing occurs because people experience the true meaning of genuine community where their quest for home is fulfilled. All these images emerge especially out of a close reading of the gospel's domestic healings. Simon's mother-in-law (1:29-31) becomes the paradigmatic exemplar of the householder in Jesus' community who is healed, resurrected, and empowered to ministry. Her story is duplicated several times in the gospel.

Significantly, the household of Jesus becomes the setting for the concrete experience and realization of the resurrection. This is an important theological antidote in a time when looking beyond or above seem to be most likely and tempting ways to avoid dealing with the tragedies of the present or emerging oneself in the grit of life. For Mark, the household of Jesus' disciples is rooted in history and culture. It is a particularized, historically conditioned and limited expression of God's *basileia*. Mark affirms categorically that the household's culturally conditioned quality and its liminality is the very reason for its experience of the resurrection. From Jesus' initial, primordial desert experience of homelessness in Mk 1 the rest of his ministry unfolds; it is the profound experience of homelessness at the end of the gospel in his sense of divine abandonment that release and resurrection emerge; it is the place of absence, the tomb, which becomes the proof of the Easter message.

All these examples of homelessness and limitation are summed up in the gospel's final verse as the women rush from the tomb in a holy silence to the mystery that they have been urged to proclaim. For Mark, the myriad of homeless experiences in all its forms which entrap or confuse the gospel's audience become the ground for disciple *metanoia* and the possibility of resurrection.

As the disciples struggle to know, see, and understand Jesus, as they fight among themselves and fail to recognize that they have the "one bread" with them in the boat, Mark reveals a household that is in need of constant *metanoia*. Jesus' household of disciples is not perfect and mirrors the household communities formed by Mark's audience. Fights over authority, rejection of the little ones, and ultimate betrayal and flight at the height of Jesus' passion reveal a household of disciples that is failed. The evangelist's intent is to encourage disciples of a later period in their struggles for community leadership, authority, and inclusivity.

Finally, Mark's story of the household of disciples reveals a community struggling with inclusion of members who have failed or rejected membership. Bartimaeus's healing (10:46-52) is the exemplary story illustrating the power of the community's leadership to encourage discipleship from the most surprising quarters or to reject former apostate members seeking reconciliation. Mark's Roman householders are being challenged to reconsider their attitude to those who are looking for a way to being reconciled back into the household. They are also being challenged to expand their limited horizons of who can belong to the Christian household.

In depicting Jesus' missionary forays into Gentile territory—sometimes with his beleaguered disciples as they cross to "the other side" of the Sea of Galilee, sometimes as he journeys a circuitous route to Tyre and Sidon—Mark raises the missionary agenda which must be the future preoccupation of every gospel household. According to Mark, such a household can no longer afford to be exclusivist, privatized, or self-centered. Its survival depends on its capacity to embrace and welcome people from other cultures, faiths, and traditions.

Jesus' warm embrace of the child in the midst of his squabbling disciples (9:36) is a poignant reminder of the embrace that the household must offer the fragile, taunted and despised. This accepting attitude becomes concretely expressed in the eucharistic gathering. This event, above all, is the quintessential moment of household nurture when the desire for community is expressed and the quest for home fulfilled.

Summary

As a way of summarizing the above, I suggest that a domestic reading of Mark's gospel invites home searchers and ecclesial leaders to consider five insights into the way we might tangibly express Jesus' household of disciples for today. Mark would encourage contemporary Christian communities to be:

- *Concerned about the present*: I have been arguing that Mark's gospel must be read with a sensitivity to the Mediterranean world which gave it shape. Domestic structures and authority patterns were part of that world. The first followers of Jesus and the audience attuned to Mark's gospel lived and wrestled with these patterns. They were involved with their world and concerned about their situation. This is clearly evident in the physical arrangement of their households which were architecturally no different than the buildings that surrounded them. The dwellings, owners, and occupants blended in with the urban landscape. In other words, Mark's Christians saw themselves as members involved in a particular society in which they exercised a civic responsibility. Their discipleship of one who revealed the presence of God's *basileia* enabled them to offer a confirmation of social good and, at the same time, a cultural critique. Out of this tension of living with an *affirmation-critique* stance Mark's gospel was born.

All this suggests that today's Christian communities need to be involved in the local, social realities that concern human beings and resist any form of fantasy flight or spiritual nirvana disconnected from the present. Mark would encourage us, with a pro-cultural attitude, to look at those values within our society and world that can be vehicles for protecting the voiceless and marginalized.

- *A social alternative:* Mark affirms the social environment of the gospel's audience. The Greco-Roman world is important. In tune with the spirit of Jesus, Mark also encourages Christians to adopt domestic qualities that are radically alternative to the patriarchal, androcentric conventions that dominated their experience. Mark's community was invited to be a social alternative. It was called to refashion its lines of authority, neutralize the organizational centrality of the *paterfamilias,* and welcome into its life the socially disenfranchized. Mark's household offered a tangible social alternative that offered an unpopular, visible critique of the dominant social structures. It would have been seen by some as a serious threat to the stability of Roman society. To remain within such a structure would not have been an easy decision to make.

  When this is translated to the contemporary church scene, a domestic reading of Mark's gospel suggests that the Christian community must offer the society in which it exists a social alternative in which people's experiences and voices are valued, patriarchal, and androcentric power structures are refashioned, and the marginalized are welcomed. The Christian household must be a living, tangible expression of real community that countcracts the alienation experienced by many in our dominant Western culture. In other words, Mark would encourage Christians to form communities that are counter-cultural.

- *An ability to recognize and address causes of division*: I have suggested that Mark's sober portrait of the disciples is a mirror of the divisions which the Roman Christian household was experiencing among its members and in relation to the wider Roman society. It seems clear that all was not well and happy in Mark's community. The romantic picture often painted by some of a "golden age" of the first-century c.e. Christian community is far from the truth. If there is any veracity in Tacitus' account of the Roman Christians, it seems that Mark's household was torn by internal divisions, betrayal, and power struggles. The evangelist wrote the gospel as a way of addressing the confusion and strife that was being experienced. Mark was able to recognize the seriousness of the division in the gospel household and sought to respond to it.

This commitment by the evangelist to naming and addressing the difficulties and tragedies that plagued the Christian community, and seemed present from the earliest years, is an important insight for today's Christian churches. The churches' focus on the social agenda, of concern for the cultural, environmental, economic and political issues is often displaced by internal division, theological witch-hunts, and crusades against the modern world. In such experiences of turmoil, upheaval, and uncertainty, some pine for a return to a golden age represented for them in a church of only a few decades ago.

Rather than returning to the "good old days" Mark's gospel encourages us to deal with the present by acknowledging the tensions and divisions that currently exist and seeking ways of addressing them. As we search for ways to respond, a patriarchal use of power has no place in Mark's perspective. Rather, from the practice of Jesus evident in the gospel, Mark would encourage a conversational approach in which people learn to hear and respond. Such dialogue is reflected in the way Jesus responds to the questions of his disciples in the house.

This approach underscores the need for the Christian household to be made up of a community of learners. Education holds the key to overcoming the tensions and divisions many in the churches suffer as they seek to deal with present pressures. The kind of education envisaged, though, is not one by which people are treated as children simply to obey the relevant ecclesiastical authority or be "brainwashed" into toeing what is considered the acceptable church line. The Christian community is a community of learners or apprentices ("disciples").

It is also a site of education in which the questions and concerns of its members is placed in dialogue with the wisdom of the tradition of believers. Through this conversation insights emerge as to how the Christian community is to live authentically in the present with an eye on the future. This conversational or dialogic educational method replicates the approach used by Mark in writing the gospel.

- *Sites of hospitality, communion, and outreach*: Mark's story of Jesus' passion and death is one of intimacy. As we have seen, Jesus' agonizing solitude in the garden, the desertion by his disciples, his betrayal by one of the Twelve and denial by its leading member, all serve to heighten the picture that Mark has skillfully painted throughout the gospel: Jesus is a solitary figure, misunderstood and rejected. This portrait is further reinforced by the kind of intimate community or household which Jesus encourages his disciples to form: open to others and united in solidarity. These very qualities desert them as his passion begins. In Mark's world, the size of Greco-Roman households, irrespective of the status of their residents, meant that people knew each other, albeit according to inherited cultural scripts. These households could be places of intimate communion. The members of Mark's households were encouraged to be welcoming of all, irrespective of social status and ethnic background. They were encouraged to form communities of hospitality, communion, and outreach.

These qualities are as important today as they were for Mark. In an era of change, uncertainty, and division, it would be easy for a Christian church to operate with a fortress mentality, building protective walls around itself. Such a sectarian attitude is hard to resist. The alternative suggested by a reading of Mark's gospel is to form a community that is hospitable, united in its diversity and reaching out to those in need.

- *Local, concrete, practical, tangible expressions of the Gospel*: Several gospel scenes of Jesus' domestic healing reveal the household of disciples as the place where the resurrection is anticipated or realized. They also become the setting for healing, forgiveness, teaching, and the expression of ministry. This ministry, it was noted, was not limited to men and its exercise enabled people to experience liberation and purpose.

In Mark's gospel the household became the place in which the Gospel, Jesus, was tangibly experienced. He was the source of its life, the agent of communion, forgiveness, and healing. This meant that while the gospel story in its early, middle and later parts pointed to the ending—to the death and resurrection of Jesus—it did more than simply anticipate the ending. The household became the concrete realization of the fruits or effects of Jesus' death and resurrection.

If Mark's readers were to look for the concrete meaning of the resurrection and its practical implications, they need to look no further than in their own communities. There the resurrection was manifest. This is an important, concluding insight that needs to be remembered and reclaimed by Christian communities today.

Rather than looking to the future to find the hopes and dreams of the Christian vision, Mark's gospel invites us to consider the importance of our present experience, especially those that seem negative and counter-productive. This is not to suggest that Mark's gospel offers what is called a "realized eschatology," that is, the fruits of the resurrection and the penultimate divine encounter can be experienced now in an unambiguous and definitive way. However the evangelist is keen to assist the audience addressed by the gospel in the last half of the first century C.E. to reflect on its present experiences. These are important and are neither to be discounted or from which it should flee.

To return to the first insight that began this summary, according to Mark, the present is important. The writer would believe that it is in this present that the fruits of the resurrection can be unwittingly experienced and recognized. Each Christian gathering, even at times despite (and maybe, because of) its limitations, imperfections, and failures, is the tangible manifestation of the power of the resurrection. This gathering expresses the Gospel in a local, culturally conditioned, historically limited moment.

Bibliography

Achtemeier, P. J. "Mark, Gospel of." *Anchor Bible Dictionary.* Ed. D. N. Freedman, 4:541–57. New York: Doubleday, 1992.

Anderson, J. C. "Feminist Criticism: The Dancing Daughter." *Mark and Method: New Approaches in Biblical Studies.* Ed. J. C. Anderson and S. D. Moore, 103–34. Philadelphia: Fortress Press, 1992.

Arav, R., and R. A. Freund, eds. *The Bethsaida Excavations Project Reports and Contextual Studies.* Kirksville, Mo.: Thomas Jefferson University Press, 1995.

Avigad, N. *The Herodian Quarter in Jerusalem: Wohl Archaeological Museum.* Jerusalem: Keter Publishing House, 1989.

Balch, D. *Let Wives Be Submissive: The Domestic Code in 1 Peter.* Chico, Calif.: Scholars Press, 1981.

Banks, R. *Going to Church in the First Century: An Eyewitness Account.* Parramatta, N.S.W.: Hexagon Press, 1985.

_____. *Paul's Idea of Community: The Early House Churches in Their Historical Setting.* Homebush West, N.S.W.: Lancer Books, 1981.

Beavis, M. A. *Mark's Audience: The Literary and Social Setting of Mark 4:11-12.* Sheffield: JSOT Press, 1989.

Best, E. *Mark: The Gospel as Story.* Edinburgh: T. & T. Clark, 1987.

_____. *The Temptation and the Passion: The Markan Soteriology.* Cambridge: Cambridge University Press, 1990.

Blass, F., and A. Debrunner. *A Greek Grammar of the New Testament and Other Early Christian Literature.* Chicago: University of Chicago Press, 1961.

Bradley, K. R. *Discovering the Roman Family: Studies in Roman Social History.* New York: Oxford University Press, 1991.

Brandt, P.-Y., and A. Lukinovich. "οἶκος et οἰκία chez Marc comparé à Matthieu et Luc." *Biblica* 78 (1997) 525–33.

Branick, V. P. *The House Church in the Writings of Paul.* Wilmington, Del.: Michael Glazier, 1989.

Broshi, M. "La Population de l'Ancienne Jerusalem." *RB* 82 (1975) 5–14.

Brown, R. E. *The Death of the Messiah: From Gethsemane to the Grave.* New York: Doubleday, 1994.

_____. *An Introduction to the New Testament.* New York: Doubleday, 1997.

Brown, R. E., and J. P. Meier. *Antioch and Rome: New Testament Cradles of Catholic Christianity.* New York: Paulist Press, 1983.

Chapman, D. W. "Locating the Gospel of Mark: A Model of Agrarian Biography." *BTB* 25 (1995) 24–36.

Collins, J. N. *Are All Christians Ministers?* Collegeville: The Liturgical Press, 1992.

_____. *Diakonia: Re-interpreting the Ancient Sources.* Oxford: Oxford University Press, 1990.

Collins, R. F. "Marriage (New Testament)." *Anchor Bible Dictionary.* Ed. D. N. Freedman, 4:569–72. New York: Doubleday, 1991.

Cook, J. G. "In Defense of Ambiguity: Is There a Hidden Demon in Mark 1:29-31?" *NTS* 43 (1997) 184–208.

Countryman, L. W. "How Many Baskets Full? Mark 8:14-21 and the Value of Miracles in Mark." *CBQ* 47 (1985) 643–55.

Crosby, M. *House of Disciples: Church, Economics, and Justice in Matthew.* New York: Orbis Books, 1988.

Delling, G. "καιρος in the NT." *Theological Dictionary of the New Testament.* Ed. G. Kittel, 3:459–62. Grand Rapids, Mich.: Eerdmans, 1965.

Derrett, J.D.M. "Contributions to the Study of the Gerasene Demoniac." *JSNT* 3 (1979) 2–17.

Dewey, J. "The Gospel of Mark." *Searching the Scriptures.* Vol. 2: *A Feminist Commentary.* Ed. E. Schüssler Fiorenza, 470–509. New York: Crossroad, 1994.

Donahue, J. R. "Windows and Mirrors: The Setting of Mark's Gospel." *CBQ* 57 (1995) 1–26.

Elliott, J. H. *A Home for the Homeless: A Social-Scientific Criticism of 1 Peter, Its Situation and Strategy.* Minneapolis: Fortress Press, 1990.

_____. "The Jewish Messianic Movement: From Faction to Sect." *Modelling Early Christianity: Social-Scientific Studies of the Second Testament in Its Context.* Ed. P. F. Esler, 75–95. London: Routledge, 1995.

_____. "Temple versus Household in Luke-Acts: A Contrast in Social Institutions." *The Social World of Luke-Acts.* Ed. J. H. Neyrey, 211–40. Peabody, Mass.: Hendrickson, 1991.

_____. *What Is Social Scientific Criticism?* Minneapolis: Fortress Press, 1993.

Esler, P. F. *The First Christians in Their Social Worlds: Social-Scientific Approaches to New Testament Interpretation.* London and New York: Routledge, 1994.

Eyben, E. "Fathers and Sons." *Marriage, Divorce and Children in Ancient Rome.* Ed. B. Rawson, 114–43. Oxford: Clarendon Press, 1991.

Feldman, L. H. "How Much Hellenism in Jewish Palestine?" *Hebrew Union College Annual* 57 (1986) 83–111.

Foster, S. M. "Analysis of Spatial Patterns in Buildings (Access Analysis) as an Insight into the Social Structure: Examples from the Scottish Atlantic Iron Age." *Antiquity* 63 (1989) 40–51.

Gager, J. G. *Kingdom and Community: The Social World of Early Christianity.* Englewood Cliffs, N.J.: Prentice-Hall, 1975.

Gardner, J. F., and T. Wiedemann, eds. *The Roman Household: A Sourcebook.* London and New York: Routledge, 1991.

Giubelli, G. *Herculaneum.* Naples: Carcavallo, 1995.

Glare, P. G., ed. *The Oxford Latin Dictionary.* Oxford: Clarendon Press, 1982.

Guelich, R. "'The Beginning of the Gospel'—Mark 1:1-15." *BR* 27 (1982) 5–15.

Guijarro, S. "The Family in First-Century Galilee." *Constructing Early Christian Families.* Ed. H. Moxnes, 42–65. London and New York: Routledge, 1997.

Gundry, R. H. *Mark: A Commentary on His Apology for the Cross.* Grand Rapids, Mich.: Eerdmans, 1993.

Guthrie, K. S., ed. *The Pythagorean Sourcebook and Library: An Anthology of Ancient Writings which Relate to Pythagoras and Pythagorean Philosophy.* Grand Rapids, Mich.: Phanes Press, 1987.

Hanson, K. C. "Kinship." *The Social Sciences and New Testament Interpretation.* Ed. R. Rohrbaugh, 62–79. Peabody, Mass.: Hendrickson, 1996.

Hare, D.R.A. *Mark.* Louisville: Westminster John Knox Press, 1996.

Harrington, D. J. "Mark." *The New Jerome Biblical Commentary.* Ed. R. E. Brown, J. A. Fitzmyer, and R. E. Murphy, 596–629. London: Geoffrey Chapman, 1989.

Hengel, M. *Studies in the Gospel of Mark.* London: SCM Press, 1985.

Holladay, J. S. "House, Israelite." *Anchor Bible Dictionary.* Ed. D. N. Freedman, 3:308–18. New York: Doubleday, 1992.

Holmberg, B. *Sociology and the New Testament: An Appraisal.* Minneapolis: Fortress Press, 1990.

Hooker, M. D. *The Gospel According to Saint Mark.* Peabody, Mass.: Hendrickson, 1993.

Horsley, R. A. *Sociology and the Jesus Movement.* 2d ed. New York: Continuum, 1994.

Horsley, R. A., and J. S. Hanson. *Bandits, Prophets and Messiahs: Popular Movements in the Time of Jesus.* Minneapolis: Winston, 1985.

Jackson, H. M. "Why the Youth Shed His Cloak and Fled Naked: The Meaning and Purpose of Mark 14:51-52." *JBL* 116 (1997) 273–89.

Jeremias, J. "Die Einwohnerzahl Jerusalems zur Zeit Jesu." *Zietschrift des Deutschen Palästina-Vereins* 66 (1943) 24–31.

Johnson, E. S. "Mark viii:22-26. The Blind Man from Bethsaida." *NTS* 25 (1979) 370–83.

Joubert, S. J. "Managing the Household: Paul as Patcrfamilias of the Christian Household Group in Corinth." *Modelling Early Christianity: Social-Scientific Studies of the New Testament in Its Context.* Ed. P. F. Esler, 213–23. London and New York: Routledge, 1996.

Judge, E. A. *The Social Pattern of the Christian Groups in the First Century: Some Prolegomena to the Study of the New Testament Ideas of Social Obligation.* London: Tyndale Press, 1960.

Juel, D. A. *Master of Surprise: Mark Interpreted.* Philadelphia: Fortress Press, 1994.

Kamp, K. A. "Towards an Archaeology of Architecture: Clues from a Modern Syrian Village." *Journal of Anthropological Research* 49 (1993) 293–318.

Kee, H. C. *Community of the New Age: Studies in Mark's Gospel.* Philadelphia: Westminster Press, 1977.

Keener, C. S. *Paul, Women & Wives: Marriage and Women's Ministry in the Letters of Paul.* Peabody, Mass.: Hendrickson, 1992.

Kelber, W. H. *Mark's Story of Jesus.* Philadelphia: Fortress Press, 1979.

Kingsbury, J. D. *The Christology of Mark's Gospel.* Philadelphia: Fortress Press, 1983.

_____. *Conflict in Mark: Jesus, Authorities, Disciples.* Minneapolis: Fortress Press, 1989.

_____. *Jesus Christ in Matthew, Mark, and Luke.* Philadelphia: Fortress Press, 1981.

Kinukawa, H. *Women and Jesus in Mark: A Japanese Feminist Perspective.* New York: Orbis Books, 1994.

Kitabevi, H. *Ancient Ruins of Turkey.* Ankara: Türk Tarih Kurumu Bastmevi, 1985.

Lacey, W. C. *The Family in Classical Greece.* London: Thames & Hudson, 1968.

Loader, W. "Challenged at the Boundaries: A Conservative Jesus in Mark's Tradition." *JSNT* 63 (1996) 45–61.

Love, S. L. "The Household: A Major Social Component for Gender Analysis in the Gospel of Matthew." *BTB* 23 (1993) 21–31.

Luz, E. "Basileia." *Exegetical Dictionary of the New Testament.* Ed. H. Balz, and G. Schneider, 1:201–5. Grand Rapids, Mich.: Eerdmans, 1990.

Mack, B. L. *A Myth of Innocence: Mark and Christian Origins.* Philadelphia: Fortress Press, 1988.

Maiuri, A. *Herculaneum.* Rome: Istituto Poligrafico dello Stato, Libreria Dello Stato, 1977.

Malherbe, J., ed. *Moral Exhortation, A Greco-Roman Sourcebook.* Philadelphia: Westminster Press, 1986.

Malina, B., and R. L. Rohrbaugh. *Social Science Commentary on the Synoptic Gospels.* Minneapolis: Fortress Press, 1992.

Mann, C. S. *Mark: A New Translation with Introduction and Commentary.* New York: Doubleday, 1986.

Matera, F. J. *The Kingship of Jesus: Composition and Theology in Mark 15.* Chico, Calif.: Scholars Press, 1982.

Mauser, U. W. *Christ in the Wilderness: The Wilderness Theme in the Second Gospel and Its Basis in the Biblical Tradition.* Naperville: Allenson, 1963.

Meeks, W. A. *The First Urban Christians: The Social World of the Apostle Paul.* New Haven, Conn.: Yale University Press, 1983.

Meggitt, J. J. *Paul, Poverty and Survival.* Edinburgh: T. & T. Clark, 1998.

Metzger, B. M. *A Textual Commentary on the Greek New Testament.* London: United Bible Societies, 1975.

Meyers, C. "Women and the Domestic Economy of Early Israel." *Women's Earliest Records: From Ancient Egypt and Western Asia.* Proceedings of the Conference on Women in the Ancient Near East. Brown University, Providence, Rhode Island, November 5–7, 1987. Ed. B. S. Lesko, 273–89. Atlanta: Scholars Press, 1989.

Moxnes, H. "'He saw that the city was full of idols' (Acts 17:16): Visualizing the World of the First Christians." *Mighty Minorities? Minorities in Early Chris-*

tianity—Positions and Strategies. Ed. D. Hellholm, H. Moxnes, and T. K. Sein, 107–31. Oslo: Scandinavian University, 1995.

_____. "What Is Family? Problems in Constructing Early Christian Families." *Constructing Early Christian Families: Family as Social Reality and Metaphor.* Ed. H. Moxnes, 13–41. London and New York: Routledge, 1997.

Murphy-O'Connor, J. "Prisca and Aquila: Traveling Tentmakers and Church Builders." *BRev* 8 (1992) 40–51, 62.

_____. *St. Paul's Corinth: Texts and Archaeology.* Wilmington, Del.: Michael Glazier, 1983.

Myers, C. *Binding the Strong Man: A Political Reading of Mark's Story of Jesus.* Maryknoll, N.Y.: Orbis Books, 1988.

Nineham, D. E. *Saint Mark.* London: Penguin Books, 1963.

Osiek, C. *What Are They Saying about the Social Setting of the New Testament?* Rev. ed. New York and Mahwah, N.J.: Paulist Press, 1992.

Osiek, C., and D. L. Balch. *Families in the New Testament World: Households and House Churches.* Louisville: Westminster John Knox Press, 1997.

Painter, J. "When Is a House Not a Home? Disciples and Family in Mark 3:13-35." *NTS* 45 (1999) 498–513.

Pantel, P. S., ed. *A History of Women in the West.* Vol. 1: *From Ancient Goddesses to Christian Saints.* Cambridge, Mass.: The Belknap Press of Harvard University Press, 1992.

Perkins, P. *Resurrection: New Testament Witness and Contemporary Reflection.* New York: Doubleday, 1984.

Perkinson, J. "A Canaanitic Word in the Logos of Christ; or The Difference the Syro-Phoenician Woman Makes to Jesus." *Semeia* 75 (1996) 61–85.

Pilch, J. J. *The Cultural World of Jesus.* Collegeville: The Liturgical Press, 1995.

_____. "Healing in Mark: A Social Science Analysis." *BTB* 15 (1985) 142–50.

_____. "Sickness and Healing in Luke-Acts." *The Social World of Luke-Acts.* Ed. J. H. Neyrey, 181–201. Peabody, Mass.: Hendrickson, 1991.

Pomeroy, Sarah. *Goddesses, Whores, Wives, and Slaves: Women in Classical Antiquity.* New York: Shocken, 1975.

Rawson, B. "The Roman Family." *The Family in Ancient Rome: New Perspectives.* Ed. B. Rawson, 1–57. Ithaca, N.Y.: Cornell University Press, 1986.

Rhodes D., and D. Michie. *Mark as Story: An Introduction to the Narrative for a Gospel.* Philadelphia: Fortress Press, 1982.

Rohrbaugh, R. L. "The Social Location of the Markan Audience." *Int* 47 (1993) 380–95.

Robbins, V. K. *Jesus the Teacher: A Socio-Rhetorical Interpretation of Mark.* Minneapolis: Fortress Press, 1992.

Saller, R. "Corporal Punishment, Authority, and Obedience in the Roman Household." *Marriage, Divorce and Children in Ancient Rome.* Ed. B. Rawson, 144–65. Oxford: Clarendon Press, 1991.

_____. *Patriarchy, Property and Death in the Roman Family.* Cambridge: Cambridge University Press, 1994.

Sanders, E. P. *Jesus and Judaism.* London: SCM Press, 1985.

Schüssler Fiorenza, E. *In Memory of Her: A Feminist Theological Reconstruction of Christian Origins.* 2d ed. London: SCM Press, 1995.

_____. *Jesus: Miriam's Child, Sophia's Prophet.* New York: Continuum, 1994.

Schweizer, E. *The Good News According to Mark.* Atlanta: John Knox Press, 1970.

Senior, D. *The Passion of Jesus in the Gospel of Mark.* Wilmington, Del.: Michael Glazier, 1984.

_____. "'With Swords and Clubs . . .'—The Setting of Mark's Community and His Critique of Abusive Power." *BTB* 17 (1987) 10–20.

Seyffert, O. *The Dictionary of Classical Mythology, Religion, Literature, and Art.* New York: Gramercy Books, 1995.

Shelton, J.A.R. *As the Romans Did: A Source Book in Roman Social History.* New York: Oxford University Press, 1988.

Spicq, C. "Βασιλεῖα." *Theological Lexicon of the New Testament.* Ed. J. D. Ernest, 1:256–71. Peabody, Mass.: Hendrickson, 1994.

Stark, R. *The Rise of Christianity: A Sociologist Reconsiders History.* Princeton, N.J.: Princeton University Press, 1996.

Stern, E., ed. *The New Encyclopedia of Archaeological Excavations in the Holy Land.* Vol. 2. New York: Simon & Schuster, 1993.

Stock, A. *Call to Discipleship: A Literary Study of Mark's Gospel.* Wilmington, Del.: Michael Glazier, 1982.

Struthers Malbon, E. *Narrative Space and Mythic Meaning in Mark.* San Francisco: Harper & Row, 1986.

Taylor, V. *The Gospel According to St. Mark: The Greek Text with Introduction, Notes and Indexes.* 2d ed. London: Macmillan, 1966.

Telford, W. R. *The Barren Temple and the Withered Tree.* Sheffield: JSOT Press, 1980.

Tolbert, M. A. "Mark." *The Women's Bible Commentary.* Ed. C. A. Newsom and S. H. Ringe, 263–75. London: SPCK, 1992.

_____. *Sowing the Gospel. Mark's World in Literary-Historical Perspective.* Minneapolis: Fortress Press, 1989.

Trainor, M. "The Divorced and Their Inclusion in Community (Mk 10:1-12)." *ACR* 72 (1995) 211–24.

_____. "The Women, the Empty Tomb, and that Final Verse." *The Bible Today* 34 (1996) 177–82.

Treggiari, S. *Roman Marriage: Iusti Coniuges from the Time of Cicero to the Time of Ulpian.* Oxford: Oxford University Press, 1991.

Van Iersel, B.M.F. "Failed Followers in Mark: Mark 13:12 as a Key for the Identification of the Intended Readers." *CBQ* 58 (1996) 244–63.

Via, D. O. *The Ethics of Mark's Gospel in the Middle of Time.* Philadelphia: Fortress Press, 1985.

Wallace-Hadrill, A. "Houses and Households: Sampling Pompeii and Herculaneum." *Marriage, Divorce and Children in Ancient Rome.* Ed. B. Rawson, 191–229. Oxford: Clarendon Press, 1991.

_____. *Houses and Society in Pompeii and Herculaneum.* Princeton, N.J.: Princeton University Press, 1994.

Wefald, E. K. "The Separate Gentile Mission in Mark: A Narrative Explanation of Markan Geography, the Two Feeding Accounts and Exorcisms." *JSNT* 60 (1995) 3–26.

Woodroof, T. "The Church as Boat in Mark: Building a Seaworthy Church." *RestorQuart* 39 (1997) 231–49.

Wuellner, W. H. *The Meaning of "Fishers of Men."* Philadelphia: Westminster Press, 1967.

Zerwick, M., and M. Grosvenor. *A Grammatical Analysis of the Greek New Testament.* Vol. 1. Rome: Biblical Institute Press, 1974.

Author Index

Subject Index

Abandonment, 169–72
Abraham, 104
Absence, 165, 169–72, 183
Affection, 181
Africa, 45
Agnates, 55
Alexander the Great, 43
Ambiguity, 171
Andrew, 26, 88
Antagonism, 101–102, 158
Antiochus' Academy, 60
Apocalyptic Literature, 161–63, 169
Apocalypticism, 83, 157, 161–63, 167, 169
Apostasy, 151, 154–55, 184
Aretas, 127
Aristotle, 38, 39, 43–51, 53, 60, 61, 180
Artisan, 97
Asia Minor, 17, 43
Atlas, grandfather of Mercury, 56
Atrium, 28, 29, 30, 32, 94, 95, 96, 179
Auditor, 8, 174
Augustus, 56
Authority *(see Potestas)*

Basileia, 24, 73, 83–84, 103, 108, 111, 113, 122, 183–85
Baucis, 56–57
Bethsaida, 25, 131, 132, 145

Betrayal, 166–69, 183–84
Blindness, 74–75, 140, 143–44, 145–46, 153–56
Boat-House Setting, 107
Boat, 113–17
Bread, 127–28, 140–41
Burial, 166

Caecilius Isidorus, 56
Caenaculum, 29, 167–68
Callides, 41
Caphernaum, 25
Caritas, 61, 62
Casa Di Bicentenario, 32, 179
Child, 149–52, 183
Christology *(see* Jesus, Nature of)
Cicero, 53–55, 59–64, 65, 67, 181
City-State *(see Polis)*
Clothing, 127
Communicatio, 61, 62
Communion *(see also Koinônia),* 41, 61, 65–67, 156, 171; between Jewish and Gentile Christians, 133–35
Compassion, 128, 131
Conflict-withdrawal, 101–102
Coniunctio, 61, 62
Courtyard—Peristyle, 28, 179
Crucifixion, 166
Cubiculum, 30, 96

Dalmanutha, 138